Winning Every Time

Winning
Every Time

How to Use the Skills of a Lawyer

in the Trials of Your Life

Lis Wiehl

BALLANTINE BOOKS • NEW YORK

A Ballantine Book
Published by The Random House Publishing Group

Copyright © 2004 by Lis Wiehl

All rights reserved under International and Pan-American
Copyright Conventions. Published in the United States by
The Random House Publishing Group, a division of Random
House, Inc., New York, and simultaneously in Canada by
Random House of Canada Limited, Toronto.

Ballantine and colophon are registered trademarks
of Random House, Inc.

www.ballantinebooks.com

Library of Congress Cataloging-in-Publication Data
can be obtained from the publisher upon request.

ISBN 0-345-46919-4

Text design by Meryl Sussman Levavi/Digitext

Manufactured in the United States of America

First Edition: May 2004

1   3   5   7   9   10   8   6   4   2

For my children, Jacob and Danielle, and for my mom and dad, Inga and Richard, who taught me to always follow my moral compass

Contents

Part II
Winning the Trials of Your Life

Foreword

The tired cliché goes: "Life is hard and then you die." And for many Americans this is unfortunately true. But it doesn't have to be. You can make your life easier if you do the basics: get educated, work hard, live honestly. But, unless you're a trust-fund baby, you'll still have a tough go until you figure out how to successfully handle the inevitable confrontations that life drops on you.

It took me decades to wise up, but just the fact that you are reading these words right now means you have an important resource within your grasp. Lis Wiehl's book is a primer on how to incorporate legal skills into your life and win battles without drawing blood. Some of her examples are as simple as convincing a landlord that you are a worthy tenant. But others are far more complicated; like succeeding in a competitive workplace or developing a relationship that lasts.

Americans are living in the most competitive society the world has ever seen. There are 300 million of us vying for a piece of that big dream: financial independence, a stimulating career, rewarding interactions with other people. These things are all attainable, but there is a price to pay. How high a price is up to you. Some of the most successful people in the country are degenerates; awful human beings who exploit others for their own gain. You can win that way in the short term. But achieving great things with dignity takes much more skill. You must understand with whom you are dealing and what it will take to get where you want to go. Only by that kind of understanding can you develop a successful life strategy.

Lis Wiehl supplies specific game plans by using the techniques that successful lawyers employ. She is insistent about defining goals and then logically strategizing to achieve them. Here is a woman who, without much help, graduated from Harvard Law School, is successfully raising two children, and is succeeding in the most intense of industries: the TV and radio media. So she knows what she's talking about.

Therefore strategy number one for you might be to listen up. Read this book slowly and apply each example to your own life. No situation is perfect, even the good ones can be improved. See if you can use the techniques taught in this book to immediately make things better in your life.

Finally, to get the most out of Lis's message, you should keep a chart. Write down the legal techniques she discusses, and then list where they can be used in your life. Make this book a game, try different strategies and keep a record on how well they work. It might take you a couple of times to perfect the techniques Lis writes about, but that is true with everything you learn. The Williams sisters didn't hit sizzling serves the first few times they picked up tennis rackets. The fun of accomplishing goals is trial and error. If everything was done exactly right the first time, there would be no drama. Life would be dull.

Rest assured this book will help you out. If you are disciplined enough to read it carefully, and shrewd enough to figure out the appropriate application to your own situation, you will acquire a distinct advantage in this world. Books are supposed to be written to enlighten. Too many of them fail on that promise. This one does not.

—Bill O'Reilly
December 23, 2003

Preface

Fresh out of law school and starting my practice in Seattle, I had finally found the perfect apartment and excitedly told the landlord I would take it. I explained that even though I was just out of school, I would have no problem paying the rent because I was a lawyer and had a job with a great . . . The landlord's face fell and he started mumbling about the unit really not being available and that he might have something *in a year or so.*

Knowing how people sometimes (okay, often) feel about lawyers, it wasn't too hard to figure out that he didn't want a lawyer living under his roof. I sheepishly told him I understood and walked back to my car, saddened by my misconception that a law degree somehow made me more trustworthy. I sat in my car and pondered my fate. Having looked at dozens of apartments, I knew this one was right for me and really wanted it. It was a good price, had lots of room, offered a great view, and was an easy walk to work.

So I decided not to take no for an answer. I got out of my car and walked back to the landlord to present my case. I explained that I had grown up in the area, I had great references who could vouch for me, and I really liked his apartment. I told him the story of how many apartments I had looked at and that this was the perfect apartment for me. Then I slipped in the comment that as a lawyer I knew that litigation was the last thing anyone looked for, and that no lawyer wanted to deal with the legal system in her time off.

The following week I moved in. I won my case not by being confrontational, but by expressing my desire clearly, understanding my landlord's fears, and explaining how I was the right person for his apartment.

*　*　*

All of us have to stand up for ourselves every day. But too often our personal insecurities, weaknesses, and hang-ups make it difficult to express—and attain—what we really want. We walk away from, rather than dealing with, difficult circumstances; we argue conclusions without presenting the premise first; we react with emotion rather than presenting the hard facts; we feel cornered and defensive when we meet up with resistance, and have difficulty making calm, irrefutable counterarguments.

In *Winning Every Time* you will learn how to employ the skills, smarts, and strategies that trial lawyers use in the courtroom to rise above the helplessness you may feel during situations of conflict at work, in life, and at home. This book will teach you how to take advantage of the valuable set of practices and strategies lawyers use to win their cases.

And let's be clear. This isn't a book to make a litigious society more litigious, telling you how to take your neighbor to court because his fence is too high. This is a book about solving problems—everyday problems—using the language, skills, and techniques that lawyers employ during conflict resolution. This is a book to help you win the trials of your life.

I grew up as the daughter of a lawyer in a conservative small town in eastern Washington State. One day, when I was seven, while accompanying my dad to see one of his far-flung clients, he stopped the car as a warning bar lowered at a railroad crossing. As we watched the train barrel by, he told me that the warning bar was something new. He had won a case against the railroad after an oncoming train killed a high school senior on his way home from the prom. The railroad had been negligent by not protecting the boy—and others—with a bar to alert drivers of an oncoming train. My dad used his legal skills to help the boy's grieving parents, and, by holding the railroad accountable, he was able to make sure there wouldn't be other people mourning loved ones because of a missing (and necessary) warning bar.

Even knowing about my father's advocacy, for years I viewed the law as a remote, intimidating force. When (much to the surprise of the people in my hometown) I ended up at Harvard Law School, I worried that they were right—that the place might be too rough-and-tumble for me, and the law too esoteric. Harvard initially overwhelmed me—the tall, heavy doors, those portraits of dead white men lining the halls, not to mention the mind-boggling task of mastering the law's language and techniques. But when it finally sank in that the law is based on cases about real people and their stories, the tools of legal advocacy seemed suddenly clear—and extremely accessible. Since then, my passion has been to make the law approachable, understandable, and usable for ordinary people.

Advocacy is a part of life, and it doesn't require a law degree. There seem to be four ways to approach situations that arise in our life:

1. Ignore them and hope they go away.
2. Assign them to someone else, such as a spouse, colleague, parent, or friend, and hope that this person will be our knight and defend us from our problems.

3. Contend with them irrationally—spontaneously combusting and grimacing at each new glitch.
4. Face our situations head-on, approaching them logically and thoughtfully, with preparedness and thoroughness.

It's option 4 that this book will help you master. As a lawyer, I believe that all of us should have access to justice—not just in a courtroom or legal dispute, but in every situation in our lives where we stand to lose something important to us or when achieving what is fair and right is at stake.

Winning Every Time will show you how to stay in command whenever life makes you feel as though you are on trial, no matter what your role is in the world, and no matter what the context—at home, at school, in the workplace, or in the boardroom. Whether you're hoping to obtain a raise from your boss, convince an insurance claim representative to reimburse your medical treatment, talk your spouse into spending less time watching TV and more time with you, or persuade a business partner to embrace a project you believe in, *Winning Every Time* will be your guide for truly practical and helpful advice about how to make the case effectively—and win it hands-down.

PART I

The Eight Steps
to the Skills
of a Lawyer

Introduction

Access to the law means access to the law's techniques—the strategies of making your case. *Winning Every Time* will demystify the jargon of the law and explain the simple truth behind its complexities so that you can relate to the law and *use* it. The idea of using the language and strategies of lawyers may seem off-putting, as it did for me as a young person living in eastern Washington State. It may conjure up images of stem-winding attorneys such as F. Lee Bailey, Gerry Spence, and Johnnie Cochran, or surly prosecutors who reduce witnesses to tears on the stand. But as we break down the strategies that lawyers employ, we'll see what was at first intimidating is ultimately empowering. These techniques will help us organize our logic, compose our passions, measure our arguments, and stay focused on our genuine goals.

I saw how effective legal strategies could be outside the courtroom in helping ordinary people advocate for themselves in my own home state of Washington, where I helped lead a program called LASER—Lawyers and Students Engaged in Resolution—in which lawyers trained middle and high school students to mediate disputes among their peers. I watched as students employed the skills of the law to resolve differences and conquer everyday problems.

When two male students were at each other's throats because one was accusing the other of "dissing" his girlfriend, we put to use such legal practices as challenging evidence based on *hearsay* ("Did you actually hear Winston dis Kyle's girlfriend, or did you just hear *about* it?"); *impeaching the witness* ("But earlier you told me that Winston said Kyle's girlfriend was a 'hottie' at the basketball game, didn't you? And weren't they all there together?"); *bias* ("Oh, I see—Jenna, you're Kyle's girlfriend's sister"); and *motive* ("Winston was upset because Kyle got into a college that they both wanted to go to and Winston didn't").

Teaching students the legal strategies involved in conflict resolution, I was amazed how many fights we were able to avert. The material LASER presented to them produced concrete, measurable results. And I witnessed how happy and empowered they were by putting these techniques into action.

Once you get comfortable with the concepts behind *hearsay, direct evidence, prejudicial evidence, direct and cross-examination*—all legal terms that have valuable everyday meanings—you can conquer your fears and get the results you want and deserve. These skills will help you access your inner advocate and bring your natural skills of persuasion to the surface.

By introducing you to eight specific steps that seasoned litigators use to offer up passionate arguments, cross-examine witnesses, and win a victory from judge or jury, *Winning Every Time* will help you become more powerful and successful in your everyday interpersonal and work-related dealings. And you'll learn how to successfully implement these eight steps in specific areas of your life—at work and in business, as a consumer, in marriage, as a parent, and in other personal relationships.

* * *

Step 1. Know What You Want: *The Theory of the Case.* We'll start with the vital importance of beginning with a central thesis that you can articulate clearly and that will serve to win you the verdict you seek. Before you begin your advocacy, you need to know exactly what your case is truly about and establish your final objective accordingly.

Step 2. Choose and Cultivate Your Audience: *Voir Dire.* Just as lawyers work hard to choose the optimal jury during voir dire (or bring a case before the judge who would be the most sympathetic to their client), so can you figure out how to choose and best appeal to your "adversary," "jury," or "judge." This step involves making sure that you bring your case to a decision maker who really can call the shots and is open to helping you. Even the most ardent and persuasive argument may go unheard, and have little impact, if you're advocating to someone who can't render you the decision you seek—or who, for one reason or another, isn't interested in assisting you. Step 2 also often entails choosing the right time and venue in which to make your case— for instance, trying to convince your bank to increase your credit line is probably more difficult right after you've bounced a few checks or when your account is overdrawn. By thinking through whom you're advocating and the setting in which you're advocating, you'll be much more likely to be successful in your pursuit.

Step 3. Marshal Your Evidence: *Discovery.* You'll learn, even before you make your argument, the importance of *discovery*— that is, of systematically gathering all the evidence you need. Your argument will gain far greater effectiveness if, like a lawyer, you assemble, evaluate, and prepare all the data you need to make your case *before* launching into your opening argument, including not only facts and information that help your cause but also data that challenge what you're trying to argue or achieve.

Then you'll be able to ensure that your case can withstand objections and cross-examination.

Step 4. Advocate with Confidence: *Making the Case.* Step 4 requires not only a change in psychological outlook—a stance of confidence rather than emotion—but also a commitment to the primary methodology of the best trial lawyers: organizing and becoming intimately familiar with all of your information before acting on it. As you begin your opening argument and offer your evidence, ideally you'll know just what you're going to say, how you're going to say it, and what you'll say or do if your opponent challenges you on any particular point.

Step 5. Counter the Claims: *Cross-Examination.* You'll learn, too, how to ask a series of thoughtfully prepared and presented yes-or-no questions designed to elicit only the information needed to affirm your key points and arguments. There's a significant difference between acting righteous and condescending (both of which are to be carefully avoided) and challenging your opponent's allegations gently but consistently through the art of cross-examination, pointing out hearsay, and making "objections" about the relevance of the evidence presented.

Step 6. Stay True to Your Case: *Avoid the Seven Deadly Spins.* Step 6 focuses on many of the manipulative techniques that creep into our relationships and negotiations. In the clutch you'll need to keep your argument authentic and avoid reacting with inappropriate emotion. You won't rely on hearsay, toss in additional charges, or make subjective characterizations. By eliminating reliance on these self-destructive techniques, you'll make room for the vastly more rational, effective strategies outlined throughout this book.

Step 7. Advocate with Heart: *Let Me Tell You a Story.* Step 7 focuses on humanizing your case. A good litigator knows that juries are persuaded not just by evidence but also by facts shaped into a story they can connect with emotionally. Using your own passion as a resource, you can shape your case into a story—and make it personal. Conveying your theory of the case using a powerful, relevant story can often help you win the heart—as well as the verdict—of that critical decision-making person.

Step 8. Sum It Up: *The Closing Argument.* Just like a lawyer speaking before a jury, once you've made your "just-the-facts" presentation and then conveyed your core message through a compelling story, you can clinch your case with a fervent and succinct closing argument. In this final step you restate your theory of the case, refer to the key evidence supporting it, remind the decision maker of the story you've related, and ask for the remedy you are seeking. If you know your theory of the case and have thoughtfully presented this theory and all your supporting evidence through the first seven steps, Step 8 will feel like a culminating moment: Having made the best possible case, you can now close the deal.

Will you have to use every step in every situation? No. But by becoming familiar with the Eight Steps, you'll find yourself reflexively using them in situations both routine and significant. Think of the steps like a well-packed suitcase—you don't wear everything you pack, every time, but if it rains you're sure glad you've got the raincoat.

The goal here isn't to teach you to become a cold, calculating legal machine who cross-examines your mother over her burned pot roast or makes "objections" to the relevance of your supervisor's requests. The goal is to help you get what you want (and still have people like you!) by providing you with the law-related tools you need to handle life's challenges, debates, and controversies rationally—and to remain, in the heat of conflict, as clear, coolheaded, and thoughtfully persuasive as the very best trial lawyers.

Chapter 1

Step 1. Know What You Want:
The Theory of the Case

> *As you approach the trials of your life, you need to find a simple but memorable theme in order to win.*

I first realized that the skills I learned as a lawyer could empower people beyond the courtroom when Jennifer, a woman with whom I worked, came to see me in tears. Jennifer is a petite, elegant woman in her fifties, an excellent paralegal who enjoys her job immensely. But after more than five years of outstanding performance reviews from the attorneys for whom she worked, Jennifer had received a negative review from her new staff supervisor, Michelle. She was stunned. Equally surprised by the disapproving review, I asked her how she had responded when Michelle presented it.

"Well," she admitted, "I was just so upset by Michelle's rating that I just signed off on it. I don't think I deserve a bad review, but it was just so intimidating." Jennifer grew up as the daughter of a hard-driving and unapproachable neurosurgeon, a man who was both demanding and controlling, so she was not used to standing up for herself. "Lis, I just don't know how to approach this," she told me. "I'm so angry, but when I even think about talking to Michelle about it, I just freeze up. I'm afraid I'll say something stupid or burst into tears."

"But," I reminded her, "if you don't say anything, the problem is just going to fester."

"I know, I know," she cried. "This bad review will sabotage my career. I could even lose my job."

I told Jennifer I sympathized with her and that we could figure this out, but that we needed to put emotion aside and approach this as if it were a case going to trial. It was one of those "Aha!" moments for me—*of course courtroom techniques can apply to everyday life.*

Jennifer wiped away the tears and we got down to the business of preparing her case.

Finding Your Key Theme

The first step toward success in the trial process is finding a theory of the case, a memorable phrase that captures the essence of the case and leads to the desired result. Besides providing a backbone for the case, this theory is your opportunity to set the stage and communicate your overall message. You can't figure out what kind of evidence is relevant or what to argue if you're running around like Chicken Little with no coherent plan or road map. It's your job to organize your information in a way that makes it accessible and clear. An effective theory of the case gives a comfortable viewpoint from which you can present your evidence—and your juror can hear it.

A good theory is easy to remember, appeals to common sense, is consistent with the evidence, and fits with your audience's concept of fairness and justice. The importance of establishing a compelling theory cannot be emphasized enough: It supports every step of the trial, just as a catchy refrain does in a song.

Songwriters know the importance of finding a theme, a chorus that conveys the central idea or emotion that the artist wishes to express in a memorable way. A songwriter has done her job if after hearing a song you're saying, "I can't get that line out of my head." Whether it's *"Raindrops keep fallin' on my head,"* or *"You're so vain,"* you can probably recognize a lyric that works (or at least one that sticks in your head). In the courtroom, a lawyer's job is to find a phrase such as *betrayal of trust, profits over safety,* or *taking responsibility for your actions* and rely on it as a songwriter would a chorus in order to convince a jury that the theme is fair and just.

In a line or two you can capture the theme of your entire case. Advertising executives know how to capture the essence or theme of their product in one line. "You deserve a break today," "Just do it," and "Where's the beef?" have all become at one time national mantras. How? The lines are catchy, are easily understood, and communicate a message. Once the ad gurus find that memorable line that works for their product, they drive it home.

As you approach the trials of your life, this book is going to help you find your simple but memorable theme in order to engage and persuade other people—and win.

*   *   *

After graduating from law school, I wanted to merge my interests in law and journalism, but instead I listened to the advice of my soon-to-be-husband and made the "responsible" decision to take a corporate law job in Seattle in order to pay back the incredible debt I had incurred while at Harvard.

I approached my new role in the "white-shoe" corporate law firm with a smile. I did my job well, learning a lot and putting a tremendous amount of effort into the tedious tasks of corporate law. But each case always came down to the same thing—money. The bottom line was the bottom line—no other considerations need apply, and I quickly realized corporate law was not going to be my life. It couldn't be. I was aching to incorporate my love of journalism into my career. That was the simple theme I kept playing over and over again in my mind. My theory of the case became "I want to write for the *New York Times.*" (Thankfully, I'm from the naive school of *I think I can.*)

From my fancy office in Seattle, I called the only person I knew who wrote for the *Times*—Pulitzer Prize–winning author Anthony Lewis, whose course on the Constitution and the press I had taken at Harvard Law. I knew him; he didn't know me (because I'd never said anything in class!). I introduced myself and told him I would really like to speak with him about writing some pieces on the law for the *Times.* After looking up my grade (one of the very few As he'd given out), he said he'd be happy to meet with me the next time I was in Boston.

"What time do you get into the office?" I asked.

"I'm an early bird," he said. "I'm always here around seven AM."

Two days later, I flew to Boston and called him at seven AM. He answered the phone, and I reintroduced myself and asked if he could see me.

"Where are you?" he asked.

"I'm downstairs at the pay phone."

What could he say?

By the end of our talk that morning, Professor Lewis gave me the name of Jonathan Landman at the *Times* (now a managing editor) and told me I could use his name. I sent Mr. Landman a letter and three story ideas. The result was success:

November 4, 1988, Friday, Late City Final Edition

Indian Courts Struggling to Keep Their Identity

---

by Lis Wiehl, SPECIAL TO THE NEW YORK TIMES

Chief Judge Elbridge Coochise never went to law school and he has never taken a bar examination. But the 42-year-old Hopi Indian is a respected jurist who presides over the sovereign courts of 16 Pacific Northwest Indian tribes in a legal system little known outside Indian Reservations. . . .

I won my case and started writing for the *Times* because I knew what I wanted. In short, I knew my theory of the case. I was able to approach Anthony Lewis and then Jonathan Landman because I was anchored by my theory of the case. It wasn't because I wasn't scared. I was petrified. I've learned that even the most self-assured, successful people feel fear, but it's how they address their fears that set them apart from those who let fear defeat them. When I face a situation in which I feel out of my league, I always come back to my current theme, the line that plays over and over again in my head.

Fifteen years later, I'm at the Fox News Channel as a sparring partner with Bill O'Reilly and cohost of his radio show. How I got there is also a story of finding my personal theory of the case, and relying on it to carry me through.

As you might imagine, meeting Bill O'Reilly and convincing him to give me—a former federal prosecutor and law school professor—a shot at Fox News seemed like a daunting challenge. Besides the fact that I was living in Seattle and the Fox studios are in New York City, there was the small detail that I had little television training. I had been providing commentary for a few local stations in Seattle and appeared on the *Factor* several times as a guest, commenting via satellite from a little square in the corner of the TV screen, but I had never met Bill.

When I was in New York on business, I arranged to meet with O'Reilly's producer, Peter Zorich, in the hope of getting a steady on-air position. After our meeting, Peter kindly offered, "Why don't we drop by Bill's office and you can say hi." My hands were shaking when I went into his office. It was very intimidating and—at six foot four—so was Bill.

As I looked around at the stacks of books in piles all over the floor, the photos of famous people, the slew of neckties, and the goodies sent by people from all across the country, I took a deep breath and reminded myself of the theory of my case: *I want this job, but I have to be true to my beliefs.*

At the time, the issue on everyone's mind was whether Gary Condit, the congressman from California, should resign over the Chandra Levy scandal. The intern, with whom he'd had an affair that he'd lied about, was at that point missing and presumed dead. Bill said, "I think he should resign. What do you think?"

I swallowed hard. Should I agree? Disagree? Then my theory: *Be true to my beliefs.* "With all due respect," I said, "who are you to take this decision away from the California voters? He's their congressman, after all. If they think he should be out, they'll vote him out." Within two minutes, we were debating so fast and furiously that a room full of producers and staff had crowded in Bill's office, all interested in the repartee. As at trial, I stayed focused on making my points with Bill.

I left Fox realizing I'd probably be knocking on a few more doors before finding a place for the next step in my career, but I was glad I had stayed true to my beliefs, rather than stepping away from them in order to please Bill.

Back in Seattle, I was experiencing the worst day of my life. My sixteen-year marriage had just been pronounced officially over, and I was standing numbly on the courthouse steps, beside my own lawyer, when my cell phone rang. It was Roger Ailes, the head of Fox News, on the phone, offering me a job in New York.

Relying on my theory had gotten me the job.

Looking back, I realize that each time I've had personal success outside the courtroom, it has been because I've had a working theory that has successfully carried me through to a winning verdict. In your life, in your own personal cases—the trials and tribulations of everyday life—try, before you do anything else, to find the theory of your case. You will be amazed by the results.

It may sound simple, but you can't win your case without knowing what you want. If you leap into the fray without clarifying your precise objective, without knowing what your goal is, you're like a sailboat without a rudder. You'll be off course from the beginning.

> *A beautiful woman entered a bar and sat next to a lawyer.*
> *"Listen honey," she said, "for fifty dollars, I'll do absolutely*
> *anything you want." The lawyer pulled fifty dollars from*
> *his wallet and said, "Okay, paint my house."*

The first step to becoming successful in any dispute or conflict, or even in life, entails stepping back from the circumstances and asking yourself, *What is this about?* followed by *What is the outcome I want to achieve?* It's the simple, clear story of what really happened. In the courtroom there are usually two competing versions of reality. Each side presents its theory of the case, hoping the jury will adopt that theory as their own. In your life, your theory of the case is the message that gives meaning to your issue and gets positive results.

How to Establish Your Theory of the Case

1. Determine What Your Position Is Really About

To begin, ask yourself how you would complete this sentence: *This is about . . .* or *What I'm really going for is . . .* Sometimes the answer is simple: "Getting money back for a defective answering machine." But often the answer is a little more difficult. If, for example, you're challenging a coworker whose nay-saying is sabotaging your joint project, your reflex may be to declare, "This case is about how impossible my coworker has been" or "I want to prove why the guy in the next cubicle deserves to be crushed like a bug." It will ultimately serve you better to say something like, "This case is about why my worthwhile project needs to be effectively implemented."

At home, instead of deciding on a short-term goal, "This is about getting my son to stop hitting his sister," you could decide your advocacy is about the longer-term "This is about respecting other people's boundaries."

If you focus on formulating your theory of the case (and don't give in to your impulsive reactions), you vastly increase your ability to change minds—and effect real change. Good trial lawyers know that they cannot represent a client effectively without having formulated their theory of the case, and they begin developing that theory the minute they take on any client. Terrible lawyers never formulate a theory of the case and just stab around in the dark—which leads to unpredictable and painful results.

2. Avoid Red Herrings

In the 1800s British fugitives would rub a herring across their trail, thereby diverting the bloodhounds that were in hot pursuit. Much like smelly fish, distracting, faulty, or shortsighted arguments subvert your true objective. Red herrings throw you off the trail of your goal.

Finish the sentence, *This case is* not *about* . . . If you phrase the proposition like this, you may be surprised at your answers. You'll realize that certain theories of the case—for example, those that revolve around sheer emotion or righteousness, such as "how angry I am" or "why I'm right"—are often counterproductive. Your case is not about "an idiotic, overpriced plumber"; it's about "a sump pump that still needs to be repaired." It's not about "the way my boss undervalues my work"; it's about "getting the raise I deserve."

Throughout the case you'll be distracted by red herrings, either those thrown in your way by others or those reeled in by your own mind. You'll need to remind yourself to return to the true theme of your case. Don't let the red herrings throw you off the trail. Follow the scent that contains the true essence of your goal. It's essential to your success.

3. Define Your Goal

What is the verdict you want? Does the theme of your case support it? So often we plunge into advocacy with a blurry, unlikely, or futile goal in mind—or no real goal at all. Yet if you begin by knowing the outcome you want, you'll be able to shape your entire case around it. For example, rather than seeking an apology from your doctor for keeping you waiting three hours, your goal may be to obtain your test results by the end of the business day. If your coworker is dousing your project with cold water, your goal is to win the project a favorable hearing, not to thwart your colleague.

Let me show you a few ways this works in the courtroom.

Look at It This Way . . .

As a federal prosecutor preparing a murder case, I would step back from the charges themselves in order to determine my position. I'd ask myself on what basis I wanted the jury to decide its verdict.

Let's say that the alleged killer was high on cocaine at the time of the homicide. I'd need to get the jury to realize that being high is not an extenuating circumstance—a red herring that I could be sure the defense would use. So I'd say to my jury, "This is a case about an innocent woman who died while waiting at a traffic light, defending her daughter when a man tried to steal her car with her child still in it. Ladies and gentlemen, this is a federal case of kidnapping and murder." Then I could declare my goal: "I am seeking a first-degree conviction."

No Excuses . . .

I have faced many defendants whose attorneys stood behind a theory of the case called the "Twinkie Defense." This theory tries to throw the jury off the trail by blaming the client's bad actions on something else—he ate too many Twinkies, for instance, and was on a sugar high when he killed/robbed/raped/molested and is therefore not responsible for his actions. In prosecuting against the Twinkie Defense, my position would have to appeal to common sense: "This is a case about individual responsibility—not trying to hide behind excuses. The defendant (not a Twinkie, drugs, or his bad mood) killed/robbed/raped/molested his victim."

The Culture Defense is also pervasive. I covered a case for Lifetime Television in which a California woman, originally from India, tried to drown her two young children because her husband was going to leave her for another woman. According to the defense's theory of the case, her motivation to murder was that her shame was too great because, in India, blame for a failed marriage falls on the woman. The way the prosecutor countered the defense and positioned his theory of the case, however, the jury would have been condoning murder had they done anything but issue a guilty verdict. The defense's red herrings were met with an impossible hurdle: Murdering your children should not be accepted in any culture.

How Irresponsible . . .

You may have heard of recent cases against tobacco companies for heightening nicotine levels in their products in order to increase addiction, or against the Ford Company for being aware of the dangers of the Pinto model's exploding gas tanks ("smoking-gun" documents proved they knew) but deciding to pay off settlements rather than change the design of their car. In both cases the companies effectively decided to take a roll of the dice, figuring it would be cheaper to pay damages to injured or aggrieved people rather than do the right thing and fix the product. And in both cases prosecutors relied on the concept of corporate responsibility in their theories of the case, appealing to each juror's concept of fairness and justice.

Don't Judge a Book by Its Cover . . .

When I took on the prosecution of a middle-class, attractive, white nursing student accused of hiring a hit man to take out her boyfriend's ex-wife, I faced an uphill battle. I knew some things about her that were inadmissible in court: When she was a young girl, she had seen her mother shot and killed by her father, for example; in addition, she had gone on to drown a cousin and a child she was babysitting (on two separate occasions). But under Oregon law the record of those murders was expunged when she turned eighteen, and she was now working at the local YMCA—teaching swimming lessons! My objective was to get her convicted, get her some psychological help, and get her away from swimming pools without referencing her previous killings.

My theory of the case had to convince a jury that beneath the cutie-pie facade of this sweet nursing student lay a sociopath who had hired a killer and fed him her homemade pasta salad while instructing him to make the killing of her boyfriend's ex-wife look like a drug deal gone bad. She gave the assassin a silencer and told him to fire two shots into the ex's head—and if their little boy was there, "to kill him, too."

Limited by my inability to use prior crimes, I made my theory of the case easy for the jury to remember: "*The book is not the cover*—beneath the surface, this defendant is a cold, calculating killer." I underlined this theme throughout the trial with the evidence of taped conversations and witness testimony regarding her uncontrollable Dr. Jekyll–Mr. Hyde temper. Although the judge and jury wanted to like her, in the end they saw her for what she was—a cold-blooded killer who had to be stopped—and sentenced her to fifteen years in a federal penitentiary.

Keep It Simple . . .

I once prosecuted a complicated white-collar fraud case that involved countless pages of paper proving that a man who owned a travel agency had bilked hundreds of people out of a lot of money. He preyed on Catholic priests and their parishioners by promising trips to the Holy Land and on World War II veterans by promising trips to Japan and Germany, neither of which ever materialized.

Rather than centering my theory of the case on the extensive, complicated paper trail, I focused it simply on the people who'd had their life savings stolen from them. "This is a case about the defendant's *betrayal of trust*. He took advantage of innocent people's hopes, dreams, and memories by having them invest their life savings in trips that he never delivered."

Though I would use selected parts from the mountains of documents as supporting evidence, I wanted the jurors to keep their minds on the stories of the individuals who had been defrauded. I kept my theme clear and easy to remember—a betrayal of trust—by persistently relying on the personal devastation this crook had inflicted on individuals (rather than the confusing mire of dates, amounts, travel documents, and destinations). By continually coming back to my theme of betrayal of trust, rather than getting bogged down by the paper trail, I convinced my jurors and clinched the case.

Just the Facts, Ma'am . . .

In the courtroom (as in life), when red herrings make you lose sight of your theory of the case, you generally lose the trail—and the trial. Perhaps this is most evident in the way in which the O. J. Simpson prosecutors lost their theory of the case, getting sidetracked for months by DNA evidence. Their theory of the case was that "Mr. Simpson, in a rage, killed his ex-wife and her friend, and what proves it is—he left his fingerprint." It was consistent with the evidence.

Unfortunately, the prosecutors committed sins that most first-year law students would have avoided—in front of a jury that wasn't very sympathetic to begin with—by trying to make the jury experts in the science of DNA. What they could have done with two quick witnesses—one to give a *Reader's Digest* version of what DNA is (two hours max) and the other a summary witness to analyze Simpson's DNA at the scene (an afternoon at most)—took months.

It was preposterous that this case could disintegrate to the point of prosecutors requesting the defendant to put on a glove, without knowing whether it would fit or not. The jury lost focus when the prosecution lost sight of its theory of the case. And I was shocked after the acquittal when Marcia Clark told the world that she'd prepared her rebuttal the night before presenting it. As an experienced trial lawyer, she should have determined her position and her closing argument—her theory of the case—months before the trial. Had she started with that, perhaps the outcome would have been different.

As the prosecutor, it was her job to establish her theory of the case from beginning to end, not wing it by responding only to what the defense had done. If she had remembered that everything flows from the theory of the case, she would not have been sidetracked by DNA and the glove debacle. Without following a defined goal, she was on the defensive, rather than the offensive—and that's suicide for prosecutors, who bear the burden of proof. The defense changed its theory of the case, its chorus, to "If it doesn't fit, you must acquit." The defense "Dream Team" was able to change—and strengthen—its theory of the case because the prosecution had gone off on the trail of smelly red herrings.

Real Life. Real Theories. Real Important.

Real life often presents situations in which the theory of the case is far less cut and dried than it is in the courtroom—which makes fleshing out Step 1 crucial to a successful result. Ellen, a college friend of mine who works for a small telecommunications firm, was told by her boss that the company's disastrous financial condition required that she share her formerly full-time assistant with a coworker. Ellen resisted the urge to go to her boss and say, *It's clear that you don't respect my work*—even though she felt that was true—or, *This move will sabotage the company further because it will slow our billing turnaround to molasses.* Instead she took this setback as the opportunity to establish her theory of a winning case: that the company needed to outsource its billing to release employees from unproductive tasks.

She made that case and won—the billing is now outsourced, and Ellen's happiness and productivity have increased exponentially.

A work-related issue might actually have to do with greater job efficiency, or a new job title you have wanted for a long time. If you can set aside your emotional reactions (or use them positively) and forget the extraneous issues that can sometimes seem like the real issue (your boss forgot to invite you to his departmental barbecue), like Ellen, you might find yourself getting exactly what you want.

Establishing your theory of the case is vital not only in work dealings and business and consumer negotiations (you don't want Sprint PCS to apologize—you want a new phone) but also in your personal affairs. And given the complex psychological and emotional framework that most of us bring to our friendships, romances, and parenting, it is painfully easy to be distracted from the true nature of our case and the goals we really seek.

Megan, one of the mothers in my daughter's play group, was angry that her husband twice forgot to pick up their little girl, Charlotte, from day care. The second time it happened, she was livid; her first inclination was to bite her husband's head off and, as she put it, "prove his general uselessness as a human being." But Megan decided that rather than lashing out at her husband, she'd take a long walk around the neighborhood and think about what the real issues were.

After a few deep breaths, Megan realized that her goal wasn't to belittle her husband. Though it would be momentarily satisfying, she knew it would do neither of them any long-term good and certainly wouldn't be beneficial to Charlotte. It also wasn't to save face with the day care workers, or to fret over the late-pickup charges she had to pay. When she really thought about it, her case wasn't about Charlotte being left waiting at day care at all, as heinous as that was.

The real issue was that the level of communication between her and her husband had deteriorated to such a level that their life together had become one big frustration. Megan returned to the house knowing what was really going to make the difference. She had her theory of the case—that she and her husband needed to discuss their respective roles and duties as parents. When they sat down together and she stated her theory, her husband didn't launch into his litany of excuses. There was no *You told me the wrong time* or *You didn't remind me*, and she was surprised he didn't once pull out his old favorite, *It's not my fault*. Instead, he said, "You're right."

The conversation led Megan and her husband to seek couples counseling, where they learned to better communicate. They've developed a more equitable, balanced, and reliable relationship—and therefore created a more harmonious home for Charlotte.

Sometimes You're Just Plain Wrong

Developing your theory of the case is about focusing on a desired goal. We all want and deserve fairness and justice, so I'm assuming that you want to win your case because it's fair and right, but sometimes you may realize you're just flat-out wrong.

My brother, Christopher, reminded me recently of such a story—a time when our dad, in the interest of fairness and justice, helped Christopher realize his theory was wrong. Today Chris is a successful actor—currently starring on ESPN's *Playmaker* and a regular on CBS's *CSI*—but when he was nineteen he got into a little trouble. On a winter break from college, he and three friends dropped by our hometown of Yakima in eastern Washington State before heading off for some skiing in Sun Valley, Idaho.

After having a bit of "fun" and too much to drink, the foursome was pulled over while weaving down a back road and cited for "MIP" (minor in possession) and "MUC" (minor under consumption). Christopher's retort went something like, "M . . . O . . . U . . . S . . . E." The officer dropped them off at the house and told them to be in court promptly at nine o'clock the following morning to face the charges. That sobered him and his friends up a bit; still, they figured they had a "get out of jail free" card since our dad had been practicing law in this small town for thirty years, and our grandfather was an esteemed retired judge in Yakima. All the judges and attorneys knew our family, so Christopher was sure the fix would be in to get him off.

The next morning Chris and his friends (still a bit hung over) packed their bags and put their skis on the roof rack, working on the theory that they'd make it to Sun Valley by noon and be on the slopes by early afternoon. They'd be in another state laughing about this minor inconvenience they had put behind them.

That morning the courtroom was packed. There were many cases to be heard in front of this municipal judge, but as Chris figured would happen, the judge waved to our dad and said, "Richard, why don't you come on up first and get your case over with." Chris was delighted. What could be better? The judge was on a first-name basis with our dad. Their case would be over and done with first. He could almost feel the snow under his skis.

My dad, my brother, and his friends approached the judge. "Richard," the judge asked, "what happened here?"

"Good morning, Judge," Dad, their advocate, began. "My son and his friends—" Pause. "—are complete idiots—" Pause. "—and deserve a night in jail." It went downhill from there. Chris turned as white as the snow he wasn't going to be skiing on. The bailiff escorted them out of the courtroom to spend twenty-four hours in the clink.

Now my family laughs about this story. Thankfully, it was my brother's only brush with the law. My dad's theory of the case was that Christopher needed to learn a lesson about taking responsibility for his actions and not expecting to always be bailed out when he was wrong. Certainly Dad could have "advocated" for my brother and made a case that might have gotten him off, but, knowing the law in Washington, he knew these circumstances would not leave my brother with a criminal record, and realized that a night in jail in the short term might prevent Christopher from repeating his mistake in the long run. As my dad constantly reminded us, it's better to be right by admitting you're wrong.

In times when you're wrong, you may be tempted to use a theory of the case that my friend in the FBI refers to as "Deny, deny, deny, demand proof, and make counterallegations." If the facts aren't for you, argue the law; if the law isn't for you, attack the other side's tactics. In other words:

- You didn't see what you said you saw.
- If you did see what you said you saw, you didn't see me.
- If you did see me, I wasn't there.
- If I was there, I didn't know what I was doing so I really wasn't "there" at all.

I heard the story of a lawyer defending a man accused of burglary who tried this creative defense: "My client merely inserted his arm into the window and removed a few trifling articles. His arm is not himself, and I fail to see how you can punish the whole individual for an offense committed by his limb."

"Well put," the judge replied. "Using your logic, I sentence the defendant's arm to one year's imprisonment. He can accompany it or not, as he chooses."

The defendant smiled. And with his lawyer's assistance, he detached his artificial limb, laid it on the bench, and walked out.

These, however, are all legal maneuverings. They are not theories on which to base your life decisions. Yes, you can occasionally use tactics to get away with something, but the questions you have to ask yourself are: *Is it worth it in the end? Will I feel good about the victory?* If the facts and the morality of the situation aren't really in your favor, it's time to get off your high horse and admit you're wrong. Happiness is a by-product of achieving a just result, not achieving a desired result at the cost of justice.

Is your real theory of the case to "win" at all costs? Are you acting like a defense lawyer by pulling out all the stops and arguing alternative theories of the case, knowing that not all of the theories can be truthful or right? Or is it to maybe lose the fight, but keep a friend, seek forgiveness, or be a better employee? Only you know the answer.

My hope is that the Eight Steps will be your tools to gain confidence, overcome challenges, and face life's obstacles with a plan and a smile.

Work Through It

Your theory of the case might not be immediately apparent to you—but figuring it out could open new possibilities for effective advocacy. Taking the time to thoughtfully consider *What is this about?* and *What do I really want?* will lay the groundwork for a win.

For Jennifer—my paralegal friend who got the bad performance review—getting to her theory of the case was quite difficult. Jennifer's history with an overbearing father who discouraged her from standing up for herself made it hard for her to pinpoint her theory of the case.

1. We Determined Her Position

At first, Jennifer decided she didn't want to say anything. She'd rather accept a bad review than cause any trouble within the firm.

She hoped that if she ignored the bad review, it would go away and no one would be the wiser. I pointed out that the review would always be in her file, and would be consulted for pay increases or could be used as the basis for termination. Then she suggested that I go speak to the partners about Michelle, but I pointed out that this could easily backfire—Michelle would then just dislike her even more.

"What is it you want?" I asked.

"I want to know why Michelle gave me a negative review. What was it based on?"

"There, that's your position!" I congratulated her.

2. We Avoided Red Herrings

Jennifer's initial inclination was to doubt herself and believe that the negative evaluation was merited. She couldn't stop crying and asking, "What's wrong with me?" and "How could I be better?"

Then tears turned to anger and her emotions clouded her judgment: "Michelle obviously doesn't know what she's talking about. I'm going to take this to a partner myself." But making an enemy out of her supervisor would do nothing for her case and would likely lead to further problems. Jennifer ultimately realized that questioning Michelle's overall competence was a red herring she should absolutely avoid.

3. We Defined Her Goal

Jennifer needed to stand up for herself without venting her anger and frustration at Michelle, and hopefully get Michelle to reevaluate Jennifer's effectiveness as a paralegal.

So her theory of the case became: "I'm good at what I do . . . so I need to know, first, how this review came about, and second, how to get it changed."

Once she had her theory down—that she was doing a good job, so she needed to know why her evaluation did not reflect this—Jennifer was ready to move forward with her case and get what she wanted.

It's About You

What is your case? And what is your theory of it? Is it a bigger position at your job? Is it a better relationship? Or is it just getting your doctor to see you on time? Once you've determined what you want, identified the red herrings, and defined your goal, make sure it's worded as clearly as a *TV Guide* show synopsis: *An ill-fated ship's survivors are marooned on a desolate island and must deal with setting up a society while looking for a way home.*

Now imagine a herd of reporters gathered on the courthouse steps waiting to pounce on you and riddle you with questions. "What do you have to say about this case?" one of them shouts, shoving her microphone into your face. Are you ready to answer? If you can't state it in a fifteen-second sound bite, it's probably not honed enough. (I've been given less time by judges to tell them why my case needs to be sent to a jury.)

Your theory of the case is your home base. When it's secure, you're ready to carry the case forward.

SKILLS OF A LAWYER FOR THE TRIALS OF YOUR LIFE

LEGAL BRIEF: STEP 1

THE THEORY

1. Determine your position.
   a. What is the broad, general situation, or conflict, you are experiencing?
   b. What was the chain of events that led to the situation?
   c. This is about what?

2. Avoid red herrings.

a. What angers, saddens, or frightens you about the situation?

b. What is this situation *not* about?

c. List the red herrings.

3. Define your goal.

a. What is the realistic outcome you want to achieve here?

b. Now, what's your theory of the case?

c. What is the theme you can use to drive this theory home?

Chapter 2

Step 2. Choose and Cultivate
Your Audience: *Voir Dire*

> *There are tricks of the trade that will help you shape your case based on what you know about the people you're dealing with.*

Perhaps it was the O. J. Simpson case that finally brought to light what trial lawyers have known all along: Who gets selected for the jury can decide the outcome of a case before the opening statements even begin. We all are a package of personal experiences and history, including factors such as our race, gender, religion, sexual orientation, and economic background. It would be naive to say that these experiences don't inform who we are. When lawyers are selecting jurors from the jury pool, they are looking for the people whom they think will be most receptive to their side's evidence. When you're trying to make a case in your personal or professional life, being sure that your audience, or "juror," has the power and predilection to help you is just as important.

In the Simpson case, the defense picked a jury from a pool of mostly African Americans, whom they hoped would be sympathetic to their theory of the case: that Mr. Simpson was the victim of law enforcement's rush to judgment because he was African American. When the jury was picked, the defense lawyers were able to put their celebrity defendant in the hands of nine African Americans, two whites, and one Hispanic, trusting that a predominantly black Los Angeles jury would hold resentment for law enforcement and acquit their client.

Since Simpson was charged in Los Angeles County rather than the white, upper-middle-class neighborhood of Brentwood, the jury pool was largely African American. Prosecutor Marcia Clark knew that no matter how many people she struck during voir dire, she was still going to have a jury sympathetic to an attractive African American sports star. And indeed, the jury ultimately consisted of people who, at one time in their life, had themselves perceived racial bias in the LAPD, or had heard firsthand accounts of racist behavior from friends or family. And O. J.'s lawyers skillfully exploited this racial mistrust.

Putting aside whether you think Simpson killed his wife or not, you have to appreciate his counsel's rapport with the jury. It was as if Johnnie Cochran were having the jurors over for a cookout in his backyard. He joked. They laughed. He was warm. They responded. He struck a balance between probing and listening. And that balance won his case.

*   *   *

In the courtroom, the judge and jury begin in theory as impartial participants, but from the moment they walk into the room, lawyers are trying to sway them to their side—to get them to sympathize with, and be persuaded by, their theory of the case. In real life, however, you may not always have a mediator available, or a jury of your peers may not be appropriate. In many cases your judge or jury might be the very person with whom you have a conflict, such as your boss, spouse, or the plumber. And if you're in a fight with your spouse, it's not really appropriate to call your neighbor over for a cup of coffee—and *oh, by the way, could you act as our judge and preside over the airing of our dirty laundry?*

Still, even though you can't always select your "jurors" in the trials of your life, there are certain tricks of the trade practiced in the courtroom that will help you work successfully with the jurors you are dealing with and pull them to your side.

Voir Dire 101

If you've ever served jury duty, you've been involved in the judicial process of *voir dire*—a French term meaning "to see and say"—in which prosecutors and defense attorneys interview prospective jury members about their beliefs, opinions, jobs, and life experiences. Each side wants to help win the case by choosing a jury made up of certain types of people—those whom it believes will favor its case.

In court the defense and the prosecution are allowed to eliminate, or "strike," jurors from the jury pool with either "peremptory" or "for cause" challenges. Both sides get an unlimited number of "for cause" strikes, but only if they prove to the judge that there is a reason why a potential juror should not be on a jury. The lawyers have to show that the potential juror has a bias against their side—a bias that would not allow the juror to keep an open mind in hearing the case. For example, if a juror knows someone involved in the case, or if the victim in a rape case is the same age as a juror's daughter who has also been raped, there would be "cause." It is the lawyer's burden to ask the questions of potential jurors that convince the judge that a potential juror has such biases.

Defense attorney Mickey Sherman told me that during the voir dire for the Michael Skakel trial (the trial of the Kennedy cousin accused of bludgeoning his neighbor to death with a golf club when he was a teenager), he realized that most of the prospective jurors wanted to be on the case, which is not unusual for the "big trials." One juror in the original pool was an airline flight attendant who was, in his interpretation, "rather arrogant." She knew of the case, had read a lot about it, and thought Skakel was probably guilty, but said she could "try real hard" to be impartial. The judge, upon Mickey's challenge for cause, said the juror should not be excused for cause since she could be fair—she'd declared that she would "try real hard" to be impartial.

He asked permission from the court to ask her one more question. "Ms. Prospective Juror," he posed, "suppose I'm a passenger on your flight to London and, just as in the movie *Airplane!,* the pilots get sick from food poisoning and can't land the plane. Let's say I raise my hand and volunteer to land the plane. I've never flown a plane before, but *'I'll try real hard.'* Would that be okay with you?" She never got to answer. The judge excused her for cause.

In a peremptory challenge, lawyers aren't required to give any reason why they are striking the potential juror: they need only state that they are excusing the person from duty. Each side can use its set number of peremptory challenges just by telling the judge that "The defense"—or the prosecution—"would like to thank and excuse Juror Number 3." Typically, a prosecutor gets three such peremptories and the defense can get five, so attorneys have to be very careful how they use them. I used peremptory strikes prosecuting a rape case to remove two older women whom I felt might be too judgmental, but kept several of the older male jurors, guessing that they might see the victim as their daughter/wife/sister and would feel protective of her. It was a good use of my peremptories. The rapist is now behind bars.

Good Picking

Selecting the jury is one of a lawyer's most challenging tasks. It's a tightrope act, balancing the need to dig for information with the need not to offend, while carrying the burden of the law. Remember, jurors are the ultimate decision makers. They hold the fate of a client or cause in their collective hands, and they will operate as a patchwork family (hopefully a not-too-dysfunctional one) to come to a decision.

Every living, breathing person has biases, opinions, and life experiences that inform the decision-making process. We lawyers want to find people whose biases and life experiences make them more prone to buying our side of the story. So we need to ask the questions designed to elicit information about these biases without distancing the potential juror from our side.

If I see from the jury questionnaire that a potential juror dropped out of high school before graduation, but has a GED, I would not ask the embarrassing: "Why did you drop out of high school?" (Translation: You are dumb.) Instead, I'd ask: "What's the process you go through to get a GED?" My aim is to get information, not back people into a corner. If I question someone's work history knowing he was probably fired, I don't ask, "Why were you fired?" (Translation: You can't keep a job.) Instead, I ask, "I see you worked for Acme? How was that experience?" I want to determine whether the person has an attitude, or trouble with authority or deadlines, not to alienate him. The answers to these types of questions will give me a good, quick read on someone.

When I question a homemaker with, say, three kids, I must realize that she may feel alienated from a workingwoman lawyer. I always say something like, "My two kids have such different personalities and characteristics. Tell me about your three. Are their personalities different from each other?" (Translation: I'm a mom, too.)

In voir dire, I don't want to alienate or embarrass potential jurors—these people might end up on the jury, and even if they don't, the other jurors are watching. I always remind my students at the University of Washington Law School that at least one of the jurors will be watching you at any given time. At the back of all trial lawyers' minds is the knowledge that they can blow the case before it has even begun by picking the wrong jury. In order to end up with a jury that favors their theory, trial attorneys must have a clear vision of their case and the issues to be discussed during selection.

During voir dire, an attorney must not fall victim to generalizations and stereotyping, which can generally and stereotypically lead to trouble. In Seattle, where I worked as a federal prosecutor, the white, middle-aged Boeing engineers who often show up in jury pools have been branded as notoriously difficult jurors for the prosecution. As a general rule, engineers are very precise and almost mechanical in their application of law and facts. They demand an often unattainable level of proof to convict a defendant. But beware of generalizations.

In a criminal drug case I prosecuted with a young African American male defendant, I saw that the defense lawyer was eager to keep several older African American working people on the jury. He incorrectly generalized that African Americans would be more sympathetic to a member of their own race. Boy, was he wrong. The defendant was convicted on all counts, and leading the pack were the older jurors whom the lawyer thought he'd had in his back pocket.

I did not object to these jury members because I had a hunch that their life experience was not just about being African American; it was about working hard all their lives for the American dream and believing that hard work would lead them to a good life. Their experiences of coming home to a neighborhood filled with young people doing drugs and seeing the devastating effect the drugs (and dealers) had on their American dream led them to be angrier than any of their white counterparts on the jury. They had seen firsthand what havoc people like the defendant had inflicted upon their own neighborhoods and families; their anger with people like the defendant led them to side with my case. It was a successful result because in voir dire I looked beyond my knee-jerk reactions and generalizations about where jurors' first loyalties would lie.

In selecting people to support your case, it is necessary to avoid tunnel vision. Being inflexible about what you think you want is just as dangerous as generalizing and making false assumptions.

In prosecuting a white-collar criminal case that involved an extensive paper trail, I incorrectly assumed that a man with a PhD in economics would sympathize with my case because of his high level of education. In a trial that involved numbers, money changing hands, and fraud, I thought this man would be able to guide the other members of the jury through the complicated intricacies.

I was so tickled at the prospect of getting this guy on the jury that I didn't do my voir dire job well. Had I questioned him more about his own personal history, I would have learned that he had a poor credit rating because he often "forgot" to pay his bills. This from an economist. What I realized later is that, although he was well educated, the guy just didn't have any common sense. Had I asked the correct questions, I would have known this and kept him off the jury. My tunnel vision told me that an economist would be beneficial, and it kept me from seeing the reality of his character. Luckily, I got the conviction, but only after the other jurors educated him about the case.

I have found that in the courtroom, as in life, you've got to surround yourself with people imbued with common sense—that's more important than the number of diplomas on their wall. After all, they may misplace the diplomas, but they carry their common sense with them wherever they go. These are the people you want in your corner.

And let's be honest. We lawyers say we are trying to find a fair and impartial jury panel, but that's not really true. No trial attorney wants to end up with an impartial juror. I want a juror who's biased in my favor and receptive to the issues I'm going to present.

The First Date

Voir dire is like going on a first date—you want to find out as much as you can about your date in a short amount of time so that you can figure out whether you want to see the person again. If you've ever been on a first date, you know it's more of an interview than a fun event. You want to get your date to like you and have a sense of what you're about, but you don't want to be off-putting with a bunch of nosy questions. Think about the last bad first date you were on. You formed an impression very quickly, probably within seconds of your first conversation.

Just as everything someone does on a first date is noticed, everything lawyers do and say during voir dire conveys a message. You notice if your date is on time, well dressed, has any nervous habits, is nice to the waiter, and has clean fingernails. Similarly, in the courtroom, from the time the panel is brought in, they are studying the lawyers and the participants with a keen interest. Just as on a date, while the lawyers are picking the jurors, the jurors are picking the lawyer whom they like and trust.

The trial attorney's three purposes of voir dire are quite similar to the goals of a first date (and to yours for your personal case):

1. You want to present yourself in the best light.
2. You need to learn about your date's (the juror's) beliefs and attitudes.
3. You must familiarize your date (juror) with the facts about you and your issues (facts of the case and legal matters that may arise).

Present

First, you want to make a good impression, while also being (and trying not to look) overly conscious of each move your date, the juror, makes. You want to be yourself—your best self—sharing something that makes you real without showing vulnerabilities and insecurities. The first date is not the time to share the story of how you had a messy divorce and are still fighting over the furniture. Though this is your real self, it's probably a little *too* real to help you move to the second date.

Fresh out of law school, in my early years as a federal prosecutor, I watched as potential jurors realized the young woman behind the table was actually the lawyer. I could tell that many of them thought, *There's no way she's going to convince us.* But I did. And I think I did it by being true to my own voice, my personal theory of the case, and by not trying to be something I wasn't—a big tough guy.

I became sister, daughter, granddaughter to many of the jurors, not by pandering, but by saying, "I will tell you what I know, and I think you will agree with my theory of the case." I never was manipulative or self-serving by proclaiming to a jury, *I'm honest,* or *Just trust me,* but I would say with confidence and sincerity, "I will not tell you anything I don't believe to be true," or "I will present the facts of this case as clearly as possible."

During my first case, I was so scared that my knees were knocking during voir dire. So I told the jury pool: "I have to confess that my knees are knocking because this is my first trial. But it is important that justice be done. I promise to deliver the evidence, if you promise to listen to it."

I've learned that in picking a jury, as in picking someone to listen to you in life, the focus should be on getting people to respect and have empathy for you. You get honest answers by creating a comfortable environment and revealing something about yourself before asking others to do the same.

Learn

Second, you want to be a good listener. If you're doing all the talking, you're never going to find out about your new acquaintance. Dates want to share information about themselves, if you let them.

You don't want the night to be over and not know anything about your date because you haven't listened. If you are someone whose dream in life is to be a father of three, and your date admits to not wanting to ever have kids, that's valuable information. Just as if a juror says she could never vote for the death penalty in a death penalty case, that's something I need to know.

Voir dire is the only time during a trial that lawyers can have a dialogue directly with jurors. It is the opportunity to find out who they are, how they feel, and how they can help your case. When it's time to select jurors, I want to know as much as I can about them, but still ask only six or so questions. From the jury questionnaires, I know their gender, their sex, their race, their age, and maybe their occupation. From there, my task is to ask a few questions that tell me whether or not they are going to see the validity of my case.

To accomplish this, I ask open-ended questions to elicit narrative responses rather than yes or no. After I ask the question, I listen to the answer. I don't just go mechanically from one question to the next. It's not about asking the question, it's about discovering something from the answer. I remember a case where my co-counsel was nervous during a witness exam and asked a man what date his birthday was. The man couldn't remember, but my co-counsel continued asking questions as if the man had answered. The fact that my colleague didn't hear that the man couldn't remember his birthday indicated to me that we needed to back up and clarify a few things.

I then ask follow-up questions based on what I've heard. "Sir, you just said that you have never been on a jury. Have you wanted to be picked before and not been picked, or have you just gotten lucky and never been called?" By picking up on what the person has said, I'm showing that I care, and moving the ball forward with another question based on the answer. The trial advocacy term for this is *looping*—linking the next question to the answer the person has just given. "After you saw the driver of the blue car hit the woman, what happened next?"

I always ask a prospective juror, "Anything I should know about you that I haven't thought of?" This has brought responses such as:

- "My sister/daughter/mother/wife was raped."
- "I was once accused of murder and acquitted."
- "I was once beaten up by a cop and believe nothing they say."
- "I am dying of cancer, so I might not be here for the whole trial."
- "We went out in high school, but you don't remember me."

Familiarize

And finally, if on a first date you pretend to be someone you're not, it's not going to serve either party in the future. If you have a two-pack-a-day habit and pretend you hate smoking, it's not going to help either of you when the truth comes out that you smoke like a chimney. The same is true in court. If there were drugs in my client's system and I don't address drugs with the jury during voir dire, it will come back to bite me later and do nothing but hurt my case.

People don't like to be kept in the dark about what's going on. Jurors want to know what the case is all about, so if they aren't given some of the highlights during voir dire to familiarize them with the case at hand, they will use their imaginations to fill in the blanks.

Who, What, When, Where, Why, and How

Most of us seldom stop to ask if we can select—or affect—the person who will hear our case, who will act as our juror. But in work and consumer negotiations—where you may have to deal with a higher-up on the job, talk to a salesclerk's supervisor, or get a broker to give you the best rate on a mortgage—you can often ascertain which of the potential arbiters of your case will be the most receptive and sympathetic. Even in situations where you can't choose your juror—say, dealing with your spouse or kids—you can still shape your case based on what you know will work best with your audience.

- *Who* is your juror?
- *What* should you ask?
- *When* should you make your case?
- *Where*?
- *Why* are you making it?
- And last, *how* should you act?

Who

In any situation, whether it be in the courtroom or in your dentist's office, you need to ask and answer the question, *Who is most likely to give me what I want?* Often you can choose your juror in a conflict. We could be talking about which school administrator you want to deal with about your child's problem in school or which guy at the transmission shop you want to talk to about your car being screwed up by his employees.

As you prepare your case, you can perform your own voir dire and assess your potential jurors to see who might be biased against you. Who might possess ulterior motives or become easily provoked or confrontational? Who would respond rigidly or illogically? If you stop to think about the jurors available, you might find that someone lacks the authority to give you the outcome you want. Find someone better to hear your case.

In a work conflict, for example, it may be more effective to go to your human resources manager if you know your supervisor is going to give you an unsatisfactory response, even if you worry that you are going over her head. You always have the right to make an appeal, just as a lawyer can appeal to a higher court. We all do this sort of thing when we ask to speak to a service representative's supervisor when we get an unsatisfactory response. This same strategy can be used in many areas of our lives, whether at home, in the classroom, or at work.

Even when you think you can't choose your juror, there may still be options. Each year, Darlene, Don, and their two kids took a two-week vacation with Don's family to stay in a rental house on the New England coast. Because they were on a limited budget, it was Darlene and Don's one vacation each year. Their kids loved it because they got to play with all their cousins at the beach, and it also meant a lot to Don's family to have them come.

Darlene's dilemma was Don's large family. Though she knew it was important for Don and the kids to spend time with his family, all of them being under one roof for two weeks was a little overwhelming, especially since it was their one and only vacation for the year. She tried to approach Don about doing something else without his family, but he was greatly insulted that she would even suggest it, and the discussion quickly led to a dead-end argument. Darlene desperately wanted to spend quality time with Don. She felt it was important for their marriage, because his work schedule had become so hectic. She had to appeal to someone in Don's family to help her, without insulting the family or their generosity. But whom?

She ruled out Don's mother. The two of them had never quite seen eye to eye. Darlene was slightly overweight, and Don's mother always seemed to be judging her; several times she'd made comments about the "pretty girls" Don had dated in high school. Darlene concluded she couldn't get an impartial hearing from her mother-in-law. Don's older sister was a possibility in that she had a strong voice in the family and liked Darlene, but she wouldn't want Don and Darlene not to come because she counted on their kids to keep her kids occupied for the two weeks. Don's younger sister and two brothers wielded no power in the family, so even if they agreed with her, what good would it do?

Darlene chose her father-in-law. They shared similar senses of humor, they always had good talks, and he regularly remarked how great a wife she was to Don and how wonderful a mother she was to their two kids. She decided to call him on a Thursday night, when she knew Don's mother went to her garden club meeting. "Hi, Dad," she said, and then got right to her theory of the case: "I was hoping I could get you to help me figure out how I could spend some quality time with Don during our vacation this year."

The conversation was a success. She chose the right juror to entrust with her case. Don's father came up with a brilliant idea and subsequently shared it with his wife, then helped Darlene put it into action. That year, and every year since, Don and Darlene's kids fly out the first week by themselves, and Don and Darlene join them and the family for the second week. This leaves everyone happy. Don's parents love having a week with their grandkids all to themselves, and Don's sister still gets to have her kids distracted by their cousins. Don and Darlene's kids love flying by themselves and seem to be more responsible for having been allowed that independence. Most of all, Don and Darlene get to take a romantic week by themselves—one year they stayed in a cheap motel and hung out by the pool, another they went camping, and last year they stayed at a bed-and-breakfast at Niagara Falls—joining the family later for a week together.

By picking the right juror, Darlene made and won her case.

* * *

Sometimes you may realize that you've picked the wrong juror. What should you do then? Back in the late-1980s, when I had just graduated from law school and was working in corporate law, AIDS was still a relatively new disease, and I wanted to do something for the people whose lives were being forever altered when they tested positive for the virus. I thought I could do the most by volunteering to draft wills for AIDS patients, in order to give those who couldn't afford to hire a lawyer at least a sense of dignity in death. But wills weren't my area of specialty, so I decided to ask a trust and estate lawyer in the firm to help me out.

My first inclination was to go to the senior partner in the firm for help, but when I broached the subject he said, "Well, I'm okay with it, but there may be others in the firm who would want to burn your furniture after you have one of *those people* in your office." I realized immediately that I had chosen the wrong juror. He was obviously couching his own feelings, so I said, "I hadn't thought of that kind of reaction. I'd better give this some more consideration."

In rethinking my idea, I asked myself who would be more receptive. I realized that someone like me, recently out of school, might think a little more progressively and be more willing to help me (and others) out. So I approached a new hire in the trust and estate department and explained my idea, my theory of the case. He told me he'd love to be involved. Together we set up a program that within five years was firm-wide, and is still up and running today. I started out by picking the wrong juror, but in realizing my error, I tactfully decided to look elsewhere rather than getting into an unnecessary philosophical debate that would have done nothing to further my goal.

* * *

Sometimes you aren't able to choose your juror—you can't exactly appeal to a different child to clean up his room—but you can customize your strategy by taking into account your juror's temperament, situation, or attitudes. Just as prosecutors and defense attorneys tailor their tone and delivery, so you can customize your case to suit your audience.

When evaluating your juror, consider using the types of evaluation techniques that a defense attorney might use to determine whether this is someone who may be sympathetic. Defense lawyers look for signs or "tells" in the behavior of a prospective juror that often let them know how the individual may feel about the case, the client, or the lawyer.

Some of these signs are very basic, others a bit more subtle. Does the "juror" look at you or does she look down or past you? Avoiding direct eye contact is often a sign that someone really doesn't want to hear or really care about what you have to say. Does your juror physically react as you speak? Does he, for example, smile at you? It's often a defense attorney's goal to make a juror actually nod her head in agreement to questions. That's not necessarily the surest way to learn someone's disposition, but it is a start. Certainly, if the person looks at you as if you have leprosy, it's not a good sign.

What is he reading or what is on his desk? Does he have pictures of his children or wife? Do these visual cues provide for you any commonality, something to talk about?

Whom do you want your juror to judge? You? Someone else? That makes a big difference in your selection process. If your child did something inappropriate, you want a juror who has children so that she can appreciate the predicaments and variety of situations kids find themselves in. If you want lower phone rates, you might select three jurors—a customer service supervisor at each of the largest phone companies.

Throughout this process, keep in mind that jurors cannot be fooled easily. Juries sniff out fakery instantly, and so do children, coworkers, bosses, and rental car representatives. You ought to assume that your juror is not stupid. Don't insult his intelligence by making absurd claims or statements. Being polite is helpful, but sucking up can be both nauseating and totally ineffective.

What

Once you've set your sights on the juror whom you believe is most likely to give you what you want, what do you say or ask to convince him to be your advocate? I have found that with my ten-year-old son Jacob, praise works better than beseeching or ordering him to do something. By positively approaching what I ask him, I get better results. As you phrase your questions, remember that most adults are like children in that we respond better to praise than to direct criticism—*if* the praise is honestly delivered and not overly manipulative.

If you plan your questions carefully *before* you begin your discussion with your juror, you will be comfortable enough to depart from your prepared questions if issues pop up that need further illumination. People who appear as if they are winging it are really just well prepared. I always have my questions written down, even though I don't actually read from my list. Writing them down reinforces them in my mind and also allows me to be less concerned with them and more concerned with the juror's answers and the body language she exhibits while conveying those answers.

The open-ended question allows the answerer to chat. This type of question invites the juror to say what's really on his mind because it doesn't suggest what you think the answer should be. For example, rather than asking a job applicant, "Will you commit to us for at least two years?" you might ask, "Where do you see yourself in five years?" And similarly, questions like, "I think I'd like to have a big family. How about you?" indicate the answer that would make you happy and tend to yield a less-than-honest answer from your juror, in this case a potential spouse. "What do you see your life like in ten years?" might be more illuminating.

Asking a juror, "Do you believe in the death penalty?" will yield a yes or no answer, but asking her "How do you feel about the death penalty?" gives you the opportunity to find out a lot more. And questions such as, "Do you think we should replace this worn-out sofa?" instantly signal the answer that you're gunning for. Try, "Have you thought about what we could do to make the living room a little more comfortable?"

If you don't get an answer to the question you've asked, make sure to either repeat the question or rephrase it, but do ask it again.

There is often something hiding beneath an evasive answer or a pregnant pause.

By preparing your questions ahead, you can stay true to what's important to you—your theory of the case.

When

Even if you can't choose your juror, you can often choose the circumstances of your advocacy by deciding when to make your case.

If you arrive at the returns department the day after Christmas or call customer service late Friday afternoon, your case won't be heard as well as it would if you arrive when things are less rushed and people are not tired and testy.

When to present your case is just as important in your personal relationships. My real estate agent, Sam, told me he learned long ago that *when* to appeal to his wife was as important as *how*. "If I want to get a drama-free hearing on some issue between us," he told me, "whether it's what color to paint the house or who is going to handle child care the next day, I know not to do it just before dinner. And whether I like it or not, my wife is a heavy smoker and long ago I learned not to ask for anything when she's nicotine-deprived."

It's probably not a good idea, for example, to pepper your children or spouse before they've had a chance to get inside the door, take their shoes off, or hang up their coat. When I come home from work, my kids know not to inundate me with questions or requests until I've had a chance to wash my face, put my hair in a ponytail, and change into my favorite sweats.

We can enjoy better results if we think about the timing of our advocacy. As they say, timing is everything.

Where

The *where* of your advocacy is important, too. Assessing the best possible place and situation for your advocacy will allow you to find the most harmonious location to present your case. Confronting your daughter at school in front of her peers might be counterproductive, just as cornering your boss in the midst of a loud meeting might short-circuit your case before it begins.

During a particularly stressful day in court, I received a voice mail from my son's principal detailing an altercation he'd had with another boy at recess. My first inclination was to race home to confront him as he walked through the door and lecture him on the virtues of "do unto others as you would have them do unto you." What I soon realized, though, was that, besides being the wrong time to discuss it, he would be more receptive to talking about negative behavior away from the house—say, on a bike ride in the park. And I would have a better chance of winning my case. My mom always makes a point of not initiating important conversations in the car, where one party (namely my father) may very well feel trapped.

People are generally the most comfortable in environments that are familiar to them. If you want to find your juror the most relaxed, meet in her office, at her house, or at her favorite restaurant. If you need to be in control of the situation, you might want to pick a place where you are the most at ease, perhaps in your office or perhaps "let's take a walk in the park."

When you create an environment for a great conversation, you give yourself a big head start toward achieving what you want.

Why

Remember why you're approaching this juror—to push forward your theory of the case. Quite simply, if your words or actions with your juror aren't supporting or reinforcing your case, you are spinning your wheels. My friend Susan and her husband, Joe, consistently spin their wheels and seem to argue for the sake of arguing. They argue again and again about his "irresponsibility" and follow-through on domestic matters. No matter what the issue—Susan's purchase of an impractical suede jacket to wear in Seattle, the rainiest city in America, or Joe forgetting their anniversary—the argument always flows back to the irresponsibility theme.

"But the more we fight, the more we don't get anywhere," Susan complained to me over coffee one morning.

"Have you ever thought about why you're fighting?" I asked.

"What do you mean?"

I suggested to Susan that rather than just throwing mud at Joe, she needed to decide in each instance why she was arguing—her theory of the case—and that once she had something specific to argue about, they might be able to make progress.

The following week, she told me, "You're not going to believe it, Lis. Our fights have turned into discussions. When I approach Joe with why I'm arguing, rather than just arguing, we actually talk. Last night, when I felt like I was losing a discussion we were having on changing our 401(k) plans, I was tempted to bring up the fact that Joe didn't pick up the dry cleaning, but I realized that was a different argument. We stayed on track and actually came to an agreement—he's calling our financial planner today."

If you get off track on why you're speaking to your juror, you'll be headed to nowhere in the rest of your case.

How

How you dress, talk, and present yourself will lead your juror to develop an impression of you and therefore support—or hurt—your position.

Look in the mirror. When I'm in the courtroom, I'm very aware that my image is being studied by the jurors. I typically wear my "trustworthy" blue suit, low pumps, and little makeup. After fifteen years of watching Barbara Walters conduct interviews, I've noticed that she dresses to fit the person she's interviewing and the environment in which she's conducting the interview. If she's interviewing a famous tennis player, she loops a white sweater around her shoulders. If she's speaking with a politician, she'll don a conservative blue suit with scarf. Remember first dates, and how you fretted over what you wore? When you're presenting your case, your dress and style are conscious choices that you can control.

While talking with your juror, you want to keep a moderate tone to your voice. Generally, a loud voice is intimidating and used to control others. None of us like to feel that we're being controlled. Tape your voice. Ask yourself a few questions and state your theory of the case. If you don't have a tape recorder, call your answering machine and leave your theory of the case as a message.

Set the mood. Don't allow anything to come between you and your juror during the conversation. You want to relate directly to your audience. If you're in a restaurant and there's a centerpiece obstructing the view of your juror, move it. If you're in your office, make sure your desk is free of clutter. You don't want your mess to be the center of attention. Turn off harsh fluorescent lighting and turn on a table lamp. If you're outside, take off the sunglasses. People need to see your eyes in order to know if they trust you. If your presentation is on the phone, stand up and smile. You will have much more power and control if you're standing, and the smile will be heard in your voice.

* * *

You've now set the stage for your case. You have an audience (your juror) and a title (your theory of the case). The next step is to discover and rehearse your lines so that you, as the star (and director) of your case, will be able to deliver a winning performance.

SKILLS OF A LAWYER FOR THE TRIALS OF YOUR LIFE

LEGAL BRIEF: STEP 2

THE JUROR

1. Who are your potential jurors?

a. Whom will your juror be judging? You? Somebody else?

b. Do you have more than one choice in your jury pool? If so, who has the power and is most likely to give you what you want?

c. Does he or she possess ulterior motives or have any reasons to dislike you? If so, what are they?

d. Will he or she listen thoughtfully to your case?

e. Do you know and can you deal with his or her temperament?

f. Are there any signs or "tells" that let you know where your juror is coming from?

g. Who is your juror?

2. What are you going to ask?

a. What can you say to encourage your juror to identify with you and your case?

b. What can you ask to find the juror's hot buttons or biases?

c. What questions can you ask that praise, rather than intimidate or criticize, your juror?

d. Do your questions suggest what you might like the answer to be? If so, what can you change about the question so that it doesn't?

e. Do your questions allow for conversation? Do they give room for the juror to tell you what's really on his or her mind? Or will the answers be limited to yes or no?

f. Write out your list of questions.

3. When are you going to make your case?

a. When is it most convenient for your juror to talk?

b. When do you feel the best?

c. When will your juror be most receptive? Most relaxed?

    d. When is the worst time to talk?

    e. So, when is the best time to make your case?

4. Where are you going to make your case?

    a. Where would your juror feel most comfortable?

    b. Where would you feel the most comfortable and in control?

    c. Where will you have the undivided attention of your juror?

    d. Where would you *not* want to talk?

    e. Where will you make your case?

5. Why?

    a. Why are you talking to this juror?

    b. Why are your words with this juror important?

    c. Write down, once again, your theory of the case.

6. How?

    a. How will your juror be dressed?

    b. How are you going to dress?

    c. How will your voice sound?

    d. How can you remain calm during your presentation?

    e. How can you adjust the environment to make it more welcoming? Is there clutter? Will there be open views of your juror? Are there comfortable chairs?

Chapter 3

Step 3. Marshal Your Evidence: *Discovery*

> *Make sure you've done your homework before you launch into your argument.*

When my son Jacob was in kindergarten, he'd come home and complain to me, "Mom, I want homework." I'd explain that he'd get homework when he was a little older, but for now he should just be happy that he could spend the afternoon playing. In first and second grade, he often came home with the same complaint. He wanted homework!

Then, in third grade, he got homework. "Aw," he complained every afternoon, "homework! Do I have to do my homework? Can't I go out and play?"

"Yes," I'd say, in unison with thousands of other parents daily, *"after you finish your homework."*

Jacob doesn't realize it now, but those few homework-free years could possibly be the only ones of his life. Homework doesn't end in high school. There's always more to learn, and if you're going to win every time, you have to do your homework before you go out and play. If you don't have all the facts, there's no way you deserve an A. For instance, if you think your plumber overcharged you for repairing your kitchen sink, you'll do a much better job challenging his fee if you find out both what he charges other people, and what other plumbers in your area charge.

During one of my recent forays in investigative reporting for *The O'Reilly Factor*, I learned that Denise Rich (whose ex-husband, wealthy financier Marc Rich, was granted a pardon by President Clinton on his last day in office in 2001) was being sued by James Hester, a former employee of hers, for thirty million dollars. Among other things in Hester's suit, he charged that Ms. Rich had pressured him to contribute money to Hillary Rodham Clinton's 2000 senatorial campaign because she had reached her maximum contribution. Since it was rumored that Clinton's people were going to refund his donation, I called Hester's lawyer to find out if he'd received the money before I called Clinton's office. So when I called Senator Clinton's office and was told the "check was cut last week," I was able to ask more specific questions and then say, "That's interesting, because Mr. Hester hasn't received it."

In the trials of your life, discovery is about doing your homework—and what you learn while doing it will make the difference between a winning A and a losing F.

Doing My Courtroom Homework

My first trial as a young federal prosecutor was a bank robbery case. The defendant, John Edward Miller, was accused of multiple armed robberies in which he would go into a bank with a pistol in hand and start shooting at the ceiling. He'd order all but one teller into the bank vault, where he would bind their mouths and bodies with duct tape; the one remaining teller would be instructed to gather all the money from the vault and stuff it in the bags he'd brought. Then he'd lock the tellers in the vault and make off with big bucks. He was very "successful"—he completed a string of bank robberies in five states over several years, netting well over a million dollars in nontaxable income—and he was one mean dude.

Since lesser criminals get tried in the state system where the penalties are much less stiff, this bank robber, like so many of the criminals who end up in federal court, was the worst of the worst, a bottom-of-the-barrel offender. He required tightened security, because he had escaped from a federal courtroom before by viciously biting his prior attorney and holding him hostage. In this case, and most of the others I would take to trial, I was asking for life in prison for the defendant, and I knew that the jurors, rightly so, would take their job very seriously.

My problem was that, unfortunately, all the evidence was circumstantial. Circumstantial evidence is a trail of cookie crumbs left on the countertop with cookies missing from a cookie jar. It does not definitely mean that your son took them, even if he was the only person in the house. "Perhaps," a defense attorney representing your son would argue, "you have mice."

In my bank robbery case, I had no direct evidence that the alleged robber actually committed these crimes. I had no eyewitnesses who could identify Miller as the robber because his disguise was fairly standard for bank robbers: a black nylon stocking over his face, a ski cap, and gloves that prevented scanning for fingerprints.

A former girlfriend of Miller's testified that he would often disappear on "business trips" at the same time as the robberies and would always come back with presents for her daughter. "I really didn't know what he did for work," she testified. "He would just say, 'I'm going to work.'"

The tellers agreed to testify about what happened during the robberies—though they were, understandably, traumatized by the ordeal. I remember one teller saying she couldn't go into hardware stores anymore because she "freaked out" when she saw duct tape.

But they helped me establish a pattern, a modus operandi, common to all the robberies, so that I could argue that all of these robberies were committed by the same person: Mr. Miller.

All of this was good circumstantial evidence that Miller was the robber, but "beyond a reasonable doubt" is a high standard of proof, so I was worried. I didn't have a smoking gun. Two FBI agents were working on the case with me: Dave Sousa, who, like me, was on his first case, and wanted to prove himself, and Dean Steiger, a senior agent, who helped us explore all our options.

During a pre-interview, I asked a teller from one of the banks if she could describe anything, from head to toe, about the assailant. "Well," she said, "he was wearing white Avias, size ten or ten and a half."

"How can you be so specific?" I asked her.

"Before I was a bank teller," she explained, "I was a shoe salesperson, and I was trained to know shoe sizes and brands." And when it came to a stressful moment in her life, she focused on shoes.

We went back and looked at the bank surveillance photos. Sure enough, they showed that the robber was in white sports shoes, and when Miller was arrested he was wearing size ten Avia sports shoes.

I studied everything I could about Miller—where he lived, whom he hung out with, where he worked. In looking into his work history, I learned that he had made an insurance claim for a work accident, in which he had lost his right forefinger, and received a loss and injury payment. Driving home that night, I had an "Aha!" moment and called Dave, begging him to blow up all the bank surveillance photos of the robber's right hand. I went back in the middle of the night and lined up the pictures on the floor in the hall of the U.S. attorney's office. I used a magnifying glass and, with no one in the office, pored over the photos. Then I discovered exactly what I needed.

During the trial, I first built my case by laying out all the circumstantial evidence, and then I called FBI agent Dean Steiger to the stand. We decided that Agent Steiger should be the one to testify because—at six foot three and muscular, with graying slicked-back hair, he looked like everyone's conception of a wise, clean-cut FBI agent. He took the stand in his blue suit and white shirt.

"Mr. Steiger, what do you do for a living?"

"I work for the Federal Bureau of Investigation, the FBI."

"And what does that work entail, sir?"

"I specialize in criminal investigations and the gathering and analysis of crime scene evidence."

Then I qualified him as an expert in firearms. "Where were you trained?" I asked. (I knew the answers already from my discovery process, following the credo: *Never ask a question you don't already know the answer to.*)

"I was trained at Quantico," he told the court.

"Were you trained in firearms?"

"Yes."

"Do you carry a firearm?"

"Yes," he said, "but not in the courtroom."

Through my line of questioning, I could tell the jurors were mesmerized by Agent Steiger's demeanor. He was what they expected from an FBI agent. Perception and presentation are crucial in testimony. With the right perception, jurors are able to concentrate on the content of what is being said, rather than why the person doesn't "look the part."

Agent Steiger explained that we had enlarged different sections of the photos taken from surveillance cameras at the banks, and in one of those enlargements, we had found something unusual about how the robber was holding his gun.

"Could you show the jury these blowups?" I asked.

"Yes," he said, lifting the poster-sized photographs.

"Can you tell the jury how the assailant held the gun?"

The defense attorney, suddenly realizing he had not done his homework and studied the photographs, objected on the grounds that Dean Steiger had never testified as an expert on firearms.

The judge ruled against him: "Every expert has his first day as an expert in court."

Agent Steiger went on to explain that a gun is commonly held with the forefinger, also called the trigger finger, in order to pull the trigger. "Can you tell the jury how this assailant held the gun?" I asked.

"The assailant did not hold the gun with his trigger finger," he said, circling the hand on the blowup with a red marker and pointing. "He held it with his middle finger. The assailant is missing his right forefinger."

"Mr. Miller," I said, turning to the defendant in a Perry Mason moment, "would you please show the jury your right hand?"

Given no other choice, he held up his hand to reveal only four fingers.

As a result of my discovery, nine-fingered John Edward Miller now resides at the Monroe, Oregon, federal penitentiary serving out a 104½-year sentence without parole. If there's one thing I learned from the Miller case, it's whether you're trying a case as a federal prosecutor or trying to convince your boyfriend to spend more time with you, you'd better make sure you have your evidence *before* you launch into your argument. You'll be a lot more effective if you've done your homework.

Getting Down to the Nitty-Gritty

In litigation, prosecutors are required to hand over all their evidence to the defense attorney. Unfortunately, no such requirement exists in real life. Your phone company is not going to tell you the name of another company that has better rates. But as you prepare your case, you can find a surprising amount of evidence that will help you win—if you know what to ask for.

When your boss mutters that a client called to complain that you didn't do a good job on a project, you can ask for details of the conversation before discussing the problems that occurred. This may remind him of your contributions to the company, and help you stand your ground. If a mail-order company tells you its shipment might arrive three weeks after Christmas, before canceling the order, try asking for a copy of the standard terms and conditions stipulating their shipping policy and any compensation that may be due you. You might find an alternate solution that benefits both parties—say, a gift card being sent announcing that the gift is on its way and a big discount as compensation for your trouble. You might discover that the company prefers these options to losing the sale and a relationship with a good customer.

We often have powerful evidence at our fingertips. We simply need to learn how to find it and then employ it.

Jennifer's Discovery

My friend Jennifer, the paralegal who had gotten a negative review from her supervisor and came to me for advice, spent several days gathering information in order to make her case. She took the company's employee manual and looked up the criteria that go into performance evaluations. In studying the manual, she discovered that only attorneys were supposed to evaluate paralegals, not supervisors.

Jennifer also learned what the definition of the unsatisfactory grade given her by Michelle actually meant: "Unsatisfactory performance does not meet the requirements of the position. Staff in this category should be identified and counseled regarding their performance prior to issuing an unsatisfactory annual review as they may be denied salary increases or terminated." She had never been told her work was anything but outstanding.

She asked for a copy of each attorney's evaluation, as well as the overall evaluation, which lumped Michelle's comments with those of the attorneys for whom she worked directly. She asked to have a copy of the numerous letters of commendation written about her during her ten years with the firm, and also asked if there were any letters of complaint. There were none.

In short, she discovered what she needed to make a strong case and push forward her theory to find out how the review came about and how to get it changed.

Erin's Discovery

There is another famous paralegal you may have heard of, whose discovery "brought a small town to its feet and a huge company to its knees." Erin Brockovich was a twice-divorced woman with three children, who had no money, no resources, and no formal education, but single-handedly put together a case that was awarded the largest settlement ever paid in a direct-action lawsuit in U.S. history—$333 million.

How'd she do it? She was persistent and did her homework.

Following a car accident in which she was not at fault, Erin found herself even worse off when her attorney failed to get her a settlement. With nowhere else to turn, Erin relied on her theory of the case ("I just want to be a good mom") and pleaded with her attorney to give her a job at his law firm. ("I'm smart, hardworking, I'll do anything, and I'm not leaving here without a job.") After getting the job, Erin stumbled upon some medical records placed in a pro bono (a case which the lawyer is representing for free) real estate file. And that's when her discovery began.

She questioned the connection between medical records and real estate, and decided she should go:

- Talk to the family who was being asked by the power company to sell their property. There she learned about chromium in the groundwater and strange illnesses in the family.

That led her to:

- A university chemistry lab, where she learned the properties of chromium—that it's used as a rust inhibitor in power plants, and that there are different types of chromium. She discovered that chromium 6 is highly carcinogenic.

The university researcher told her to:

- Consult the county water board, where she collected records documenting well tests proving the existence of chromium 6 in groundwater.

She gathered:

- Water samples from various sites around the town.
- Dead frogs from runoff.

She learned:

- That the power plant's cooling towers, kept rust-free with chromium, dumped their excess water into ponds, which weren't lined as mandated by law.

She documented:

- Buyouts of properties by the power company.
- Health problems among the families who lived there.
- The paths of groundwater and the contaminated wells.

Bottom line: When it was time to present her case, she was confident enough to declare, "There are no holes in my research."

Your case doesn't have to be for $333 million; it might involve a better position in your company, a better relationship with your spouse, or a better cell phone plan. Whatever it is, it's your homework that will help you obtain it.

Your Discovery

In gathering evidence, you can:

- Ask questions verbally of people who can help you *(interviews)* or in writing *(interrogatories)*.
- Order documents you need *(requests for production)*.
- Follow leads.
- Solicit other testimony from people involved *(witness interviews)*—from work colleagues if it's a job matter, or from bystanders if, say, you're defending your position after a car accident.
- Accumulate and assess evidence that might damage or undermine your case, so that you don't find yourself blindsided by negative evidence that you overlooked or decided to ignore.

Ask Questions

One of the most important things a lawyer does when preparing a case is to ask questions so that no stone goes unturned. To excel at discovery, you have to be a good student of people in order to analyze what will make them talk. Appeal to people's egos, get them to brag about what they know, or find other people who know something and may be willing to talk (exes are notorious for telling all).

My FBI friend Dave Sousa points out that there are five ways to get people to "spill the beans":

1. **Incentive.** Offer a reward. Criminal cases are often settled by plea bargains in which a less guilty party agrees to tell all on the more guilty party in exchange for less or no prison time.
2. **Appeal to a sense of morality.** Speak to the person about the importance of doing what is right, or the heavy burden of secrets and the need to get things off the chest.

3. **Minimize what the person has done.** Often used in child porn or rape cases, this technique says to the perpetrator, *Everyone's had these kinds of thoughts; what you did was only human.* Leading to: *You can tell me what happened.*

4. **Shift the blame.** By blaming the victim—"She was asking for it with what she was wearing!"—you, the questioner, emphasize that the defendant really had no choice.

5. **Bluff.** Act as if you know something that you really don't. Dave once told a robbery suspect that he had sent the mask the robber wore into the lab and they were able to get a "facial print" off the mask (totally impossible). The defendant said, "Oh s**t, I didn't realize you guys could do that" and confessed. In another case an agent told a murder suspect that he knew the victim and he was a son-of-a-gun, and that he'd like to shake the hand of the guy who killed him. The murderer stood up and proudly shook the agent's hand.

Not everyone is as dumb as some criminals, but the lesson here is that if you don't ask questions, you won't get answers. And the smarter you are with the questions, the better you're going to find the results. If you're too busy (or timid) to ask questions personally, write them down. Lawyers call these *interrogatories*. When I'm asked to comment on a case or event on television, the producer sends me a list of questions that the anchor might ask me in advance. It makes us both feel more comfortable, because I've gotten a chance to think over the answers, and the anchor won't be caught with dead "um" airtime.

You can also talk to experts to make sure you are armed with evidence. For instance, if you're applying for a new job or undergoing salary negotiations, call people who do the same kind of job and ask them what salary range you should expect. Asking their advice and giving them the flexibility of a range will make them feel comfortable providing you with the knowledge. When you're negotiating your own salary with this information, you are informed and will know if the salary offered is unreasonably low or excitingly high.

Todd, a business executive, was refinancing his New York City condominium in order to take advantage of low interest rates. While awaiting a closing, he received a call from his mortgage broker saying that because the mortgage company hadn't received a document from his managing agent, Todd was probably going to have to "buy a point" since the rates had changed. Todd smelled something fishy, and rather than addressing it with the mortgage broker right then, he asked if he could call him back.

He called two other mortgage brokers to ask if this was a trick of the trade, and also called his condo's managing agent to ask what he knew about the missing document. What Todd learned was that the managing office's fax machine had been out for a week and that they never received the request. He also learned that the document should actually come from the appraiser's office anyway. When he called his mortgage broker back, he was able to ask whether he'd actually tried to get in touch with the managing agent personally (rather than just fax), and learned that he hadn't. He also asked if the form could be obtained from his own company's appraisal office. The mortgage broker said, "You're right, I could just get it from them." By doing his homework, Todd was able to save himself thousands of dollars and the anguish of fighting with his mortgage broker.

Discover information that can give you the juice to power your winning case.

Order Documents

If your case involves written facts, aim your discovery at pulling together any and all transaction information that can bolster your case. If you're in a dispute over an electric power bill, you want to have prior power bills to show comparative usage. If your insurance provider has decided that a composite filling at your dentist is "cosmetic" rather than necessary, you could consult your plan book regarding "elective" surgery and have your dentist write a letter explaining how, as normal procedure, he uses white composite fillings rather than silver because they are just as strong, are less noticeable, and the costs are only slightly higher.

Companies—from your insurance provider to your credit card company—are required by law to provide the terms and conditions of their agreements with you. Otherwise known as the "fine print," these documents inform you of your obligations and theirs. If you're putting your credit card payment in the mail late, you want to know the grace period you have before you incur late fees. And if you do incur late fees and are calling to ask for a reimbursement, you should have prior bills (to show how you're consistently on time), the date you mailed your check, and the date it was processed. Perhaps if you take the time to check the dates, you'll discover that the company took an unusually long time to process your payment.

There are numerous resources available to support your case, if you're willing to do your discovery. You can visit your local tax assessor's office to weigh your taxes against those of properties in your area of similar size and quality. You can visit the building code office to learn whether the fence your neighbor is constructing is up to code. If you see the owner of a convenience store looking at the property next to yours, you can consult your town zoning officer regarding approved uses.

Journalists and now many computer users know the secrets and the power of finding information on the Internet. The Internet is an amazing tool that can help you do everything from comparing prices to planning a vacation to finding your high school best friend. One of the best search engines is www.google.com. If you're on the way to make your case (as I was yesterday) and your car goes dead, sites such as this can help you remember whether to hook up the black or the red clamp first and to which of the batteries, the good or the bad. I knew one sequence worked and the other risked explosion. I went to Google and typed "How to Jumpstart"; several sites popped up and gave me specific instructions, which I could then cross-check for accuracy.

Another great resource for a variety of government-related documents is the federal Freedom of Information Act. All records of government agencies are available to you, upon written request, guaranteeing your right to inspect a storehouse of government documents within twenty days. Journalists use the FOIA to discover and identify everything from government waste to complicity in safety problems to the salaries of public employees.

You can use the FOIA to discover any governmental information that isn't classified. If you live near a nuclear power plant, for example, you can submit a FOIA request to find out the extent of emergency planning, the existence of safety violations, or whether tests have been performed on the surrounding environment. During the presidential election ballot debacle in 2000, there were numerous FOIA requests issued in Florida to examine the ballots, both from the media and from private citizens. And I read of several residents in my neighboring town who used the FOIA to find out details of street reconstruction being started on their block. Using this information, they were able to halt the work because the design plans were both inadequate and inappropriate to the zoning laws of the area.

The possibilities with FOIA are endless—you can petition the Consumer Product Safety Commission, Commission on Civil Rights, Council on Environmental Quality, Food and Drug Administration . . . For further information and a sample letter of how to file a FOIA request, please consult "How to Use the Freedom of Information Act," designed by the Reporters Committee for Freedom of the Press at www.rcfp.org/foiact/index.html.

Follow Leads

If you've ever done work around your house, you know that when someone gives you the name of a great contractor, the great contractor might know a great electrician, the great electrician might know a great plumber, and the great plumber might finally be able to stop your leaky kitchen faucet. Discovery also works that way. One source can lead you to another source that can lead you to another source that can lead you to your answer. I've found that in my life as in my court cases, if I keep looking, I usually find the answer.

But be warned, not all leads pan out. Some leads head right to a dead end. During the Unabomber case, thousands of FBI agents around the country were sent scurrying to find anyone by the name of "Nathan R" because a scrap of paper was found near where one of the bombs went off with "Nathan R" written on it. It proved to be totally meaningless, but nonetheless required many hours of investigation and countless interviews with "Nathan Rs" around the country.

During a spate of local bank robberies in Seattle, the FBI began to notice a coincidence. Every time a white Ford van was stolen in the area, a gang of bank robbers would hit one of three banks: Olympic, Seafirst, or Key Bank. They would take over the bank and get away with big money. At least one witness remembered seeing a white van speeding away from the crime scene, so the FBI decided the two events must be connected. Every time a white van was stolen, then, agents would immediately stake out those three banks. It happened several times to no avail. Finally the FBI realized one had nothing to do with the other. It was pure coincidence.

Sometimes the dots don't connect, but when they do, they can make a winning picture.

Solicit Testimony

Soliciting testimony from people who may have been involved indirectly might be able to shed light on your case. If a customer has complained about you, for example, you'll want to get assistance from colleagues who witnessed the encounter. Did it happen as the customer suggests? Or was it that the customer came in already enraged? If you're in a car accident, bystanders can be your best defense in a he said–she said situation. Unless of course, they didn't see it the way you experienced it.

My friend Scott tells the story of how he was in a car accident when he was fifteen years old, slamming his dad's truck into the back of an elderly woman's brown Pinto. Remembering the advice from a friend's father that "if you're ever in an accident, get witnesses," Scott ran over to a gas station right next to the crash site to get the attendant's eyewitness testimony.

"Did you see what happened?" he asked, his hands shaking.

"Yep," the attendant said as he pumped gas.

Great, Scott thought, *I have my witness.*

"Yep," the attendant continued, "you slammed into her hard."

Which brings me to my last point about evidence—sometimes you discover things that might not be in your favor.

Assess Damaging Evidence

While you're garnering evidence for your cause, very often you can discover what evidence the other side might use against you. If you don't, you may be caught like a deer in headlights. I always tell witnesses that I can deal with anything—no matter how bad—if they just come clean and tell me everything. (I instruct witnesses testifying on behalf of my side that the other side knows all their warts and secrets because often my witness is the defendant's former girlfriend, wife, business partner, what have you.)

I was prosecuting an illegal-alien smuggling ring in an immigration case. I had a witness named Sunita on the stand, who testified to paying a fair sum to be smuggled over the border, only to have the defendant, Mr. Singh, come to her and extort more and more money. Sunita did a great job on direct examination. Then on cross, the defense attorney stood up and said, "Isn't it true you were having an affair with Mr. Singh?"

"But we were in love!" she wailed.

The jurors' perception of her changed from being the victim of extortion, to being a rebuffed girlfriend.

When you discover something that the other side can use against you, you want to bring it up before they do. If you don't acknowledge it, guess who will? The other side! The best way to do this is by "sandwiching it" into your case, not headlining it. For example, I once had a crucial government witness who'd previously been charged with perjury. During his testimony, I said, "Bill, is it true you've been charged with perjury once?"

He was able to respond, "Yes, when I was eighteen, and my mother was faced with bankruptcy, I lied in order to try to help her keep her house. It was the worst decision of my life." It rendered the other side powerless in trying to use the issue against us.

If you've been late in your rent payments before, but this time the check really was lost in the mail, you'll want to say, "Mr. Landlord, I mailed my check in plenty of time before the first of the month. I know that I've had some trouble paying on time in the past, but this month is an honest mistake. I'd be happy to come right over with a new check, and you can tear up the other one when it arrives."

*　　*　　*

As you do your discovery to make your winning case, most likely there will be people who try to put roadblocks in your way. They will attempt to make your job more difficult or run you off your course: Be aware and prepared for this.

I was working on a big case for a civil law firm, and the partner trusted me to take a key deposition. It was my first. (*Taking a deposition* refers to taking sworn testimony from someone who will be a witness at trial. Besides the deponent, the lawyers for both sides are there, as well as a court reporter to swear in the witness and record what is said. There is no judge to monitor fighting or make legal rulings, however, and no jury, either.)

So in my first deposition, I was pitted against a very senior lawyer who took to tapping his knuckles on the table and sighing as if terribly bored every time I asked a question. At first I was distracted and intimidated. After all, I was a young lawyer, he an experienced partner, and I figured I must be screwing things up. Then it hit me: He was doing this to get me off my game, to make me nervous, and without the court reporter making a record of it. Instead of getting mad, I got even. I said to the court reporter, "For the record, let it be known that the defense counsel is rapping his knuckles and sighing at all of my questions." He turned beet red, and the behavior stopped.

Take control of your discovery and you take control of your case.

Straw, Sticks, and Bricks

Discovery is absolutely critical to your case. It provides the materials for building your house. Once you have the materials—the mass of facts, guesses, opinions, and interpretations—you must determine if each piece of evidence is:

- *Prejudicial.* This evidence may be true or relevant, but is likely to push jurors to make a rash or misguided decision based on their own irrational biases and prejudices instead of the hard facts at hand.
- *Circumstantial.* Evidence involving suppositions or conclusions that are second- or thirdhand, without incontrovertible observation, and usually not admissible in court.

- *Direct.* Evidence arising directly out of fact.
- *Evidentiary killers.* Such evidence is unusable because it is tainted by bias, motive, or hearsay. It must be identified early in the process and challenged if used against you.

Figuring out what kind of evidence you have is as simple as remembering the story of the three little pigs.

Prejudicial Evidence—"Grasping at Straws"

The first little pig built his house out of straw because it was the easiest thing to do. Prejudicial evidence might be easy and it may even be true, but it is so pernicious or provocative that it undermines your theory of the case. I call it "bite-your-tongue" evidence because it stirs such animosity in your adversary, or is so distracting, that it doesn't serve your cause.

If your husband had an affair ten years ago (which you forgave him for) and tonight he forgot to go to the supermarket again, it's not relevant to bring up his infidelity. It's just grasping at straws. It may also be damaging not just to your husband, but also to your theory of the case, because it will make your husband angry and possibly keep you from achieving your desired result. However, pointing at the empty refrigerator may well be relevant, and so might mentioning that last Friday the fridge was empty, too. Even though these statements may seem prejudicial to your spouse, they are true and relevant to your case.

Anna, an international banker, had to confront the issue of relevant versus prejudicial evidence in confronting a coworker. This colleague, Shelley, prided herself on her no-nonsense honesty—to the point that she would sabotage Anna's projects by haranguing other countries' banking officials, waving in their faces a tally of their outstanding loans, and making disparaging remarks about their national work ethic. Shelley thought she was practicing "tough love"; Anna thought Shelley might provoke an international incident.

Anna gathered her evidence: angry cables from foreign governments, unfavorable news items, and an accounting analysis showing that despite Shelley's tactics, loans were defaulting at a greater rate than ever. Because she knew something of Shelley's parenting habits, she decided to add to her list of evidence the fact that Shelley's twelve-year-old son was so rough on other kids that he was considered a friendless bully at school. Anna decided that Shelley's son was her secret weapon to prove that Shelley's human relations strategy always backfired.

When Anna brought Shelley's parenting into her argument, Shelley was infuriated. "My son doesn't work at this bank," she seethed. "How dare you try to use my parenting against me!" Anna had ruined any chance of getting through to Shelley with all her positive evidence and instead put a fissure in their relationship that ruined the work environment.

If you rely on prejudicial evidence, the other side will huff and puff and blow your case down.

Circumstantial Evidence—"Stick by Stick"

The second little pig built his house out of sticks, certainly stronger than straw. Like sticks, circumstantial evidence—evidence that works to prove a fact through inference—can sometimes be very strong, if the evidence is stacked together the right way. It can even convince the wolf to change his mind.

When Sara, the mother of a sixteen-year-old boy, received a two-thousand-dollar phone bill listing a host of calls to Indonesia, she called one of the phone numbers on the bill. It turned out to be a phone sex line. Once she got over her shock, she was able to correlate the calls with times when her son was home unsupervised. She presented this circumstantial evidence to him. Squirming under the gently persistent questioning about the days and times she was gone and he was there, he finally admitted that he'd made the calls.

Sara was able to use the same evidence, together with her son's admission, to challenge the long-distance phone provider—which had channeled all the calls through Jakarta to accumulate international charges. Ultimately, she went to her state's consumer fraud agency in an attempt to get her money back, stop the scam, and protect her son with parental control on such numbers. (Her son was grounded for a month and forced to pay back the cost of the calls with twenty dollars a month deducted from his allowance.)

Another way circumstantial evidence can be of use is if it allows you to make a clear deduction. If you wake up in the morning to find snow on the ground, you can assume that snow fell overnight even if you didn't see it doing so. This type of circumstantial evidence can be very useful when dealing with your case. You just need to be aware of how you stack it.

A judge friend of mine, "Judge Bill," once told me the story of a murder case he had tried. The victim was a young mother who'd vanished while purportedly out on a walk—her body was never found. Her husband was charged with the murder, but the case was completely circumstantial. During the closing statement, the defense lawyer argued that because her body had not been found, it was possible the victim was still alive. Judge Bill described the great flourish with which the defense counsel finished his argument, saying: "In fact, ladies and gentlemen, Darcy might walk through that door right now." Everyone in the room, jurors, gallery, and even the prosecutors, turned and looked at the door. The only person who didn't turn to look was the defendant (and Judge Bill, who was watching the defendant), who obviously knew that his wife wasn't going to walk through the door. (Exactly why some circumstantial evidence is inadmissible in court.)

Circumstantial evidence does not come with a 100 percent money-back guarantee, and from time to time throwing it around can get you in trouble. That lipstick on your husband's collar may honestly be attributed to a hug from a departing coworker at her good-bye—and *good luck with married life*—party, not evidence of an affair. That's why you don't want to damage your personal case by using exclusively circumstantial evidence to make important points.

In the Miller bank robbery case, in which I used the robber's shoe size and type, I had to be aware that during cross-examination the defense attorney could ask the former shoe salesperson–bank teller, "Isn't it true that size ten is a very common size for a man's shoe? In fact, is it the most common shoe size? So, many millions of men wear shoe size ten, and not just my client?" Or let's assume that the robber drove a blue Chevrolet sedan from the bank as a getaway car, and Miller owned a blue Chevrolet sedan. This again is circumstantial evidence, and during cross-examination you will discover there are "X million Chevy sedans now on the road in the United States, and X million of them are blue."

Connect the dots, add your intuition, and then conclude. But don't ever base your case on one piece of circumstantial evidence; you will get blown away.

Direct Evidence—"Brick House"

A piece of direct evidence is as solid as a brick house. It bolsters your theory of the case and allows you to confidently declare, "Not by the hair of my chinny chin chin." The wolf can huff and puff all he wants—direct evidence will still stand strong. When you gesture at Exhibit A—the full kitchen trash bag—and then point at your husband, you've marshaled direct evidence and used it. Your husband can't deny that the kitchen bag is full. He can still argue, but he can't deny.

My colleague Bill O'Reilly knows how to use direct evidence to prove his case both on his program and in his personal life. Late one winter night after taping *The O'Reilly Factor*, he was driving home from the Fox Studios in New York City to his home in Long Island. A few miles from his house, he tried to stop at a stop sign and slid right through it. As luck would have it, there was a police officer encamped directly on the other side of the street.

A few blocks later, with sirens and flashing lights, Bill was pulled over. A big Irish police officer, coincidentally named Officer O'Reilly, came over to his car and gruffly instructed him to get out. Bill followed directions and tried to politely explain that he knew he had not stopped at the sign, but if the officer would please go back with him to the sign he would be able to see that there was ice on the road; that was why he'd slid through the intersection.

Officer O'Reilly wouldn't hear any of this and told Bill he was just trying to make excuses, adding that he was going to make the fine even bigger because he didn't like Bill's attitude. Bill quickly sized up the situation. He could have used prejudicial evidence—the "don't you know who I am" approach—or pointed to the circumstantial evidence that it was freezing cold, it had been raining, and the cop was just waiting for someone to slide through the stop sign. Instead, he realized that both approaches would do more harm than good and decided not to pick the grumpy officer as his juror. He wanted the traffic judge to serve that role. He also decided, as he took the ticket and wrote down the officer's badge number, that his theory of the case would be to get excused from the ticket and make sure the cop knew his hostility and unwillingness to listen was wrong.

Bill went home, then came back later that night packing a camera with a date and time meter on it. He did his discovery by taking pictures of the scene—the stop sign and the ice on the road—and later through the Freedom of Information Act pulled the officer's "sheet" to find that numerous citizen complaints had been lodged against this Officer O'Reilly.

Armed with his evidence, Bill went to the court hearing and told the judge his story, complete with photos, weather reports, and the cop's sheet. Thanks to Bill's careful review of his direct evidence, Officer O'Reilly was reprimanded and the ticket was dismissed.

Nothing withstands the other side's huffing and puffing like direct evidence.

Evidentiary Killers

Once you've discovered your evidence, you need to ask yourself some questions in order to assess that the evidence is not tainted. Evidence based on hearsay, bias, and motive is generally inadmissible and should not be used to support your case or make a case against you. These are "evidentiary killers" and may either kill or incapacitate your case.

To determine if a piece of evidence is an evidentiary killer, ask yourself:

1. Is It Hearsay?

Hearsay is a statement, other than directly from the source, offered to support the truth of an assertion. Basically, hearsay is the case equivalent of a rumor. If a piece of evidence requires the words *he said* or *she said* to support it, it is hearsay and therefore unreliable and should be challenged.

> Q: Jim, what did Frank tell you about the accident?
> A: He said he saw the ladder set up next to the hole.

Though this question might lead you to talk to Frank, Jim's statement of what Frank said should not be used in your case.

Sometimes hearsay is admissible in a courtroom under what's called the "hearsay exception." An excited utterance someone says at the time of a traumatic event—like "He hit me!"—technically is hearsay, but we allow it as evidence because the person who made the statement had no time to invent or fabricate the statement. "Dying declarations"—what people said on their deathbeds or at the scene of an accident—are also allowed because those who know they are dying are deemed unlikely to be making things up.

2. Is There Bias?

Does the person or institution that provided this piece of evidence have an ulterior motive that might challenge or undermine its veracity? Bias is any tendency that prevents a person from being impartial. Sometimes this is because there is a personal relationship.

> A: Bobby would never hit another child.
> Q: You're Bobby's mother?
> A: That's right, and I know him very well.

3. Is There Motive?

Does the "witness" in your case have a predisposition or reason to skew the evidence or deliver testimony that might not be truthful? Motive is the urge that prompts a person to think and act in a certain way—often based on greed, love, hate, and revenge. Motive taints the credibility of a witness.

> Q: Are you sure you saw me take money out of the cash drawer?
> A: Absolutely.
> Q: If I quit, would you want to be manager?
> A: Sure. It'd be great to be making what you're making.

After you've found all your evidence and assessed its merit, you're ready to organize how you want to present it. As you move forward toward a win, you need to carry with you your *order of proof* and formulate your *trial plan.*

The Order of Proof and Trial Plan

An *order of proof* is a list of which exhibits (tangible things) you will present as evidence at trial and which witnesses you are going to call. It gives you and your judge a road map of how you are going to make your case—the sequence of the evidence you will present. In a murder case, for instance, your order of proof would list all witnesses along with the evidence they will present:

- The butler will introduce the murder weapon (a knife).
- The detective will introduce the autopsy records.
- The victim's assistant will introduce the perfume bottle she bought for the victim to give to his girlfriend that the wife found.
- The wife's tennis pro will say she was not at the club for her usual Tuesday-evening lesson, though she told police she was.

The order of proof is your step-by-step walk-through of your witnesses and your evidence. When planning your personal case, you should do the same thing—laying out (on paper, on index cards, or on your computer, if necessary) your evidence and the plan for most effectively presenting what you've discovered, even though you're not going to give it to your judge or juror. This will help you organize your case, stay focused during presentation, and remain on a winning course to success.

Just as trial lawyers know their closing argument before they enter the courtroom, it's critical that before launching into your argument, you organize and plan out your entire case—including things you want to deal with before cross-examination and what evidence you want to withhold until later—to give your case even more conclusive power in Step 8 when you sum it up in your closing argument.

In addition to your order of proof, craft your trial plan using your theory of the case, and how the law and evidence support that theory. The *trial plan* outlines an overview of the facts of the case according to your side, describes how the law supports your facts, and then sums up how you are going to win your case based on facts, law, and common sense.

*   *   *

If your case were a term paper, you would now have your thesis, you would know who's grading it, you would have done your research, and you'd have made your outline—now it's time to write the paper. It's time to make your case.

SKILLS OF A LAWYER FOR THE TRIALS OF YOUR LIFE

LEGAL BRIEF: STEP 3

THE EVIDENCE

1. What techniques will you use to gather your evidence?

    a. Ask key individuals to "spill the beans"—supervisors, employers, professionals.

    b. Order documents.

    c. Follow leads.

2. Using one or more of the techniques above, identify your evidence.

    a. List each piece of *direct* evidence—pieces that arise directly from fact.

        i. What you already possess:

           1. Your paycheck.

           2. Your invoice.

           3. What you and your juror witnessed.

        ii. What you find when you research:

           1. Freedom of Information Act (for instance, your colleague's paycheck, if you are a public employee).

           2. Terms and conditions.

           3. Photos you take.

           4. Weather reports.

           5. Previous invoices, invoices from your neighbor who had the same plumber fix an identical problem.

b. Identify and write down your *circumstantial* evidence—pieces that arise from conclusions or suppositions.

    i. Stack your evidence—build your case:

        1. Connect the dots.

        2. Add your intuition.

        3. Conclude.

    ii. Avoid basing your case on one piece of circumstantial evidence.

    iii. When you connect your dots, avoid grasping at straws—make sure your argument is logical.

c. Identify and write down your *prejudicial* evidence.

    i. What facts about your case are irrelevant?

        1. Most of these (for instance, your husband's affair) are emotion-based.

        2. With each piece of evidence, decide if it serves your cause or not.

d. Identify and write down your *evidentiary killers.*

    i. What pieces of information exist (direct, circumstantial, or prejudicial) that will not serve your theory?

    ii. Of the evidence you've already collected, what pieces are hearsay, biased, or motivated by greed, revenge, or the like?

3. Develop your *trial plan.*

a. Sequence your evidence—your order of proof.

    i. What are your two most important pieces of evidence? Start with one and withhold the other until later.

    ii. Begin with a bang—start with your most attention-grabbing fact. This tells your juror that you have something important to say.

    iii. Sequence the rest of your evidence; sandwich it between your two smoking guns.

    iv. As you sequence, arrange your evidence so that each piece builds on the previous; stack them to build a strong case.

    v. Conclude with a punch. The last piece of evidence in your presentation should give your juror no choice but to agree with you.

b. Write it all down.

Chapter 4

Step 4. Advocate with Confidence:
Making the Case

> *Think of each piece of evidence as a brick for a wall that you're now going to stack up so that there's no way through, around, or over.*

JUDGE: Are both sides ready?

PLAINTIFF'S LAWYER: Ready, Your Honor.

DEFENDANT'S LAWYER: We're ready, Your Honor.

JUDGE: Members of the jury, we're now going to hear the opening statements from each side. The opening statements should give you a general overview of what the lawyers expect to show you in terms of witnesses and other evidence throughout the trial. This should help you understand the actual evidence when it is presented to you. Plaintiff, you may proceed.

Once you've established your theory, chosen your jury, and gathered your evidence, you're ready to make your case. Whether you are confronting your boss about staff favoritism, going over an invoice with your contractor, or countering your teenager's declaration that Ecstasy really isn't such a bad drug, you now have the tools to build your case with confidence and command.

By the end of this chapter, you will feel confident making an opening statement—one that is based on your theory of your case, laying out your direct evidence (to your insurance company: "This weather report says it was snowing the night of the accident") as well as the circumstantial evidence you've chosen to use ("Here is the receipt for the plowing service I hired that morning to clear my driveway"). Moreover, you will feel confident to ask direct questions of your juror—questions that, when answered, solidify your case—and learn how to anticipate and deal with issues of bias and motive in your adversary.

Recently, I found myself on my second phone call to the cable company attempting to cancel my "premium channels"—a relatively simple task, you'd think. But it wasn't that easy. First, there was the frustrating self-service telephone menu absent the option to speak to a human representative, followed by "we're experiencing high call volume and lengthy wait times." By the time I actually got to speak to someone, I was already perturbed. Adding to this was the fact that the customer service representative I had spoken with the previous month (after going through the same rigmarole) failed to accomplish what she had promised. As a result, a simple request had become a case.

After establishing a theory ("this is not about how annoyed I am, but rather canceling the channels and procuring a refund for last month"), picking a jury ("May I speak to your supervisor, please?"), discovery of the facts (to whom I spoke and when, and the current cable bill), it was time to make my case.

Opening Statement

"You only have one chance to make a good first impression," as they say. In court, as in real life, the opening statement is the most powerful few minutes of an attorney's presentation. From research, we know that the majority of jurors reach a judgment of the case by the end of the opening statements. Why? Basic conditioning. Since the beginning of time, all creatures have been forced to make quick assessments in order to survive. ("Is that *Tyrannosaurus rex* an herbivore? Should I run or just stay here and continue to pick these delicious berries?" *Chomp.*)

As we go about our lives in the twenty-first century, the sheer volume of information thrown our way makes quick decision making a necessity. Who has the time, or inclination for that matter, to digest and process the thousands of bits of data thrown our way on a daily basis? Similarly, jurors, in the courtroom and out, will assess any situation in the manner to which they have grown accustomed: *quickly.*

Jurors are constantly attempting to make sense out of the environment they are in, and skillful attorneys assist them in doing so. Your juror will be listening to your information, sorting it, and rejecting what doesn't fit with her belief system.

Be well aware that during your statement, your juror is reading as much into nonverbal communications such as clothing, eye contact, expressions, and even the characteristics of your voice, as he is your words. But he is expecting something important to be said. Seize the opportunity! Use this time to clearly, and pleasantly, state your theory, establish your themes, and demonstrate the facts that will entitle you to a favorable verdict. In addition, don't forget to request the outcome you want.

It is crucial to the success of your case that you project confidence, energy, and a firm belief in the importance and virtue of the theory you're conveying.

Set the Tone

The "opening statement" of your discussion will set the tone for the favorable outcome you are requesting. Whether you're attempting to convince your spouse to spend more time at home or the cable company to cancel your service and refund your money, if you start with a negative tone, you can be sure you'll get negative results.

In the cable TV instance, my opening statement could make or break my case: I had the supervisor's attention for only a few moments (you can imagine how many calls are in queue for a supervisor handling complaints for a cable TV company), so I had to use those seconds wisely. In my opening statement, it was crucial that the tone of my voice wasn't threatening.

If you are prepared, you will be relaxed. If you are relaxed, your juror will relax. I always rehearse my opening statement aloud several times, so that I don't have to rely on my notes. That way, I can be in the moment with the jury, maintaining eye contact and projecting my belief in the case. If I move, I move with purpose, and if I gesture, I'm aware I'm gesturing. I'm also careful to avoid distracting mannerisms.

As a prosecutor I would sometimes encounter a certain defense attorney who would, throughout his case, twist his neck in an attempt to "crack" it. It never failed that I would see people in the jury rubbing their own necks during his discourse and, it never failed, he would always lose his case. I don't think the jury could listen to his words because they were too busy watching his actions.

State Your Theory

Jurors tend to remember what they hear first and last. It's therefore important to state your theory up front, much like a headline.

- "Members of the jury: This is a case about recklessness and how it ruined another person's life."
- "Good morning. This case is simple. John Evans wasn't there when Joe Williams was stabbed. He wasn't within ten miles. He was home with his family. This is a case of mistaken identity."

Or in my personal case:

- "Thank you for taking my call, Ms. Supervisor. I canceled my premium channels last month, but it seems they are still active and I've been charged for them. I have the dates, times, and people I spoke with, and I'm hoping you can take care of this, and I can get a refund."

In the courtroom, a consistent theme woven throughout the case will evoke powerful images that, most often, transcend the facts of the case. Good themes are based on:

- *What we know to be true.* "This is a case about the underdog."
- *People.* "This is a case about Ms. Smith's responsibility for her own actions."
- *Situations.* "This is a case about inappropriate sexual conduct."

A compelling theme will help your juror organize the thousands of pieces of information that head her way, provided the theme is consistent with the juror's preconceived notions and life experiences. Most of all, an effective theme will evoke powerful images in the juror's mind and encourage him to "do the right thing."

Establish Your Story

Successful trial lawyers often use their opening statement as an opportunity to tell their client's story to the jury. A good story contains the characters, the facts, and an emotional appeal, and is often the most powerful vehicle for delivering a compelling message and persuading the jury.

As many of us recall, we learned as children through stories—who doesn't remember the lesson to "never cry wolf"? Although he doesn't realize it, I still teach my ten-year-old valuable life lessons through telling tales. Whether it's the fact that I wasn't crazy about math when I was in the fifth grade or how I saved my allowance each month as a child rather than spending it on candy so I could buy myself the best bike, I always couch the lessons in the context of a story. (Fortunately for my son, I never walked five miles to school through blowing snow.)

Developing a story probably won't be necessary in all situations of conflict. A complex "fox-and-hound" analogy will probably only confuse the issue when convincing your plumber not to charge you overtime for his second visit to fix a leaky pipe. It would probably be counterproductive to begin the plumber's visit with a curt, "This is a case about doing the right thing. There once was a hound plodding along . . ."

"Sure, lady, whatever you say. Can you move out of the way?"

But a story would work with my customer service representative: "I canceled the premium channels last month because my ten-year-old son was watching some things on those channels that are okay for adults, but not for kids. I felt like I wasn't doing my job as his mother."

Since most jurors see the world through emotional eyes, focus on the people, not the problem. Personalizing your case is important because jurors want to help people they like. If your client (or you in your personal trials) is likable and sympathetic, the jury is more likely to return a favorable verdict.

Preview Evidence

Much like a movie trailer, the opening statement is your opportunity to give a preview of what you will be presenting later. Besides telling your juror what the case is about, this is your opportunity to announce what you are going to show. Just as a movie trailer wouldn't give away the end, you don't want to give away your evidence. You want to indicate you have it, and that the jury will be able to see it, but the opening statement is not the time to launch into all the evidence. Your goal is to entice the jury to see your "movie" in order to see your evidence.

Request the Outcome You Want

I once witnessed a long-winded opening statement by a veteran public defender. Thirty minutes after she began her monologue, in which she threw unnecessary data at the jury, she summed up her presentation. With the average person's attention span being twelve minutes, the jury was already mentally exhausted, and she hadn't even mentioned what she wanted them to do. Did she want them to acquit? Convict? It simply wasn't clear. From her opening statement, the jury lacked direction, which ultimately cost her the case.

From the beginning, whether you're in the courtroom or in your boss's office, you must establish credibility by revealing your honest wishes. Simply put, ask for what you want:

- "He had his wife's blood on him from head to toe. We will prove that he killed his wife in the basement of their home because he was enraged over an affair he thought she was having with another man. This is a case of a jealous husband who firmly believed 'till death do us part.'"
- "I want to show you proof of productivity increases, letters of praise from both colleagues and customers, and proof of my enduring commitment to this company. No one deserves this new position like I do."
- "When I called on March 5 I spoke with Operator Number 523, and she said my service would be canceled immediately. As you can see by my records, it wasn't canceled. I'd be happy to fax you my statements and canceled checks. It's very clear that a minor mistake was made and that a refund is appropriate."

Keep in mind that your opening statement—no matter how simple or complex the issue—will set the tone for the rest of your case. And research has shown that once a juror has determined what she *thinks* has happened, she will then filter every piece of information presented to corroborate her version.

Presenting Your Evidence

Once your opening statement has set the tone and your intent, begin to lay out your case rationally and clearly. During discovery you have developed a trial plan, sequenced so that your case builds logically. Nothing is more ineffective than an illogical rant that goes all over the board.

I once saw an irate customer attempting to return a well-worn pair of shoes to a teenaged cashier at a department store. "These fell apart," he said. The teenager explained the return policy of "no returns after thirty days," adding "And sir, we haven't sold these since last year." The customer raised his voice and began to grasp at straws: "This store is the worst. You make everything so difficult. I'm never going to shop here again." Between sentences, he highlighted his irritation with audible huffs.

Why was he getting nowhere? Because he came unprepared, and like a cat backed into a corner, he adopted a losing posture, hissing and batting uncontrollably. Aside from the fact that he was making his case to the wrong juror (after all, what authority does a seventeen-year-old have to return his money?), he ended up sounding more like a lunatic than a faithful customer. He did not receive his money back as a result of his ranting, and he left the counter with his year-old shoes, only after making a complete fool of himself. Regardless of the ethics of returning a well-worn pair of shoes, this guy could never have gotten what he wanted; he simply didn't have his case planned out.

Had he laid out a trial plan for a winning case, he would have approached the situation quite differently. He would have asked to speak to the supervisor of the shoe department, and once he had her attention he would have explained his problem with the shoes rationally rather than emotionally:

"I love this store and have shopped here for years. As you can see by this stack of receipts, I'm a very loyal customer. Unfortunately I'm missing the receipt for this particular pair of shoes, but I purchased them about a year ago. I'm not one to complain, but if you look at the stitching on these shoes, it is defective. I have several other shoes by this maker and each of them has held up remarkably well. In fact, the shoes I have on are from here, and I've had this pair for more than three years. I know your policy is a thirty-day money-back guarantee, but I'm hoping you will examine the defective stitching and issue me a store credit for the purchase of a new pair."

I would be willing to bet that the situation would have turned out quite differently, and both sides would have felt good about the results.

Evidence Building

When I'm laying out my order of proof, I think about how each piece of evidence can be put together to paint the whole picture. I decide what evidence (both verbal and tangible) each witness will be responsible for introducing and how I can set the scene (through a bank teller, case agent, victim, what have you). Then I lay out the story.

I build my case the way a mason builds a wall—one brick at a time. I think of each witness, each piece of evidence, as a brick that's going to stack up against my opponent, such that there is no way through, around, or over. The mortar that holds my bricks together comprises things like bank records that show a pattern of deceit, or weather reports that confirm icy roads. These facts serve as reinforcements and join together the evidence and the testimony from witnesses.

As I'm putting my evidence in order, I remind myself that I have lived with the case for months, maybe years, and know all the facts inside and out, but the jurors are coming in knowing nothing about the case. I have to paint the picture, tell the story, while obeying the rules of evidence and meeting the burden of proof. Sometimes the most logical way to tell a story is chronologically, but that isn't always the most effective way. For example, in a fraud case, I would instead start with an overview of the crime through the testimony of an FBI case agent and then let individual victims tell their stories against this backdrop.

Let's look at evidence building in real life:

Deena joined a gym only to discover it was not at all what she expected, and she decided she wanted out of her contract. Before going on an I-want-my-money-back rampage, she decided to gather evidence supporting her theory that she deserved a partial refund. She dug out her credit card statement in which she was charged the enrollment fee and the first six months of dues. She asked her doctor to put in writing his suggestion that a steam room would be good for her muscle spasms. She pulled a flyer off the bulletin board that said the steam room would be "closed for repairs" and got out the membership guide listing the weekly classes offered. She also brought her membership contract on which she had circled the gym's services she wanted, including the "steam room" and "on-site babysitting weekdays during morning and evening hours."

She decided not to speak to the commission-based "enrollment counselor," because she knew he would try to talk her into staying. Instead, she made an appointment with the general manager, a woman she'd seen in the gym carrying a diaper bag.

Deena opened her case by saying that when she'd joined the gym, she was very excited. The last couple of years had been difficult for her. Ever since her daughter, Sophie, was born, she had been having chronic back problems. In fact, it was her doctor's advice that made her come to the gym. "He thought the steam room and the Pilates class would be good for my back." Then she explained her disappointment, without getting angry or emotional. "I've brought my daughter with me a few times only to get here and find that child care wasn't being offered that night, so I've had to turn around and go home. Also, the steam room has been closed since the day after I joined."

"We're waiting on the parts," the general manager interjected. "I'm told they should be here next week."

"I understand," Deena said, not letting this throw her off track. "But I've also been disappointed that the Pilates program was canceled."

"We unfortunately didn't have enough interest."

"I was interested. In fact, besides the steam room, that was one of the reasons I joined here rather than the gym closer to my house. I suppose the bottom line is that I don't think I've gotten the things I was promised, and I'd like a refund of my initiation fee and the four months I haven't used."

"I certainly understand your concerns," the manager said. "I have to say I'm shocked to hear we didn't have child care. That is a program I started when I had my daughter, and since I'm typically here during the daytime, I wasn't aware we were having staffing problems at nights. Thank you for bringing it to my attention." Then she agreed to issue Deena a full refund, and offered her a month free "in the hope that during this time we can make improvements that will change your mind."

Deena won her case by being prepared and thinking through her presentation from start to finish. As you move through the presentation of your case, keep focused, assured, and "on message" just as Deena did. Remember, you are confident about your decision to make a case and have your evidence in good order—any result other than your objective is undesirable.

Direct Examination

Building a logical case involves more than just laying out the evidence gathered in discovery. It also incorporates asking questions of your adversary in an intentional manner, allowing you to further your case.

When I teach trial advocacy, I tell my students to forget about being a lawyer when they're asking questions and instead to think like a newspaper reporter. In direct examination, you need to find out who, what, when, where, why, and how. When you're asking a question that starts with one of the *w*'s or the *h,* you know the answer is going to elicit a story. You must make your case on direct, convincing your juror by his own answers to your questions.

Take my daughter's direct examination of me concerning pets:

DANI: Mom, what animals can be pets?
ME: Dogs, cats, and fish.
DANI: Can hippos be pets?
ME: Not usually.
DANI: Why not?
ME: They're too big for a house.
DANI: But you can get a baby hippo and then give it to the zoo when it gets too big.
ME: I suppose so.
DANI: I'm not saying I want a hippo . . . wouldn't a dog be a lot easier?
ME: Ugh!

She got her point across with her direct line of questioning. Direct examination, as my questioning by Dani illustrates, allows someone else to tell a story in her own words and, if well constructed, goes to reinforce your case. In Dani's case, my answers proved that a dog is a pet, and is a lot easier to keep than a hippo.

Let's say you notice a scratch on your car after having it washed. When you question the manager of the car wash, you want his answers to form a story and that story to support your case that the car wash scratched your car or at least agrees to investigate:

Q: Who is responsible for the quality control on the wash equipment?
A: The exterior supervisor.
Q: Where is he during the operation?

A: At check-in—he took your money and asked you to put your car in neutral. He makes sure your antenna is retracted and checks for loose luggage racks and that type of thing while your car is given its hand rinse.

Q: Why does he retract the antenna?

A: So that none of the equipment is snagged on it.

Q: What does it mean to have "touch-free washing"?

A: That the equipment stays off the car.

Q: Are there any parts that do touch the car?

A: Well, the brushes and the drying flaps, but they're made of nylon and cloth.

Q: When was the equipment last serviced or checked?

A: Every morning or if there's a problem.

Q: What kind of problems might occur?

A: Equipment that gets stuck or comes loose. That sort of thing.

Q: Could you check to see if there's any equipment stuck or loose now?

A: Sure.

While not evoking an "okay, we did it," confession, this type of questioning moves toward finding answers. After the search of the car wash for malfunctioning equipment, you might ask the manager about the nature of scratches. For example, "How long does it typically take for rust to form?" or "What's the difference between a scratch and a dent?" Your goal is to help the manager realize there's a greater probability that the car wash scratched your car than that you scratched the car and came in for a car wash.

One warning as you ask your questions: *Be careful about how you lay out your evidence and phrase your questions.* You don't want to allow room for surprises. A famous example of a damaging ambush occurred during the drug trial of former Panamanian dictator Manuel Noriega. When the defense attorney sought to discredit a government witness, he asked, "How many drug deals would you say you've done?"

"With your client or without?" the witness retorted.

Noriega was convicted of eight counts of racketeering, drug trafficking, and money laundering and sentenced to forty years in prison. Perhaps he would still be living in the presidential palace in Panama City if his attorney had thought through his line of questioning. Although this gaffe probably wasn't the sole reason the defense lost the case, it certainly couldn't have helped.

Ask Not, If You Know Not

As you plot out your questions, always follow the lawyer's dictum: *Never ask a question you don't already know the answer to.*

My friend Andrew Hamilton, who is now an attorney with the Department of Justice, once represented a man whom the state was trying to involuntarily commit because of mental illness. He had been locked up for seventy-two hours, and the state was trying to keep him in for an additional fourteen days. Andrew's task as an attorney was to try to get him out. According to Andrew, "The guy looked perfectly sane and perfectly harmless, so I decided to emphasize this to the judge. I asked my client how he was doing in the facility and he said, 'Fine, except when the lights go out.'" Then Andrew committed the absolute no-no and asked his client a question he didn't know the answer to. "I asked him what happened then because I thought he was going to say the staff mistreated him. Instead he said, 'That's when the bats come out of the ceiling and attack me.'" That's when Andrew realized his client *was* totally crazy and probably needed to be kept where he could get some therapy.

Make It Personal

The first thing I do when I begin questioning a witness is personalize him so that the jury feels as if they know him and trust him. I get him to tell a little about his background—something about his family, where he's from, what he does. In asking these questions, I maintain eye contact and, in a courtroom situation, I will have instructed my witness to maintain eye contact with the jury. This makes the witness comfortable, but also makes the jury comfortable. In your personal cases, of course, your witness might in fact be your juror, so this makes the personalization part of direct all the more important.

You want your witness-juror to trust that you really want to know what she thinks. By asking these questions, you are not looking to offend. You're asking because you value her opinion and know that she has the power to give you what you want. "Now, what do you think was wrong with my report?"; "Has anyone else complained about my performance?"; "How can I fix the problem in the future?" Asking these types of questions allows the person answering to feel empowered.

Balance Your Questions

Remember: Clearly and logically presented arguments are your building blocks, so it is important to remember to ask only one question at a time. Asking questions that entail multiple points or throwing too many requests at your juror at once will only cloud your issue, create confusion, and ultimately cause you to lose control of your case.

Asking carefully planned leading questions encourages short, factual answers that build one upon another, each giving you the response you anticipate. ("Was it light or dark out?" "Was there blood on the floor or wasn't there?" "Isn't it true that other employees are paid forty dollars an hour?") These questions provide short, to-the-point answers.

Open-ended questions are riskier than leading questions, but are generally more effective if planned correctly. The witness is no dummy; he can tell when he is being manipulated in a certain direction ("Was the woman five feet tall and about thirty years old?"). By suggesting the answer in the way the question is phrased, the impact of having the juror volunteer the information himself is diminished. Open-ended questions allow the juror to volunteer the information himself, making it more effective in your case because he is more likely to find it believable ("Please describe what the woman looked like").

Let the Witness Tell the Story

On direct, the witness is the "star," the storyteller. (On cross-examination, the opposite will be true. You as the questioner will be the star, and it will be your questions that grab attention.) This is not to say that you want to ask questions that are so broad that your witness or juror tells her entire life story, starting in kindergarten. You want to be open with your questions, but focused. You want to entreat your witness or juror to tell you what happened or what he's feeling, and use your questions to keep him on the right track—yours.

Think of yourself as a sweet, elderly aunt—a caring person who really wants to hear the story and know the facts. When something isn't clear, she asks, "Who were you with?"; "What was he doing?"; "When did you get back?"; "Where did you buy that?"; "Why did you get a tattoo?"; or "How are you going to explain that to your parents?" By asking the five w's and the h, she finds out the real scoop.

Ask questions that help focus the conversation. For example, rather than, "Do you ever eat out?" and "Do you like fish?" try "On the night you got food poisoning, where did you eat?" and "What did you eat?"

The trick with open-ended questions is to phrase them in such a way that they elicit a descriptive response. This accomplishes two objectives: First, open-ended questions allow your juror to remember the facts and explain details himself. Second, they minimize the feeling that you are dictating how things were or will be done.

As your juror gives you the answers that support your case, in her own words, your argument will begin to make sense to her. By letting her tell her side of the story, you will have made it possible for her to think that she came to the decision for herself, rather than you forcing it upon her—which almost always encourages defensiveness.

As you are asking your questions, open-ended or not, remember the power that listening has on your juror. Effective communication is 30 percent talking, 70 percent listening. Be interested in your adversary's answers. Maintain eye contact with him. Nod your head to let him know you are on the same page and that you are on the same side. Listening accomplishes two objectives: First, it eliminates the feeling that the presentation has been scripted in advance, and second, it keeps you alert to the unexpected answers that will inevitably appear.

Direct examination is also the time to admit into evidence any facts that undermine your case, so that you can present them in a way favorable to your argument. If you don't admit them into evidence, your opponent will ambush you with them later. Not all cases are cut and dried—there is always evidence unfavorable to the client. The way this evidence is presented is the difference between an average lawyer and a brilliant one.

Challenges

The most challenging and necessary part of presenting your case is to maintain control of your presentation at all times. From your adversary's often defensive or distracted reactions to your own natural tenseness, you will find yourself surmounting all kinds of roadblocks, some of which you will have anticipated and others that you deal with on your feet.

When Nicole spoke to a school principal about getting her thirteen-year-old son, Brad, transferred to a classroom with a more experienced teacher, she had to make sure she didn't let herself become provoked when he went off on tangents. "The guy kept interrupting me and spinning off into these long speeches about school choice and how parents and kids could make any situation work if they just tried hard enough. This had nothing to do with what my kid was experiencing—his teacher was ignoring him in class!—I had to hold my temper and steer him back onto the topic. The evidence I had—what other parents said about this teacher, the disaster I had documented over his test preparation—helped me remember why I was there, which was to get Brad out of that classroom."

In my court cases prosecuting criminals, even when witnesses were prepped, they often became nervous being in the spotlight and forgot what they were going to say. I'd cringe when I heard, "I don't recall." The solution is to go back to your discovery (all the research and evidence you've compiled) and "refresh the recollection" of your witness. "Ma'am, I'm showing you your earlier sworn testimony. Would you please read that to yourself and then answer my question?"

Sometimes you have to call a "hostile" witness for your side— someone who can help your case, but doesn't want to (for example, the mom, sister, or girlfriend of a criminal defendant). In court, you can ask the judge to deem her "hostile," and then you can "lead" the witness. If she still dances around your question, you can ask it again and persist until you get an answer. If the witness refuses several times to answer your question, the jury will realize that she is trying to hide something from them, and will distrust whatever she has to say.

The process of presenting your evidence and asking questions to support your case will not be as cut and dried as it appears in the pages of this book. Rarely does an adversary sit idly by as a case is presented—human nature causes a fight-or-flight response. You can count on the fact that your juror will try to turn the tables on you.

As the inevitable challenges come your way, stick to your plan. It is not necessary to jump ahead to respond to a challenge; you can do it in your own good time. As your juror tries to sideline your points, keep asking the same questions, making the same point gently and persistently, to stay on track and reinforce your point (and make your opponent look silly and bullying in the process).

If I know the answer to a question, and I know the witness knows the answer to the question, I will not change my course. For example, in a vehicular homicide case, if I know the defendant has had ten beers at The Tavern that night—eyewitnesses have testified to it, the defendant has earlier confessed to it, the bar tab says it—I will say, "Sir, isn't it true you had ten beers to drink on the night in question between eight and ten PM?" Defendant responds, "I might have had a few." My follow-up: "Before you got in the car at ten fifteen and before you plowed into and killed Mrs. Clark, you had ten beers, didn't you?" Defendant again responds, "I might have had a few." I continue, "You had ten beers, sir. Let me draw it on the blackboard for you. 1, 2, 3, 4, 5, 6, 7, 8, 9, 10. Ten beers." I stick with my line of questioning until he has no choice but to admit his "few" is really ten. If he keeps saying "a few" even after I point out the evidence, I have made my point and the jury realizes he is lying by not answering my question honestly. You cannot always get liars to tell the truth, but you can expose them as liars.

Asking yes-or-no questions when you are being challenged during your presentation is also an effective way to stay on track. And by all means, avoid engaging in argument over evidentiary points. You are presenting, not arguing.

The Do's and Don'ts of Presenting

Before you launch into the presentation of your case, do your legwork, so that you won't get ahead of yourself—establish your theory, select the juror, the time and place for the discussion, and gather your evidence. Above all, don't allow emotion to dictate your argument and encourage the tendency to jump ahead of yourself with a passionate argument.

Just like Nicole, the mother who made her son's case to the

principal, it is important to remember exactly why you are presenting your evidence. To ensure that your emotions don't get the best of you and to reinforce your confidence, consider the following do's and don'ts of making your case:

- **Do** keep your voice low and steady.
- **Do** go slowly.
- **Do** be pleasant—you don't need to act like a prosecutor to succeed like a prosecutor.
- **Do** present yourself as a thoughtful teacher. You are not arguing; you are gently educating.
- **Don't** forget to breathe deeply and calmly—and **do** remember that you are more prepared than your opponent.
- **Don't** use over-the-top legalese. Unless you really are in court, legalese and stiff arguments will be ineffective.

Only after you have laid the groundwork should you plan your case, solidly building it into a clear and concise presentation. With careful and pointed planning, the case will be so clear that your adversary, juror, or judge will have no choice but to agree with you and give you what you want.

But make no bones about it—this will not be easy. Very rarely do you sit down to make your case only to hear your juror declare, "You're right! You deserve a refund. Would you like cash, or can I give you a check?"

In a perfect world, the outcome we seek would be the one we receive. Most often, however, we present our case to our adversary only to have him turn around and discredit our theory.

When I was a freshman at Columbia, I took a job as a nanny to a family on the Upper West Side of Manhattan. It was basically the only way I could afford to live in New York and attend a college that was out of my reach financially. After a semester with this family, I realized I wasn't being treated fairly. In addition to a small salary, I had been promised room and board. The conditions were dreadful: I had to sleep in a cold, damp basement (even though there was an empty guest room upstairs), I wasn't invited to eat with the family, and my salary was far less than what other nannies I had talked to were receiving. I decided to ask for a raise and better living conditions. Even though I didn't realize it at the time, I was actually making my case.

I wanted to continue working for them, but under better conditions (Theory of the Case). I decided to approach the couple together rather than individually, and one night, after the children went to bed, I asked if I could speak with them, knowing that would be the best time to have their full attention, and they'd be the most relaxed (Voir Dire). After telling them how much I enjoyed the children (Opening Statement), I presented my evidence of what other nannies were making, their duties, and their benefits (Discovery). I asked them, "What am I doing right?" "What could I do better?" (Direct Examination) and suggested ways I could help them more—with the laundry, for instance.

I concluded, "And with those responsibilities, I think I deserve better compensation and living conditions." I can remember waiting confidently for the answer. Naively I was convinced they had heard my concerns and would readily give me the guest room and a better salary. Instead, the husband stood up and declared, "That's absolutely ridiculous. We're giving you what you're worth, Lis."

Uh-oh. I hadn't anticipated such a strong no. I slunk out of the living room, defeated. Retreating to the mildewy basement, I comforted myself with a Ritz cracker, thinking, *What just happened?* I had been so confident, so sure, but now I doubted myself. He had actually convinced me with his dismissal that I didn't deserve any better. He had turned the tables on me, and I had fallen for it.

What could I have done differently? At the time, I was stumped, but had I waited until I finished law school, I would've listened to his response, then calmly countered with a valuable trial lawyer technique: cross-examination.

SKILLS OF A LAWYER FOR THE TRIALS OF YOUR LIFE

LEGAL BRIEF: STEP 4

MAKING YOUR CASE

1. Refer to the trial plan you completed in Step 3.

    a. How did you arrange your evidence?

    b. What is the fact that gives "the bang" with which you can begin?

    c. What is your "smoking gun"—the strongest piece with which you can end?

2. Establish your theme, tone, and demeanor.

    a. Establish a theme.

        i. Is a theme effective for your advocacy? Or is using one inappropriate?

        ii. In terms of choosing a theme, what is your case about?

            1. Is your theme the underdog? Responsibility? Justice?

            2. Is your theme logical?

            3. Is it phrased in a way that will align with your juror's life experiences and preconceived notions?

            4. Does your theme effectively ask your juror to "do the right thing"?

    b. Set your tone.

        i. Decide on the tone of your voice and on your mannerisms before you present your case, and stick with your choices when emotions run high.

        ii. No matter what tone you choose, it must be nonthreatening and positive.

        iii. What will your juror respond best to—being firm? Authoritative? Gentle? Or will playing dim-witted and requesting help serve your purpose best?

    c. How will you present yourself (if you are meeting your juror in person)?

        i. What clothing will you wear?

    ii. Does your hair, makeup, or accessories send a message that is consistent with your theme, tone, and theory? (For example, what does a Rolex watch say about your financial status?)

    iii. Make a commitment to relax during your presentation.

    iv. Remember to make eye contact, avoid distracting mannerisms, and adopt an open posture (keep your arms uncrossed, for instance).

3. Plan your opening statement.

    a. What is the case about?

    b. Keeping in mind that jurors best remember what they hear first and last, what do you want to begin with?

    c. Combine your "big bang" with what your case is about to write your opening statement—the theory you will state as you begin your presentation.

    d. As you write your theory sentence, remember to make it consistent with your theme, tone, and presentation.

    e. Preview your evidence—state what you have that will support your request.

    f. Request the outcome you want.

4. Sort your evidence.

    a. What evidence will be most effective as a statement of fact? (For example, "You charged me twenty-five dollars per hour on last month's invoice.")

    b. Knowing that information is more powerful when jurors state it themselves, what evidence will be most effectively phrased as a question?

       i. Leading questions. ("Doesn't this invoice say that you charged me twenty per hour?")

       ii. Open-ended questions. ("According to this month's invoice, how much did you charge?")

    c. What evidence will undermine your case?

5. Write the statements and questions you will use during direct examination.

    a. Write your open-ended questions.

    b. Write your leading questions.

    c. Present the evidence that undermines your case in the best way to minimize its impact. ("It's my fault that I didn't request a bid for your services, but since you didn't say anything to the contrary, I assumed you would be charging the same hourly rate as last month.")

6. Present your case.

    a. Open with a statement that grabs your juror's attention and explains your theory of the case.

    b. Tell your juror what evidence you have that supports your theory.

    c. Walk through your evidence as planned, ending with your strongest piece.

    d. Directly address your juror. Ask questions that, when answered, will support your case.

7. Finish with your summary.

    a. Write your summary sentence using your strongest piece of information. ("Your invoice stated that you spent June 24, 25, and 26 working on my kitchen, but I was home sick on the twenty-sixth and you never arrived—so unless I'm mistaken, you worked only sixteen hours total.")

    b. Repeat the outcome you desire. ("Therefore, the invoice should be adjusted, don't you agree?")

Chapter 5

Step 5. Counter the Claims:

Cross-Examination

> *Use cross-examination to get the other side to agree to evidence that supports your case.*

PROSECUTOR: I'll ask you one last time, did you kill the victim?

DEFENDANT: No sir, I did not.

PROSECUTOR: Do you know what the penalties are for perjury?

DEFENDANT: Yes sir, I do. And I know they're a lot better than the penalty for murder.

Once trial lawyers present their case and finish the direct examination part of the trial, they utilize cross-examination as a response to witness testimony to either have witnesses admit to evidence that supports their theory of the case or to ask questions that discredit a witness favorable to the other side. Cross-examination involves asking two types of questions: Yes-or-no questions and leading questions (those that encourage a particular answer).

Translating this to your personal case, once you and the person with whom you're dealing have both made your cases clear to one another, you can use cross-examination to get the other person to agree to evidence that supports your theory or to point out where he is mistaken.

But here's a sage word of advice for cross-examination in your case: *Tread lightly.* Remember that cross-examination involves asking pointed questions designed to get a witness or your opponent to say what you want. The witness is not free to explain her answers—which, of course, is very frustrating. In the courtroom, it is not a technique that engenders warm feelings between the lawyer and the witness, and the best lawyers use it at trial in a very responsible way. Bullying a witness on the stand is something to be reserved for rare instances.

When Sam Waterston, who plays a talented and seasoned prosecutor on *Law & Order,* pressures witnesses to admit they're lying, we're thrilled by the surrender. In the midst of a conflict, we all imagine ourselves cornering our adversaries through our skillful questioning and, in a final dramatic moment, trapping them into admitting wrongdoing. But in real life, this type of questioning is dangerous. As for dreaming of becoming a skilled cross-examiner of everyone from your spouse to your boss, forget about it. The dream is nice; the reality is a nightmare. People married to lawyers will tell you they hate it when their spouse uses cross-examination in a family argument.

SPOUSE: Honey, I really think we need to get a new car. Ours is really starting to fall apart.

LAWYER: But just last week, you said you enjoyed driving it, isn't that true?

SPOUSE: Well, honey, what I meant was—

LAWYER: Answer the question: Yes or no.

SPOUSE: Look, there's more to it than—

LAWYER: It's a simple question. I think you can give me a simple answer.

SPOUSE: Yes, I can: I want a divorce.

The kind of forceful cross-examination you see on TV is appropriate only when you're trying to prove someone is lying or when you want to make someone squirm. It puts the other person in a defensive, hostile position. So you certainly wouldn't use this approach with anyone with whom you want to have an ongoing relationship. It could prove very destructive to the relationship.

That said, cross-examination—and asking simple yes-or-no questions to nudge the person you're dealing with to get to the truth of the situation—can, in many circumstances, be useful to you. When done sensitively, cross-examination does not need to be a poisonous process. Used to gently lead your adversary and encourage him to see the validity of your theory on his own, cross-examination can be an effective way to move your case forward.

For instance, I know a trial lawyer in Atlanta who uses this technique with her teenaged daughter when she wants to help the girl see something she's avoiding or denying. The lawyer alternates between leading questions and open-ended questions—but only when there's one logical answer. She uses these to gently nudge her daughter in the right direction, so there's only one conclusion:

KATIE: Joshua likes me, but my friend Tiffany won't let him talk to me. She's always putting me down and trying to make him like her.

MOM: Your feelings are hurt by what Tiffany is doing, right?

KATIE: Yes.

MOM: But you don't think you can talk to her about it?

KATIE: No.

MOM: Because you don't want to make her feel bad?

KATIE: Right.

MOM: Okay. Well, you've told me in the past that a lot of kids don't like Tiffany.

KATIE: Yes.

MOM: She's bossy?

KATIE: Uh-huh.

MOM: Isn't what she's doing with you and Joshua an example of the kind of thing that makes people not like her?

KATIE: Yes.

MOM: But Tiffany doesn't understand why people don't like her.

KATIE: No, she doesn't.

MOM: And if nobody ever tells Tiffany that what she's doing is hurtful to them, and makes people not like her, then she won't be able to change her behavior, and she won't have any friends.

KATIE: Well, I guess so.

MOM: Okay, and right now you feel terrible about what she's doing. And if you talk to her, she might feel terrible.

KATIE: Yes.

MOM: But if you tell her, you might feel better if she stops doing it.

KATIE: Yes.

MOM: And if Tiffany learns from it, it'll help Tiffany in the long run because she'll have more friends.

KATIE: Yes. You're right.

To the extent possible, Katie's mother wants these questions to help Katie take the journey herself, from her starting position—"I could never say anything to Tiffany!"—to the logical end position—"Talking to Tiffany is good for her and for me." It's done gently and without any accusations or browbeating. Her mom guided her into seeing something important, but without any of the dramatic questioning—*Isn't it true, Katie, that Tiffany is making your life miserable? Just yes or no!*—that would only make Katie run to her room in tears.

Break Down Your Opponent's Arguments

Having to deal with your adversary's response is by far the most nerve-racking part of making your case. However, you can ease the anxiety of presenting your counterargument by employing the legal tools of cross-examination to keep you on course. By asking yes-or-no or leading questions, designed to confirm information that you know is true, you maintain control and are able to keep your eye on the prize: winning the case.

As you did in Step 3 when you gathered your evidence and planned your line of reasoning, you can use the strategies of cross-examination to assess an opposing case and break it down point by point in order to point out flawed facts or gaps in logic.

Central to the process of discrediting your adversary's evidence is to catch nuances and weaknesses in his arguments—in other words, to listen. As obvious as it sounds, we often forget to do just this, concentrating so wholeheartedly on the next set of questions we have planned that we miss an opportunity to support or refute evidence crucial to our case.

Sitting opposite Bill O'Reilly on his nationally syndicated radio show is sometimes a test of listening and then bringing out the cross-examination skills to challenge Bill's arguments. Recently Bill and I debated the death of Jessie, a girl who had gotten a bad heart transplant at Duke Hospital. Bill's position was that the parents of this girl should not be able to sue Duke Hospital or the doctors who performed the surgery because she and her parents had come into the United States illegally.

O'REILLY: She's a Mexican, and her parents smuggled her across the border from Mexico so that they could get her heart surgery. The hospital tried to save her life, but they couldn't. So, Jessica's parents are going to sue the hospital. I think that's absolutely wrong!

WIEHL: Why?

O'REILLY: Because the hospital tried to save her life when it didn't have to. The hospital didn't have to perform the operation.

WIEHL: But once they took on the responsibility to perform the operation, they took it on to perform it correctly, not negligently.

O'REILLY: And you believe they did it on purpose?

WIEHL: No, they made a mistake. The surgeon made a mistake.

O'REILLY: Absolutely.

WIEHL: But that's negligence.

O'REILLY: Jessica's mother made a mistake by bringing her here illegally.

WIEHL: I'll grant you that. But once the hospital took on this little girl, they had the obligation to do the right thing by her.

O'REILLY: They didn't do the wrong thing, they did the incompetent thing. I think it's morally unacceptable for the mother to sue the hospital. The hospital did the family a tremendous favor by doing what they didn't have to do, by trying to save this girl's life. The laws of this country dictate that the girl didn't have the right to this transplant.

WIEHL: You're not going to punish incompetence?

O'REILLY: Not in this case.

WIEHL: Why?

O'REILLY: Because I did something wrong to put my daughter in the position.

WIEHL: Oh, gee. So, doctors can be incompetent when they perform operations on illegals, and they won't be punished for it?

Later, when I resorted to using the skills of good cross-examination, I made my point.

WIEHL: Wait a second, the doctors took on the patient, correct?

O'REILLY: Yes.

WIEHL: They promised to give their best care, right?

O'REILLY: Yes.

WIEHL: And yet the operating doctor used a blood type he knew to be wrong for little Jessie.

O'REILLY: Yes, but he didn't do it on purpose.

WIEHL: And so the parents shouldn't be allowed to sue? In other words, you'll give the doctor and the hospital a free pass based on this girl's and her parents' legal status, not on the fact that they're people.

O'REILLY: Cut her microphone!

And they did! It was the first time in the history of his show that a cohost had her microphone cut off. The next day, the e-mail had streamed in. So Bill said on air, "Well, the listeners are about 50–50 on our debate yesterday."

"Wait a minute," I interjected. "I still got 50 percent of the votes, even though you cut my mike off? Imagine if you had not turned off my mike!" Bill was speechless.

Don't Panic!

When making your case, you will inevitably encounter arguments that attempt to discredit your theory. Do not panic; instead, guide the discussion back to the items that support your theory using the following three techniques: impeaching, exposing nontruths, and discrediting hearsay.

Impeach

Impeaching a witness means showing that what this person has said just isn't true. As unpleasant as it sounds, we impeach each other's statements all the time. If your child told you she was going to do her homework before playing video games, and you interrupt her game to show her the unfinished worksheet you found in her backpack, you've impeached her by contradicting previous testimony with present reality. But beware: It also works in the other direction. Your child does the same thing to you when she interrupts your phone conversation to say, "You promised you'd read me a book right after dinner, but now you're on the phone."

Impeaching a statement or witness is an effective means of proving your case. Essentially, you are making your adversary acknowledge prior testimony and then challenging what she said with current testimony. Trial lawyers begin this technique by establishing the current testimony, asking leading questions, and then nailing the opponent on the contradiction between what was declared earlier and what is being said now.

You can employ these techniques outside the courtroom by following a similar model of impeachment. Say you want to prove your boss's tendency to say one thing, and then do another. You might make your case by asking him to verify his current stance on a situation ("No, I never gave this project the go-ahead"); follow by asking him leading questions ("Is this the memo you signed on January 28?" "Does this line say the project is 'approved'?"); and get what you want by stating the now obvious contradiction ("So, Mr. Tate, you say you never agreed to the joint project, but you signed this memo on January 28").

During the impeachment proceedings against President Clinton, I was hired by the U.S. House of Representatives Judiciary Committee to help conduct the investigation and advise the Democrats. I was consistently in a power-deficit position against the Republicans' lawyers and ironically had to use "impeachment" techniques on a regular basis. For example, one of the big questions early on in the investigation was whether both sides would be able to subpoena (call) potential witnesses to testify. On the record, the GOP lawyers were quick to say that both sides would be allowed to call witnesses if they desired. So we lawyers huddled and decided to indeed send out several subpoenas to at least interview some potential witnesses.

Our GOP counterparts quickly came back and told us that we had no right to call witnesses, and that they (the GOP) held the exclusive rights to issue subpoenas and wouldn't allow any subpoena requests from the Democrats. I had to put to them their prior inconsistent statement—that is, the public record in which the GOP lawyers said, "Both sides can subpoena witnesses on request." I "impeached" them to get them to admit that they had actually made that declaration and that they were now backing off that promise with no apparent cause. The result: We were able to send out our own subpoenas.

The impeachment during The Impeachment didn't stop there. The GOP also held the purse strings. We were a bit surprised when the five of us—there were five lawyers for the Democrats, twenty-five or so for the GOP—showed up on the job the Saturday after the Starr report was released to find that we had no offices, no secretary, and no copy machine. A couple of us trudged over to Kinko's for pens and pads, but we realized we had no place where we could talk in private, because the press was camped out everywhere. Meanwhile, Newt Gingrich had publicly declared that the Democrats would have a well-cared-for staff. So Richard Gephardt, Democratic minority leader, went to Gingrich and impeached him with his prior inconsistent statement, saying, in effect, "If you don't want this situation on the front page of the *New York Times* tomorrow, you'll remedy this problem."

The next morning we had an office, complete with cable television, copiers, computers, and a secretary. (Not quite the plush accommodations of the GOP lawyers—who got a full kitchen, snack room, and more—but still, we were much relieved.) Sometimes, even during Impeachment, impeachment comes in very handy.

It always helps to remind people of the things they've said, especially when it helps your case.

Expose Nontruths

Because you have done such thorough evidence gathering, you can impeach not just a witness or adversary's recently made contradictory statements, but facts that you know not to be true. And you can do it without losing your bearings or seeming prosecutorial.

Several years ago I bought a Ford SUV and was very excited about it. I thought it would be very safe for chauffering my kids around, but a few weeks after I bought the vehicle, the Firestone tires on many Expeditions began blowing up and causing wrecks. (This eventually led to a full recall.) Having read the initial reports, I called the dealer who'd sold me the car. He had, of course, treated me as his best friend during the sale, but now, when I said I was upset over all the news reports and wanted different tires put on my car free of charge, my "best friend" said he had no clue what I was talking about.

I asked a few more questions, and then said, "Dozens of people have been killed in overseas accidents when these tires exploded."

He blurted, "No, not dozens of people. Only a handful." Gotcha! He *had* heard the reports, and I had exposed him as a liar. The result (after I exposed his nontruth): I got my tires replaced at no cost.

Discredit Hearsay

In many common disputes, much of what people call evidence is actually hearsay, secondhand or worse. Such testimony is completely unreliable. Remember the game of "telephone"?

For several summers during childhood, I attended Camp Rogununda in eastern Washington State. Every year on the first day of camp the counselor sat us in a big circle on the lawn in front of the cabins. In an attempt to ward off gossip for camp week, we engaged in the game of telephone, in which we whispered a secret one to another all the way around the circle. The game teaches its subtle lesson when the statement *Johnny's eyes are blue* becomes, after twelve retellings, *Jenny has the flu.*

Many of the faulty cases in our daily life are built around hearsay, similar to this game. When hearsay is offered as fact, it can often be challenged quite easily. Phrases like *he said* or *my second cousin's boyfriend told me* should be alarm bells telling you that what follows should be challenged. The telltale "she said" is your cue to respond, "Did you actually hear that person say . . . ?"

If you are a sales representative and the vice president of your division tells you that sales of the company's classical music recordings are down in your territory by 15 percent, and you have no idea where he got that figure, you might just find out that the "statistic" is nothing more than something he heard from an unreliable source. When, through cross-examination, you find out that one of the sales reps for a different territory—the one who wants your job because it's an easier commute for him—is the one who told the vice president about the drop, you can establish that the evidence the vice president is reacting to is hearsay.

During the LASER program in Washington State—the program I helped lead for middle and high school students in which lawyers trained students to mediate disputes among their peers—I saw students falling into the trap of hearsay every day. I counseled many students who would start their story by saying something like, "My friend Mary told me that Joey told her that Sue said I'm fat, and I'm mad at Sue." I'd quickly ask, "Did you actually hear Sue say it?" When the answer was no, I'd send the student out to find undeniable evidence. On occasion, somebody had actually said something mean, but nine times out of ten it was a misunderstanding that was quickly resolved.

Hearsay really is quickly resolved. All it takes is getting to the alleged initial source and asking, "Did you say x?" Take the time to ask; it'll save you a lot of angst.

To Rebut or Not to Rebut? That Is the Question

Many of your adversary's responses warrant the question, "Should I rebut this counterclaim or is it more effective to ignore it?" That is, should I provide evidence or an argument that opposes what he said, showing that it is not correct or to be believed, or should I consider it unworthy of a response?

In most instances, responding with just the facts, sans emotion, will negate your opponent's attempts at derailing your case. During a rebuttal, however, it is important to discourage your adversary from explaining her position, since hostile witnesses will often take any opportunity to slip in a statement damaging to your theory.

Limiting your juror's "talk time" is an effective means to avoid explanations during cross, which can be accomplished by using short, leading questions ("Mr. Reeves, doesn't this invoice show charges that were present on last month's invoice?"). Avoid using open-ended questions at this time ("Mr. Reeves, what does this invoice say?"), because it gives your juror an opportunity to explain his position in a manner that's often unfavorable to your case.

Often, not answering with a rebuttal, but simply getting the line of questioning back on track, will do the trick. Without directly addressing your opponent's statements, carefully planned phrases such as those listed below can negate the effect they have on discrediting your argument.

- "No, what I'm asking you is . . ."
- "Let me repeat what I just presented to you . . ."
- "Did you hear the fact directly? No? Then who told it to you? And do you know what that person's source was? And *his* source?"
- "Here is why I believe that person would make that claim against me . . ."
- "Today, you are saying this . . . But as you see, on this date you said this . . ."
- "I'm sorry, but that's not the real issue. The real issue here is . . ."

Preparing Your Cross

Regardless of your intent—whether to support your evidence or to discredit the other person (or that person's witness)—the structure of the cross should be developed using the following two guidelines:

1. **Don't repeat your direct.** Keep in mind that cross-examination is *not* the time to reargue all the evidence you exhibited in Step 4.

2. **Make your strongest points at the beginning and end.** Open your cross with strength and finish with a bang, with a few lesser points sandwiched between. People will remember best what they hear first and last.

In order to accomplish your goal, remember the following three points when you prepare your cross-examination:

1. Adhere to your theory of the case even under challenge.
2. Keep command of your case when emotions run high.
3. Prepare cross-examination in advance and anticipate your opponent's arguments.

1. Adhere to Your Theory

In Step 4 you learned how to prepare a direct examination of your adversary using the evidence you unearthed in discovery. As you present your case, no doubt you will experience opposition—but the advocates who stand up for themselves under pressure and keep their goal in sight will end up getting what they want.

Similar to direct, the first few seconds of a cross-examination can make or break its effectiveness. Keep your introduction decisive and avoid weak statements such as, "Principal Howard, I'd like to ask you a few questions about my son's teacher." The only purpose these introductory proclamations serve is to show Principal Howard that you aren't really confident in what you're going to say. Instead, begin with a declaratory bang: "Principal Howard, is it true that my son's teacher failed the state proficiency exam for teachers?" (information you learned during your discovery). This makes Principal Howard aware that you are informed and ready, so he'd better pay attention.

Stick to your points and make them resolute, keeping your theory as subtext to each of the questions you pose. ("Principal

Howard, is it true that my son's teacher failed the state proficiency exam for teachers?" Subtext: I want my son out of that classroom and into the class with the better teacher.)

In cross-examination, you don't want your adversary to tell her story—you want to control her testimony so that her answers are assertions of fact that support your case. Make your points quick, informative, and without question.

2. Keep Command of Your Case

Cross-examinations can be frustrating—an adversary's answers may not be to your liking, and the tendency to argue will always exist. In terms of maintaining your credibility with your juror, arguing is a disaster. Show me a person who stoops to the level of argumentative probing, and I'll show you an ineffective advocate.

I've always said, you don't have to be cross to deliver an effective cross-examination. I learned my lesson as a young prosecutor when I lost my temper at a witness I knew was lying to me. Reaching for the Perry Mason gotcha moment where he would break down and confess the crime right on the stand, I got hot under the collar and lost my cool, blowing up at him. All I did was make myself look like an underfed pit bull. I did nothing but lose credibility. Now I know how to walk softly but carry a big stick.

Knowing you don't have to be overtly aggressive is perhaps the most liberating truth of effective cross-examination. In most instances, showing frustration and anger in communication does nothing but force your witness into a stance of righteous indignation. Think of the last instance in which you gave in to the knee-jerk reaction of irrationally attacking your spouse over something trivial the moment he or she walked through the door. Nine times out of ten, the response was immediate hostility and defensiveness—which accomplishes nothing but igniting an unpleasant evening.

Rather than give in to your emotions during cross-examination (or any step of your case, for that matter), I have found that challenging an adversary based on your presentation of the facts, without raising your voice or your ire, is the most effective road to getting what you want.

3. Anticipate Your Opponent's Arguments

If your discovery is thorough, you should not be hearing any surprises during cross-examination. When Robert found out that his sister Brenda was abusing their shared power of attorney for their ailing mother's affairs—Brenda was charging her own groceries to their mother's credit card—he was able to challenge her, carefully, on two grounds. After Robert produced the credit card bill, Brenda countered by saying she bought the groceries not for herself but for their mother. Robert, foreseeing this, cross-examined.

> Q: Was Mom in the hospital on February 11?
> A: Yes.
> Q: She finally went home on the twenty-third?
> A: That's right.
> Q: And the hospital prepared all her food up until she went home?
> A: Of course.

He pointed to the date for one of the charges and compared it to the hospital bill.

> Q: So Mom was in the hospital recovering from surgery during the two-week period these groceries were purchased?
> A: You're right, Robert. I purchased a few things on Mom's credit card.
> Q: You actually spent close to five hundred dollars, right?
> A: No, it was just a few things.
> Q: Here are three charges during that period. Do they add up to around five hundred dollars?
> A: I was going to pay it back!

Robert was able to effectively cross-examine his sister because he prepared a counterargument *in advance* of the confrontation, not as a result of the confrontation.

During cross, play it safe. This is a time to elicit responses favorable to your case or to minimize the impact of unfavorable ones, not the time to embark on a new discovery expedition hunting for new information. The questions you ask should be those for which you know the answers.

I was hired a year ago to be a legal ethics expert in a case involving the breakup of a legal partnership. At the trial, the opposing lawyer tried to grill me on my credentials. "Ms. Wiehl," he asked, "how many years have you taught legal ethics?"

"Five," I said, "plus I also taught the bar exam, and have been hired many times as a behind-the-scenes legal ethics expert." He was getting nowhere in attacking my credentials, so he decided to go ahead and bring out his smoking gun. "Isn't it true, Ms. Wiehl, that you've never testified as a legal ethics expert at trial?"

Anticipating (and relishing) this question, I answered, "That's right, sir. I get paid the same whether I testify or not, and since testifying is stressful, I've always turned down these cases. But when she [the lawyer I was testifying for] came to me, her story was so compelling and she had been so wronged by your client that I thought it was my moral and ethical responsibility to the profession to take on this case."

That ended his line of questioning, and we won the trial.

Cross-examination is almost addictive—there is always one more point to refute, one more question to ask. But be careful not to ask one question too many. During cross, you should only ask enough questions to establish the points you will make during your closing argument (Step 8). Don't let the person you're questioning end your case with an answer. If you must roll the dice and ask questions whose answers you aren't sure of, at least be sure you can handle the responses.

If I Knew Then What I Know Now

The process of presenting your evidence is only the tip of the iceberg in the comprehensive preparation of a trial. Unless your direct examination is so effective that the company you want to acquire instantly agrees to your proposed purchase terms or the guy who skidded into your car offers to buy you a new one, you're going to have to contend with your opponent's counterarguments.

As a college freshman, thinking I'd made a convincing argument for better pay in my nanny job, I unfortunately didn't anticipate that my employers might not instantly acquiesce to my requests. I was naive to the "jerk factor"—some people just don't want to listen. Knowing what I know now, I would be able to deal with their negative retort. Rather than consoling myself with Ritz crackers in a cold basement, I would have come back with this cross-examination:

Q: Mr. Marcus, when you hired me to work as your nanny, you told me the terms of the employment, correct?

A: That's right.

Q: Specifically, you told me that you had two children, Katie and Julia, and that I would be responsible for making them breakfast, taking them to school, picking them up, and taking care of them after school by taking them to the park and playing games with them. Right?

A: Yes.

Q: Then each night it would be my job to make their dinner, bathe them, and put them to bed?

A: Yes.

Q: Have I made their breakfast every day, taken them to school, and picked them up?

A: Yes.

Q: And have I played with them and taken them for fun trips in the park?

A: Yes.

Q: And have I made them dinner each night and put them to bed with a bedtime story?

A: Yes.

Q: And in exchange, you promised to give me a room?

A: Yes.

Q: And you have a guest room upstairs?

A: Yes.

Q: And in the four months I've been here, has anyone ever stayed in the guest room?

A: I don't think so.

Q: You promised me board?

A: Yes.

Q: Did you tell me that you would pay for my food?

A: Yes.

Q: So I've moved here from Washington to work for you and you've entrusted me with the safety and well-being of your two beautiful little girls?

A: Yes.

Q: And I live in the basement?

A: Yes.

Q: And all I am allowed to eat is peanut butter and crackers?

A: Uh . . .

SKILLS OF A LAWYER FOR THE TRIALS OF YOUR LIFE

LEGAL BRIEF: STEP 5

CROSS-EXAMINATION

1. Think about your cross-examination.

   a. Carry the theme, tone, and demeanor you set before your direct through to your cross-examination.

   b. Base your cross on what you already know from discovery.

2. What to do before you prepare your cross:

   a. State your objective for cross.

        i. What pieces of evidence do you want to reiterate that were stated in direct?

        ii. How about evidence that discredits negative responses from direct—those that don't support your theory?

   b. Avoid repeating the questions and statements you asked in direct.

   c. Keep it quick: Limit your questions for cross to no more than five.

3. Plan your cross.

   a. Write your cross in the same manner as your direct, keeping in mind that jurors remember best what they hear first and last.

        i. What piece of information that supports your case will you start with—your "big bang"?

        ii. What piece of information that supports your case will you end with—your finish?

        iii. All questions that support minor evidence and discredit facts working against you should be your "sandwich" questions.

   b. Finally, respond only to juror answers that are worth discrediting or supporting.

        i. What juror statements will you respond to?

        ii. Which will you ignore? For example, all statements tainted with emotion should be ignored—it's not worth getting into a boxing match.

4. Write your cross.

   a. Question types:

        i. Use only yes-or-no or simple leading questions, no open-ended questions.

        ii. Use questions only when you are 99 percent sure that you can manage your juror's answer.

        iii. Use no statements in cross, only questions—remember, the point is to have your juror's own answers support or discredit evidence.

        iv. Likewise, no new information should be presented here.

   b. Be prepared and write two versions.

        i. One set is responses to how you think your juror will respond.

        ii. The other is in case your juror throws you a curveball.

    c. Write questions that support your theory.

        i. For example, "Mr. Niceguy, do you agree that the red paint on your bumper matches that on the side of my truck where a dent is present?"

    d. Pre-plan your questions to break down arguments.

        i. Specific to your case, how will you use impeachment?

        ii. Expose nontruths?

        iii. Discredit hearsay?

5. Finish with your summary.

    a. Finish with the question that drives home the most important piece of evidence presented thus far. "Isn't it true that Ms. Smith and Mr. Neighbor-across-the-street both gave witness statements that you were driving your blue Honda when it sideswiped my truck?"

    b. Again, repeat the outcome you desire. "It's only fair, then, that you pay for the damages."

Chapter 6

Step 6. Stay True to Your Case:
Avoid the Seven Deadly Spins

> *Staying true to your case is not only a matter of integrity but also a key to the success of your advocacy.*

At this point, you may feel that you have accomplished all that is in your power: You have established your theory, picked your jury, organized and planned your case. You are feeling invincible. What could possibly happen to derail you on your road to victory?

One word: *spin.*

I spend many waking hours with the master of the no-spin zone on radio and TV every week, and the word *spin* will never mean the same to me. Setting aside whether you agree with his stance on issues, Bill O'Reilly's point on spin is well taken. If you try to veil your arguments in conclusions with premises not built on fact, or say something that you can't support, or try to divert attention from the real issue—you're guilty of spin.

The Seven Deadly Spins

There are Seven Deadly Spins in making your case that can send even a winning case out of control:

Spin 1. Abandoning, digressing from, or deviating from your theory of the case.
Spin 2. Overpromising.
Spin 3. Adding last-minute charges that prejudice your case.
Spin 4. Resorting to hearsay evidence.
Spin 5. Making subjective characterizations.
Spin 6. Making false inferences.
Spin 7. Expressing uncontrolled emotion.

These Seven Deadly Spins are potholes in your road to victory—weaknesses that, if not avoided, will throw your case out of alignment. Here's how to spot and steer around them.

Spin 1: Abandoning, digressing from, or deviating from your theory of the case.
Cure 1: Don't go there!

While presenting your case and managing your adversary's response to it, you will be tempted to deviate from your considered approach and respond in the heat of the moment—speaking off the cuff or inserting a piece of evidence that relates in no way to your theory of the case.

Take for instance, Evelyn, who was purchasing a country house in a small town. After the thirty-day grace period to close had come and gone, the owner of the house decided to pull the deal from Evelyn and sell the property to a higher bidder. Evelyn was enraged. The reason she hadn't closed was because the title search company said the house did not have clear title, so she arranged for a meeting with the owner and came well prepared to make her case. She laid out the facts: "I've spent several thousand dollars on inspections and on an architect for his designs. I've already met with the town's building inspector and gotten plan approvals, and the contractors are ready to begin work immediately."

Then Evelyn laid out her theory of the case—she wanted the house at the price agreed to, but was told by her mortgaging bank that she couldn't close without clear title. She explained to the owner that due to some issues that he needed to clear up—the clear title—she couldn't close. When the owner mentioned that the other buyer could close right away because he was paying all cash, Evelyn lost sight of her theory. She could have said, "Yes, but our deal wasn't all cash, there was a mortgage contingency, and you agreed to provide me with a clear title and a house in broom-clean condition." But she didn't. Instead, the suggestion of "cash" threw her off course, and she completely digressed from her solid theory into mudslinging and accusations of the owner's drug use and dirty dealings.

Had she stuck with her theory of the case, she might have convinced the owner to be a gentleman and stick to his word, even though the contract was technically void. But it was too late: Evelyn had fallen victim to Spin 1, and it cost her. The owner got up, walked out of the room, and sold the house out from under her the following week.

In the heat of your argument, you will be tempted to toss in irrelevant or prejudicial evidence or divert your argument into the hot-button issues. Don't. It will only damage your case. Staying true to the ultimate goal is probably the largest challenge that people face when making arguments.

Spin 2: Overpromising.
Cure 2: If you don't have it, don't say it.

Anywhere in your presentation, from setting forth your theory of the case to your final argument, you may find yourself making large declarations about what you are going to prove or how much evidence you have.

When trying to convince a jury, it is important to make only those promises you know you can keep. As a trial lawyer, in making my opening statements to the jury—and telling them the story of the case—I only promise evidence I am absolutely sure the judge is going to let me introduce at trial. Don't promise the smoking gun unless you have it. Because if you promise—and don't deliver—the jury will wonder why you didn't produce it and will question anything else you have to say.

Once, my friend Andrew Hamilton was prosecuting gang members who had taken over an apartment complex and were dealing large quantities of crack. He had convinced one of the gang members to plead guilty and testify against the others. Andrew used this in his opening, telling the jury that "one of their own will take the stand to tell you about all their workings." Unfortunately, when it came time for the gang member to testify, he refused. So in his closing, Andrew had to explain to the jury that some of the evidence had not turned out as he'd originally anticipated. Had his case been even slightly vulnerable, his explanation might not have been accepted by the jury, and that missing piece of the promised puzzle might have been the thing that gave them "reasonable doubt."

In the case of Laci Peterson, the missing pregnant woman found dead in California, her husband, Scott Peterson, was charged with double homicide (of both Laci and their unborn son). Mark Geragos, Peterson's attorney, postured that he would find the real murderer and suggested satanic cults and unknown people named "Dave." Just as O. J. and his lawyers said they'd find the real killer and never did, statements such as this weaken a case. Jurors expect Geragos to expose the "real" killer, and if he doesn't, the question is, "Why not?" Most jurors will then see the statement as a smoke-screen, an attempt to divert attention.

In your personal cases, overpromising might not render a guilty verdict, but it might make the difference between things going smoothly and not. I arrived for my neighbor's dinner party one evening to find her very distressed. Her house was surrounded by scaffolding and covered in blue tarps. "Lis," she said, "I'm so mad. My roofer promised me he'd be done in a week. Three weeks later, and look at this mess. I'd much rather he told me it would take a month and surprised me by doing it sooner." Overpromising earned her roofer no bonuses and no future recommendations.

Susan was trying to get her son, Trevor, on the varsity basketball team. She thought his skills were above the junior varsity level, so she made an appointment to talk to the coach. "Trevor is a great player," she bragged. "He's been scoring in every game and seems to be an asset to the team." The coach explained that Trevor was indeed a great player and that he was grooming the boy for greatness, but he thought it was best to let him cut his teeth against players his own size. "I think he'd get really frustrated trying to score against guys who are more than a head taller than he is," the coach told her.

"Oh," Susan said, her mind spinning. "Don't let his height now fool you. Trevor's dad grew six inches the summer before the tenth grade, and Trevor's doctor said he's going to have the same growth spurt. I'd hate to see him stuck on the wrong team when in the fall he's going to be six inches taller." By the look on the coach's face, Susan knew she'd blown her case.

If you raise the bar of expectation, you'd better be able to jump it. It's better to hold back some of your evidence and assertions, then bring them forward late in your argument as the coup de grâce.

Spin 3: Adding last-minute charges that prejudice your case.
Cure 3: Never wing it!

Of course I want a defendant to break down on the witness stand and admit guilt—as they do on TV—but as a prosecutor I know I have to discipline myself to keep control of the examination by sticking to my original plan. I remind myself to avoid the trap of grandstanding righteousness and spontaneous "gotcha" cross-examination maneuvers since they can actually undermine my case.

So often I watch with utter frustration as attorneys lose control of their cases by abruptly switching gears midtrial and attempting to head in a different direction when their trial plan isn't going well. Throwing in some last-minute charge, they insert seemingly irrelevant information or points that do nothing but ricochet right off the heart of the argument. Even seasoned lawyers do this, especially when they are ambushed by evidence they don't expect.

Stopped by a police officer for speeding, Pete was trying to talk his way out of a ticket. Unfortunately, when he added, ". . . And my accelerator was sticking," the officer added another citation for "faulty equipment."

Inserting extraneous facts and additional charges that are not in your trial plan does not achieve your desired result. Just as complaining, "I've been on hold for twelve minutes," when you're trying to get your power restored doesn't suddenly make the operator want to rush over and help you herself.

Spin 4: Resorting to hearsay evidence.
Cure 4: If you didn't hear it yourself, don't rely on it as fact.

As a prosecutor, there have been many times when I would have liked to use hearsay, but can't (because it's not allowed in court) and shouldn't (because it is inherently unreliable). Nine times out of ten, relying on hearsay will render you not credible and will cause your case to implode. "He said–she said" should be the cue to challenge whatever follows. As you impugn your juror's counterarguments, challenging hearsay as an ineffective piece of evidence, you can bet that others will do the same to you.

My friends Mary and Tim just celebrated their fortieth wedding anniversary, and had Mary relied on hearsay, they would never even have gone out. One of her friends told her she had heard a rumor that Tim was a no-good womanizer who constantly cheated on his girlfriends. Instead of turning down the date with Tim, Mary did what good attorneys do: She went right to the source. She went out with Tim and asked him about his womanizing ways. What Mary discovered was that Tim was the victim of a woman scorned. The friend who'd told her Tim was no good was in fact a one-date girl-friend who was denied a second.

Be forewarned, of course, that actions do speak louder than words. Tim could have well said he wasn't a womanizer and have been the biggest chauvinistic pig in town. (Remember, burglars, drug dealers, and murderers don't typically volunteer, "Oh, yeah, that's me.") Mary didn't rely just on his denial to convince her; she also observed his actions.

When questioning someone regarding hearsay evidence, tread lightly. None of us like to be accused of something we didn't do. Should there be a situation in which hearsay seems plausible—when you're hearing the same thing over and over from more than one source—still be advised to investigate further. If second- or third-hand information is going to influence your advocacy, you need to make sure it doesn't torpedo your argument.

Spin 5: Making subjective characterizations.
Cure 5: Stick to the facts!

Perhaps the most prevalent of the Seven Deadly Spins is subjective characterization. Whether in direct or cross-examination, it's quite natural to deviate from your "just the facts, ma'am" resolve. Instead of establishing incontrovertible facts ("Mother, didn't you agree to be here at eight PM to babysit?"), you resort to statements that are open to interpretation and challenge ("Once again, Mom, you are so unreliable!").

If you're explaining why you sideswiped your neighbor's car coming home from work one night, you shouldn't declare, "The lighting was poor that evening." The poorness of lighting can be a matter of debate, not an absolute fact. If, however, you declare,

"There is only one streetlight on the entire block," you are being factual; no one can disagree with you.

Dan, a tutor for Blair, a troubled eleven-year-old boy attending a Passaic, New Jersey, school, nearly fell into the subjective characterization trap when he and the principal had a conference with the boy's parents. Instead of focusing on incontrovertible facts of Blair's behavior (Blair had kicked his gym teacher and spat at Dan), Dan began by saying, "Your son has seemed really angry lately. Has he been witnessing tension at home?" Aside from the fact that the first words out of his mouth were a surefire way to make Blair's parents defensive (virtually guaranteeing that they would be unwilling to accept the idea of Blair's shortcomings), if he continued on this path, Dan would have lost the battle before he had begun. While the principal glowered at him, Dan realized that if the parents were going to be persuaded that Blair had a problem, he had to set aside his own opinion and stick to the facts—the incidents of kicking and spitting.

Spin 6: Making false inferences.
Cure 6: Don't lie, even if you think it might help you.

Persuading from false inferences—statements based on made-up or false facts that are likely to "pass" as being true—is wrong both legally and morally. When I was eight years old, I wanted a pet very badly and begged my mom and dad for a cat or dog. (Sound familiar?) Both my parents worked outside the house and said I wasn't old enough to take on such a big responsibility. One winter day, another third-grader brought a whole litter of kittens to school, and I just had to ask for the beautiful black one with a white button nose and four white-tipped paws. On my way home with the kitty, I got scared and realized I needed to somehow convince my mom to let me keep her, so I stopped at the bottom of a hill near my house, took the kitty out from beneath my coat, and stuck her in a hole in the hill. I backed off a few steps and then walked by the hole, spotting the cute kitty. I picked her up and took her home.

"Where did you get that cat, young lady?" my mom demanded as soon as I got inside the door.

"I found her," I replied.

"What do you mean you found her?" my mom asked, not letting go of the subject easily.

"I found her in a hole on the way home," I said, with my most pitiful eyes. "She didn't have a collar, and it's cold and snowing outside, Mom. Please can we keep her?"

"Kiwi" was a part of our family for years, but my telltale heart always beat a little louder when I thought about not being truthful. A couple of years ago, I asked Mom if she remembered the story I told her about finding Kiwi in a hole. She said she did. Then I asked her if she'd believed me, and she said, "Absolutely not. I spotted that tall tale right away."

I was arguing technicalities. Sure, I had "found" the kitty in a hole, but not really. I had changed the facts to suit my purpose. Fortunately, Mom was forgiving, but I guarantee that jurors won't be as forgiving as my mom.

Unfortunately, false inferences sometimes turn up in court, sullying the reputation of the legal profession with each appearance. The kidnapping and murder of little Danielle van Dam shocked the nation. The San Diego seven-year-old was abducted from her bedroom while her parents were home. The frantic search for her lasted several weeks, until her body was found in the woods near her home. Early in the investigation, police suspected Danielle's neighbor, David Westerfield, a fifty-year-old design engineer, and when they searched Westerfield's home, they found child pornography on his computer as well as physical evidence, including Danielle's blood, that inexorably tied Westerfield to the murder.

During the trial, Westerfield's lawyers, Steven Feldman and Robert Boyce, argued to the jury that someone other than Westerfield had killed Danielle. The lawyers presented expert witnesses testifying that the state of decomposition of the body (the so-called bug theory) was inconsistent with Westerfield having killed Danielle.

They also pointed fingers at Danielle's parents, insinuating that they were bad parents with a "loose" lifestyle who left their home vulnerable for the real killer to abduct Danielle. Not content to simply poke holes in the prosecution's evidence, the lawyers presented their own theory of the case that an intruder, negligently let in by Danielle's parents, had in fact killed the seven-year-old.

So what was wrong with what Feldman and Boyce did in the Westerfield trial? Defense lawyers are supposed to advocate zealously for their clients, right? They argued from premises they knew to be false. Prior to trial, they had entered into plea negotiations with the prosecutor of the case. The deal they were about to strike was this: Westerfield would take law enforcement to the girl's body, and in exchange, he would receive life in prison rather than the death penalty. But before Westerfield and his lawyers could sign the plea agreement, the cops found Danielle's body without the aid of Westerfield.

Knowing that Westerfield was the true killer, Feldman went so far as to tell the jury in his closing argument that Danielle was "crying out from the grave" proclaiming Westerfield's innocence. In so doing, the lawyers crossed that ethical line between arguing that the prosecution had not met its "beyond a reasonable doubt" burden of proof, and arguing instead that their client wasn't the killer and that the real killer was still on the loose.

What did the jury say about these false inferences in light of all the physical, circumstantial, and direct evidence that pointed to Westerfield's guilt? They gave him the death penalty!

Lawyers aren't the only ones guilty of making false inferences. The media also has a way of jumping to conclusions—if there's no news to report, they simply create rumors. I witnessed a prime example of false inferences in action when I served as deputy counsel during the impeachment hearings of President Clinton. The day that Kenneth Starr, the not-so-independent counsel, testified before the House Judiciary Committee to defend and advocate for his report, which was in effect an indictment of the president, the halls were crammed with media. Journalists were asking anyone everything.

Starr was scheduled to begin his testimony at noon, and a few moments before noon he was seated and ready to go. Noon arrived, all the networks interrupted regular programming, yet no testimony. Ten minutes passed, still nothing. Representative Henry Hyde had not even brought the proceedings to order. So what did the media do? They began to draw inferences from the delay. The big national correspondents were on the air speculating that there must be some "horse dealing" going on behind the scenes between the Democrats and the Republicans. Or perhaps, some offered, Clinton was so worried about Starr's testimony that he had called in to stop it.

You know what was really going on? Kinko's (yep, the copy store) was late in delivering to us (the lawyers) our briefing notebooks for the members of Congress. Without those notebooks, the members would not be prepared for their questions and follow-up "talking points." While the networks were making false inferences, we were beating up on the folks from Kinko's.

As in life and politics, things are not always what they seem on the surface. I learned a big lesson then, and carry it with me now in television work. I strive to analyze, report, and reflect on a story, but not to speculate, jump to conclusions, or predict.

In your personal cases, fabricating evidence or using an excuse or alibi you know to be false is a way to sink your case and leave yourself morally challenged.

Matt is a great golfer. In fact, he's obsessed with the game. So much so that on nice days, he took to inventing excuses to get out of work. One Tuesday he called in sick so that he could get out on the greens. When he returned in the evening after a great day, his boss had left numerous messages on his answering machine, and wanted to know why he wasn't home. Matt called his boss and told him he'd been at the emergency room with his elderly neighbor, a story he knew the slightly befuddled old lady would happily confirm. But when his boss called the hospital and found out that Matt was there over the weekend, not Tuesday, his alibi was blown. Matt lost all credibility within his office, and then, during recessionary cutbacks, he was the first to go.

False inferences is a lawyer's way of saying "lies" or "attempts to get away with a falsehood." Don't fall into that trap. You may get away with it in the short term, but in the long term it catches up with you.

Spin 7: Expressing uncontrolled emotion.
Cure 7: Stay calm and under control.

Keep in mind throughout the case you're making that reacting with more intensity than sense will only damage the straightforward argument you have spent countless hours developing. Use your newly acquired advocacy skills to avoid hectoring your adversary or letting yourself get angry, weepy, or defensive, especially in your rebuttal or cross-examination.

There is only one Johnnie Cochran who can preach fire and brimstone and hold up the Bible as he emotionally quotes scripture. That kind of performance comes with a big yellow CAUTION flag. If I were to do that in the courtroom (or in my personal life), I would look as silly as a four-hundred-pound Hell's Angel in leotards. It's not me. I just couldn't pull that kind of performance off, and the jury would recognize instantly that they were being played.

I once watched the closing argument in a murder trial where the defendant was accused of using a gun to kill his girlfriend. The prosecutor ominously warned the jury, "You don't want to let this killer go free. If you do, he'll walk out of here with all of you. He'll get in the same elevator with all of you. He and his gun!" I turned and looked at the jury box: Several jurors rolled their eyes, others were shaking their heads.

Honest emotion works. While fighting for her clients Lyle and Erik Menendez, two brothers accused of brutally murdering their affluent parents, attorney Leslie Abramson argued vehemently for the boys. Her unbridled passion could not be faked. She truly believed in her clients' innocence, and that belief convinced the jury. Even in the face of an overwhelmingly strong prosecution case, and the brutal facts of the case that shocked a nation, the jury could not find the brothers guilty. Most analysts credit the two hung juries to Leslie Abramson's ardent, emotional defense. (The brothers would be tried again in 1995 and be convicted of the double murder.)

Both Leslie Abramson and Johnnie Cochran demonstrate that controlled emotion can be very effective. But uncontrolled emotion can absolutely destroy your case.

On Bill O'Reilly's radio show, we raise subjects over the course of the two-hour program and then take callers. As you can imagine, we get all types of listeners who call in from across the ideological spectrum. Sometimes the callers, who disagree with Bill or me or both of us, actually get so emotional that they make our case for us. Once, Bill and I were discussing nude camps for children. Both of us took a stand that it was wrong to allow children ages six to eighteen to cavort naked at camp, saying that whatever consenting adults wanted to do on vacation was one thing, but unsupervised kids should not be included, especially when the former president of the club was selling nude videos of girls over the Internet. We said we thought that 99 percent of the parents in the United States would agree with us.

Then "R. C." called in. "Well, about 99 percent of the Germans would have agreed with Adolf Hitler!" he railed at us, equating our stance on nude camps with Nazism. "You and Lis are idiots and scumbags." Bill let him rant for a little while before cutting in and saying, "Thanks R. C., you've just helped make our point. We've just heard from the 1 percent that doesn't agree."

When people become irrationally emotional, they have precious little chance of winning their case. Christie, a woman whose husband left his job as a chef just weeks before he would have earned two weeks' vacation, called her husband's employer to make the case that they needed the money. Her theory was that her husband had worked almost a year and should be entitled to at least some of the vacation pay. During the conversation, the owner listened carefully to Christie's case, agreeing that her husband was a good employee and would be missed, but he asked Christie if she knew that her husband hadn't turned in a few things that were owed the restaurant. "Owe!" Christie screamed, losing control of her emotions. "We don't owe you anything! You're a selfish, heartless, pretentious man." Then she drove the nail in the coffin of her case by threatening him with a Fair Labor Standards Act lawsuit.

When faced with a question, Christie sabotaged her own good efforts of making her case by giving in to the spin of uncontrolled emotion. Had she remained calm and listened to the owner's requests, she may have won her case. Instead, she was told that the conversation was over.

Excessive emotionality needs to be avoided. It's great to bring passion into your argument, but if you let yourself be held captive to what you are feeling, you will probably damage your case.

Avoid the Spins

If you stick to your plan, avoid the Seven Deadly Spins, and stand by your best intentions under pressure, you'll be able to maintain control of your case. Of course, even the most conscientious advocates may find themselves sidetracked once in a while. Should you find yourself falling in a pothole while presenting your case, stick to the following three techniques to get back on course: Take a time-out, remember your trump card, and translate your emotions.

Take a Time-Out

Just as a child sometimes needs to cool down, so might you in the middle of a debate need a break to regroup, collect yourself, and re-root yourself in the theory of your case. This will allow you to move forward with purpose, not anger. A time-out might also help you in cooling down an adversary and controlling the presentation of his claims.

My children and I were painting the outside of the house when, after several hours of frustrating work, the gallon of paint we needed to finish was accidentally knocked over. Just as I was about to dive into "it's your fault" finger-pointing, my daughter looked up at me and said, "Mommy, you need a time-out." I walked to the mailbox and took a few minutes to collect myself. When I returned, they ushered me into the living room, turned on Lifetime Television, and served me two scoops of fudge brownie ice cream. Two hours (and a trip to Sears) later, we were happily finishing off the paint job.

Remember a Trump Card

Knowing that you have one crucial card to play will help you keep your case on track, making it less likely that you will make damaging statements or lose control of your emotions. For example, you change dentists because your old one missed two cavities you had. In asking for a refund for your last two visits, you hold the fact that you attained copies of the X-rays that clearly showed the cavities (according to your new dentist) until the end of making your case, and hearing out your old dentist's defense. That might be the trump card that convinces him you deserve a refund.

Or if you're approaching your boss for a raise, you might also ask for more vacation time or a child care allowance. Because you've asked for more, he might be happy when you're willing to settle for less. The fact that you really just want a raise is your evidence in reserve.

Translate Emotion

It is a given that you may feel tension, frustration, or anger while making your case. But by carefully translating an emotion you feel into a statement you make, will keep the emotion from getting the best of you. Should you veer into too much emotionality, curb yourself by using *statements* of emotions that work as factual evidence—"I'm upset by your actions"—instead of *expressions* of emotion—"You're an idiot!" It is far more effective to declare as fact, "I'm angry about this," or "It frustrates me when these three situations arise," than to shout at or harangue your juror. Uncontrolled emotion makes your case uncontrollable.

* * *

As you make your case, avoid the Seven Deadly Spins. Be direct, be succinct, and be honest. Your goal is to control the presentation. If you try to argue something that isn't true, or evidence that you really don't have, or lose yourself in emotion, your case will spin out of control. Besides, straying from what is ethical and just will only bite you back; even a win will ultimately feel bittersweet.

Ultimately, you want to feel good about the tools you employed to achieve your objectives. And when you celebrate your win, you'll want to know you were tried and true.

SKILLS OF A LAWYER FOR THE TRIALS OF YOUR LIFE

LEGAL BRIEF: STEP 6

CHECKLIST TO AVOID THE SEVEN DEADLY SPINS

1. Deviating from your theory of the case.
   ❑ I'm relying on my theory of the case.
   ❑ What I'm about to say supports my theory of the case.
   ❑ I'm on course for my trial plan.

2. Overpromising.

❏ I know I can deliver what I'm promising.

❏ This is not a smokescreen.

❏ My juror will see proof of this statement.

3. Adding last-minute charges that prejudice your case.

❏ I'm in control of my evidence.

❏ This evidence is in my order of proof.

4. Resorting to hearsay evidence.

❏ This statement does not include "he said" or "she said."

❏ I know this firsthand.

❏ This cannot be challenged because it is fact.

5. Making subjective characterizations.

❏ This is an incontrovertible fact.

❏ This is not strictly an opinion.

❏ If it's an opinion, I'm stating it as such.

6. Making false inferences.

❏ This statement is true.

❏ There is no exaggeration in what I'm saying.

❏ The facts haven't been fudged to suit my purpose.

7. Expressing uncontrolled emotion.

❏ I am not hectoring my adversary.

❏ I'm not being defensive.

❏ I am not "performing."

❏ My emotions are in check.

❏ I'm breathing.

Chapter 7

Step 7. Advocate with Heart:
Let Me Tell You a Story

> *A powerful story engages the listener and works to persuade by conveying a message in a fresh and memorable way.*

The power of the story cannot be denied. Stories communicate your message and make it easy to remember. Can you tell the story "Goldilocks" or "Hansel and Gretel" or "The Ugly Duckling"? Yes. Did you study those stories this morning before picking up this book? No. Stories are memorable, and their messages long lasting. If, through a story, you can lend empathy and emotion to your logic and reason, you will prove yourself an extraordinary advocate.

Many people feel that lawyers are persuasive because they apply fancy words to logic paradigms, thereby convincing judges and juries that the view they're advocating is the only sensible one. In reality, however, the most effective attorneys are the ones who tug at jurors' heartstrings. Through themes and storytelling, they align their client's situations and facts to mesh with jurors' life experiences. They make their case personal, which results in jurors seeing the facts through the advocate's eyes.

If you are specific in your word choice, you can label in your juror's mind the people and circumstances of your case, conveying attitudes and messages. In the courtroom there is a difference between calling my party "the plaintiffs" and "elderly World War II veterans," or between calling a crash an "accident" and a "collision." There's also a way to project an image that imprints in the jurors' minds by simply reminding them of a story they already know and how the parties in the case could be characters within that story. I'll say, "Bad people prey on the innocent. Remember the Wicked Witch offering Snow White the apple? The defendant in this case is like the Wicked Witch. Over and over again he offered something to innocent people that he knew was going to endanger their lives." That seed is often enough to plant a permanent image in jurors' minds.

In your own cases, stories can also make a huge impact, helping your jury see the reasons behind and the importance of your theory of the case. Brian, whom I met through a mutual friend, used storytelling in a positive manner when making his case to the president of the medical center where he worked. A fairly hard-bitten hospital administrator, Brian was almost alone in arguing against serious cutbacks during a board meeting, until he added storytelling to his advocacy:

"Mr. Calvert, six years ago when I came to this institution it was because I knew you were pioneers in sponsoring hospice care. That mattered to me because my grandmother had just died of breast cancer and I had seen how painful it was for my mother and my uncles to have to travel ten miles across town to a cold, sterile hospital to watch her die. Like my grandmother, every one of us hopes to die in our own bed, surrounded by family. And if we can't do that, the next best thing is the warmth of a hospice. I know firsthand what a difference it makes." Ultimately the hospital did institute cutbacks, but as a result of Brian's advocacy, the cuts to the hospice program weren't as dramatic as other budget cuts hospital-wide.

Story Power

The first time my son told me he'd already finished his homework when I knew he hadn't, I recounted a story:

Have you ever heard the story of the little shepherd boy who grew bored as he kept watch over the village sheep? To amuse himself he cried out, "Wolf! Wolf! There's a wolf chasing the sheep!"

The villagers ran to his aid, but when they arrived at the top of the hill, there was no wolf. They just found the shepherd boy and he was laughing. "Don't cry 'wolf' when there is no wolf," the villagers warned the shepherd boy and went grumbling back down the hill.

A while passed and the boy again sang out, "Wolf! Wolf! The wolf is chasing the sheep!" To his delight, he watched as the villagers raced up the hill once more to help him drive off the wolf.

When they again saw no wolf, they told him firmly, "Save your cry for when there is something really wrong! Don't cry 'wolf' when there is no wolf!" The boy grinned as the villagers went back down the hill.

Later, a real wolf was prowling about the flock. Alarmed, the shepherd boy leapt to his feet and cried out, "Wolf! Wolf! There's a wolf about to attack the sheep!" But the villagers thought he was fooling them again, and so they didn't come.

At sunset, the villagers wondered why the shepherd boy hadn't returned to the village with their sheep, so they went up the hill to find the boy. They found him beneath a willow tree crying. "There really was a wolf! He got some of the sheep, and the rest of the flock scattered. Why didn't you come help me?"

"We'll help you look for the lost sheep in the morning," a wise old man said, putting his arm around the boy. "But remember, nobody believes a liar, even when he's telling the truth."

When I finished the story, Jacob looked up at me, his eyes welling with tears, and said, "I understand, Mom. If I tell you a lie once, you won't be able to believe me even when I'm telling the truth. I won't 'cry wolf' again."

My case against his lying went a lot more smoothly because I had a story to illustrate the problem. Jacob quickly identified with the shepherd boy and understood that it wasn't just about his not doing his homework; there were broader implications of his lie. Every afternoon since, he does his homework and voluntarily leaves it on the counter before going out to play (okay, almost every day—some days it's still a struggle).

Stories engage the listener and work to persuade by conveying a message in a simple, fresh, understandable way. There's a reason Jesus spoke in parables. He was a master storyteller in that his parables wrapped wisdom and truth in stories to which his listeners could relate, and he used them to speak directly to his audience. For example, a lawyer (yes, a lawyer!) asked Jesus how to have eternal life, and Jesus (knowing his audience) had the lawyer answer his own question: "To love thy neighbor as thyself." After answering, the lawyer responded with another question. (Have times not changed or what?) The lawyer, proudly thinking he was *always* kind to his neighbor, wanted to know how Jesus defined *neighbor*. Jesus answered with perhaps his most beautiful and best-known story:

A man was going down from Jerusalem to Jericho, and he fell among robbers, who stripped him and beat him, and departed, leaving him half dead. Now by chance a priest was going down that road; and when he saw him he passed by on the other side. So likewise a Levite, when he came to the place and saw him, passed by on the other side. But a Samaritan, as he journeyed, came to where he was; and when he saw him, he had compassion, and went to him and bound up his wounds, pouring on oil and wine; then he set him on his own beast and brought him to an inn, and took care of him. And the next day he took out two denarii and gave them to the inn-keeper, saying, "Take care of him; and whatever more you spend, I will repay you when I come back."

—Luke 10:30–35

Jesus then asked the lawyer which of the three passersby was a neighbor to the man. The lawyer answered, "The one who showed mercy toward him." Jesus was able to conclude: "Go and do likewise."

I'm not here to preach the gospel to you, but there are a few things to note about this parable that will help you "go and do likewise" in crafting stories that bolster your own case. First, Jesus left the injured man unidentified. Since he is stripped of his clothes and unable to speak, his ethnicity, social class, and background are not clear, and the audience was perhaps more readily able to insert themselves into the injured man's circumstances. The audience, being Jewish, would naturally assume that the man was a Jew. When you hear the story two thousand years later, you can probably relate it to your own life. Next, the parable taught the lesson of "loving thy neighbor" by comparing and contrasting three approaches to the injured man, not by just telling the lawyer, "Help anyone you encounter who is in need of help." Though valid, the statement would have had far less impact than the story. And in the end, Jesus allowed the lawyer (his audience) to decide for himself, to make the decision based on what he knew to be right.

Storytelling

When faced with a difficult trial with a circuitous trail of evidence, I like to tell the jury a story to illustrate that in a trial I present a lot of evidence through a lot of different witnesses. "Sometimes the evidence will fit easily together and make sense right then and there," I say, "but sometimes, like in this case, you might not immediately see why I'm presenting a certain piece of evidence and how it fits into my case—what the overall plan is. In the end, though, you'll see the pattern."

Then I recount a story by acclaimed Danish writer Isak Dinesen in which she tells of a Danish farmer who left his farmhouse one afternoon for a walk. He was hit by a sudden, violent snowstorm and got completely lost in his fields as he tried to make his way back home. He took this path and that—totally lost, he worried for his life. Finally, after many twists and turns, he saw the outline of his house. He stumbled inside and collapsed in bed, grateful to be alive. The following morning he awoke and climbed on his roof to shovel off the snow that had fallen during the storm. As he looked out from his rooftop, he saw the field where he had wandered. What he could see was that his tracks had made the perfect pattern of a stork, the symbol for life. Sometimes, in life as in trials, we are in a storm and can't see where we're headed, but there is a bigger plan, which will become apparent.

After I tell that story, I know the jury will not worry that they aren't catching on to my evidence or feel dumb because they are missing something in my logic. When they hear things that seemingly don't fit in the puzzle, they trust—through the lesson of my story—that the pieces will fit together. Even though I'm presenting a storm of information, they know that in the end they will be able to connect the dots and see the big picture. And I know my storytelling works, both by the look of understanding I get from the jurors when I tell it and also by the verdicts I get at the end of those cases.

Allowing stories to help make your case will work well for you if your advocacy is built on a foundation of fact and sound reasoning. Just as children are persuaded by stories, so, too, are the decision makers—the grownups. When it is appropriate (especially in certain workplace-related and personal advocacy situations), the effective advocate reinforces a fact-based argument by telling a story that:

- Allows your juror to empathize with you and your situation.
- Logically relates to the case at hand.
- Isn't threatening to the listener.
- Places you, the advocate, in an honest but positive light.

You don't want to begin with a hotheaded statement of righteousness, but once you've presented your evidence (direct) and rebutted your adversary (cross), you can afford to make it personal. It can be incredibly powerful—and empowering—to round out your advocacy with a story. But it is important to make sure that the story works as a piece of evidence and is developed in a way that allows your juror to empathize with your theory.

Karen had been at her Web design company since it opened. She was a good employee—smart, creative, sociable, and clients loved her work—but each time a better job within the company became available, Karen was overlooked. At first, she was fine with it, knowing that eventually her loyalty would pay off. After three or four slots opened up and were filled with her coworkers, Karen decided she at least needed to bring the owner's attention to the hope she had that, one day, he'd recognize her contributions to the company and give her a promotion.

Karen went to him and made her case. She told him how much she loved her job with the company; how she felt her compensation was respectable in the industry; and how she saw herself continuing to grow within the company. Then she said, "But I feel a little like that frog that was hopping around the farmyard and fell into a pail half filled with fresh milk. Did you ever hear that story?"

"No," her boss laughed.

"Oh, it's cute," Karen continued. "The frog tried and tried to reach the top of the pail, but the sides of the pail were too high and too steep for him to hop out. So he tried to touch the bottom and spring out, but it was too deep. Nevertheless, the frog didn't want to give up, and optimistically decided that he'd just keep swimming around. Eventually, his swimming churned the milk into butter, and he was able to sit right on top of the delicious butter, ready to jump out."

Karen's boss got the point without her having to whine, make threats of leaving, or complain about the other people who were given positions ahead of her. Her story worked powerfully—the next month she got a promotion, and she has now worked her way up to vice president.

Your presentation of facts and evidence will have more punch if you pair it with a forthright and evocative story. Bruce owns a restaurant on the Main Street of a small town in upstate New York. His business was good, but parking had become a problem—there were only a few spaces available on the street, and after he opened the restaurant, five other businesses had followed suit. When a property down the street came available, Bruce went to the town board to make his case that the town should acquire the property and put in a municipal parking lot.

Bruce presented the evidence he had found in discovery. He told the board members there were currently enough spaces in the business section of Main Street for only thirty cars, and that many of those spaces were occupied by employees of the six businesses and town hall, leaving only a handful of spaces for visitors to the town hall and customers of the six businesses. He presented a petition, signed by the merchants of Main Street, expressing the need for more parking. He explained the principles behind "economic multipliers," telling the board how each dollar spent in a local business grew exponentially before leaving the town, and referenced studies from around the country showing that towns that invested in the infrastructure of their downtown areas experienced remarkable revitalization and a great increase in their tax base.

The board members seemed interested, but Bruce's real success came when he shared his own story. "All my life I've wanted to own my own restaurant, and when I came to this town two years ago, I knew this was the perfect location for me. I wasn't scared by the fact I would be the only business here. When I was a child, my grandfather owned a five-and-dime on a main street in the South. His business was great. Next to his store there was a vacant lot, and people who came to his store parked in that lot for many years. Without him knowing it, the lot was sold in a tax sale and the new owner closed it off to parking. For a couple of years, my grandfather fought to keep his business open, but eventually people got frustrated at trying to find a place to park and shopped elsewhere. His business, as well as the others in town, folded. He was heartbroken. His life's dream didn't survive the hardship. My customers are telling me that I should move to Stone Brook where there's plenty of parking. They tell me that many days they come by Main Street, but can't find a parking place, so they head into Stone Brook. Please don't let our town become a ghost town. There are six great businesses here. We just need your help in finding a place to park for the people who want to spend money here."

Shortly thereafter, the board voted to purchase the property, and Bruce's restaurant is now thriving. When you reinforce your strong evidence with a compelling story, you've made a winning case.

Logically Relates to the Case at Hand

Storytelling is effective because it "tricks" recipients into learning something without realizing that they're learning it. But beware: Just because the story has "a lesson" doesn't mean that the lesson will work for your case. No matter what the moral of a story is, it is ineffective unless it shows the passion of your position and speaks to the case at hand.

Your waiter doesn't want to hear you tell the tale of "The Milkmaid and Her Pail" in order for you to find out when your food will be ready, but it might be the right story if your daughter is bragging to her friends that she's only applying to one college because she knows she's going to get in; the theory of your case might be that she shouldn't put all her eggs in one basket and should instead apply to several schools. Along with your evidence—the statistics on the number of applicants versus the number of acceptances, the reassurance that it's not that you aren't confident in her grades and abilities, and the fact that other colleges also have great programs in her major—you tell the tale of Patty the Milkmaid.

Patty the Milkmaid was going to market carrying her milk in a pail on her head. As she went along, she began calculating what she would do with the money she would get for the milk.

"I'll buy some fowls from Farmer Brown," she said, "and they will lay eggs each morning, which I will sell to the parson's wife. With the money that I get from the sale of these eggs, I'll buy myself a new dress and shoes; and when I go to market, all the boys will want to talk to me! Polly Shaw will be jealous and I'll look at her and toss my head like this."

When she tossed her head back, the pail fell, and all the milk spilled. So she had to go home and tell her mother what had occurred.

"Ah, my child," said the mother. "Do not count your chickens before they are hatched."

My bet is that the story would communicate the lesson to the daughter far more powerfully than hours spent lecturing, ranting, and talking about what "other kids are doing."

Isn't Threatening to the Listener

When the story is applicable to the theory of your case, and communicates in a nonthreatening way, the listener will be brought in. If your story makes you an angry blowhard, the listener wants to turn away. I remember Captain Kangaroo telling the story of "The North Wind and the Sun."

The North Wind boasted of great strength. The Sun argued that there was great power in gentleness.

"We shall have a contest," said the Sun. Far below, a man traveled a winding road. He was wearing a warm winter coat.

"As a test of strength," said the Sun, "let us see which of us can take the coat off that man."

"It will be quite simple for me to force him to remove his coat," bragged the Wind. The Wind blew so hard, the birds clung to the trees. The world was filled with dust and leaves. But the harder the wind blew down the road, the tighter the shivering man clung to his coat.

Then the Sun came out from behind a cloud. Sun warmed the air and the frosty ground. The man on the road unbuttoned his coat. The Sun grew slowly brighter and brighter. Soon the man felt so hot, he took off his coat and sat down in a shady spot.

"How did you do that?" said the Wind.

"It was easy," said the Sun. "I lit the day. Through gentleness I got my way."

Gentle storytelling allows the listener to put herself into the scenario and identify with the characters, feeling part of a common—if not universal—experience. When a listener is not feeling personally picked on, she will approach a story with an open mind and be much more likely to see your point and give you what you want.

Places You, the Advocate, in an Honest but Positive Light

Jurors notice when people seem honestly engaged with the case they make, and even your most stubborn adversaries might find their opposition melting if you expose a sincere heart. Speaking from the heart with the disciplined fire of a good courtroom lawyer—not one of those cool, aggressive litigators who rely so much on clinical facts that they alienate juries, and not one of those stem-winders who populate Hollywood movies—will enable you to include in your case the passion of your position.

In one case, I prosecuted thirteen defendants who ran an illegal-alien smuggling ring. Over the course of several years they smuggled thousands of people into the United States. I illustrated just how despicable these men were by telling the story of an individual, Jin, who was the victim of the ruthless immigrant smuggling gang I was prosecuting. I mentioned his wife, Lin Xiun, and told the story of how these smugglers came into Jin's community and made lavish promises of the good life in the United States, and how his entire family worked for a year and gave all their meager savings in order to pay for his passage in the hope that he would be able to bring them to the United States, only to have him enslaved and starved on a crowded boat. Then I said, "Jin can't be here today. He didn't make it to the United States. He, like so many other victims of these smuggling operations, died of dehydration on his journey. But today I'm here for him to make sure he gets justice." By telling the story, I made all the victims' stories come to life for the jury.

As you speak from the heart, you can slow down, lower your voice, make your narrative points one by one, and allow your urgency to show—defusing your persona, getting past the cross-examination mentality, and maybe even bringing a tear to the eye of your adversary. With a story, you are no longer a pushy competitor to your juror; you are human.

Recipe for a Good Story

When I was in law school, I realized that law always comes down to stories. Your case contains within it your story. What happened? Or what should happen? Who did it happen to? Or should it happen to? When? Where?

When I broke my cases down to their story form, the task of presenting them seemed much less daunting.

Several ingredients go into making a good story, one that works:

- It focuses on the people, not the problem.
- It must be vivid and set a scene.
- It has a beginning, middle, and end.

Focus on the People, Not the Problem

Your juror is human and will most likely view your case through emotional eyes. It's natural for a human to be interested in what has happened to another human. Though it's rather morbid, think of the last time you drove by an accident. Whether you looked or not, I can guarantee there was a slowdown of cars because of other drivers interested in what happened. It's a phenomenon known as rubbernecking, and it occurs because people are interested in what happens to other people.

As you prepare to tell your story, this means that you want to focus on, and personalize, what happened to the people involved. You want to make your main character easy to relate to and give her something to overcome. Suppose your case is about getting your mother into a nursing home. The story you tell the administrator should involve the events that your mother (or you) have been a part of, not the mundane facts and figures of Medicare or insurance or the costs of her medicine—the administrator hears that with every patient file that crosses her desk. But there's only one you and you have only one mother:

"I'm afraid for my mother," you might say. "I'm in my last year of college two thousand miles away, and I'm getting calls from her neighbors saying she's doing things like not being able to get the door unlocked when someone visits, going to the mailbox without her top on, and now she can't even remember how to use the phone. My mother has always been such a strong woman. She worked two jobs after my father died in order to make it possible for my sister and me to have a good life and get a good education. I am overwhelmed by the thought of putting my mother in a nursing home, and I just need to know that at your facility someone kind will take care of her . . ."

Personalizing your story is particularly important because your juror will want to help someone he likes or at least feels for. The objective of telling a story is to get people to care. If the characters in your story are likable or sympathetic, your juror will be more likely to give you what you want. It's human nature.

Be Vivid and Set a Scene

One of the interesting things about storytelling is that every time a story is told, it changes a little. We remember the pictures and emotions that the story made us feel, and we store these images in our brain rather than the actual words spoken. It's important to remember this when telling a story to your juror. You want to create images that are positive for your case and stick with your audience, so that when your juror goes to make a decision, he remembers the images that you've created.

A good storyteller will present her account so that it supports the facts and the theory of her case while also forging a connection with the person she's trying to persuade. The message should be easily accessible, but the scene must be remarkably vivid and bring the listener in. Dramatic storytelling is memorable and grabs your juror's attention by letting him relive the event or visualize the outcome from your perspective.

Clement Clarke Moore could have said:

I was asleep, my wife was asleep, and the kids were asleep. Suddenly, there was a noise outside, so I got up to see what it was.

Instead, he wrote:

’Twas the night before Christmas, when all through the house,
Not a creature was stirring, not even a mouse.
The stockings were hung by the chimney with care,
In hopes that St. Nicholas soon would be there;
The children were nestled all snug in their beds,
While visions of sugar-plums danced in their heads;
And mamma in her ’kerchief, and I in my cap,
Had just settled down for a long winter's nap.

When out on the lawn there arose such a clatter,
I sprang from the bed to see what was the matter.
Away to the window I flew like a flash,
Tore open the shutters and threw up the sash.

My point here is the importance of detail, not that you should recite Clement Clarke Moore's famous Christmas tale to your juror. Your goal in storytelling is to make your juror interested, not bored. When I'm telling a story to a jury in the courtroom, I conscientiously choose my words much the way a screenwriter would choose his to entice the moviegoer to watch and listen with undivided interest.

Rather than telling my jury:

Olivia was startled by a noise in the middle of the night. There was a robber in the house.

I might say:

After graduating from college, Olivia had just gotten a job as an event planner for a large hotel. She had taken an apartment on her own, in an old Victorian house near the hotel. On March 23, after a late event at work, she went home around two o'clock in the morning, washed her face, and climbed into bed. Shortly after she closed her eyes, her nightmare began. She heard a noise. At first she thought it might have been her neighbor's cat in the garbage cans outside, but then she recognized the sound as the creak of the floor in her living room. Someone was in her house . . .

By telling a story, rather than just sharing the facts, I have grabbed the jurors' attention. They want to know what happened to Olivia, and then, hopefully, how they can help her. As you make your case to your juror, you, too, can set the scene in a way that makes your juror interested and brings him in.

A Beginning, Middle, and End

Your story needs to have a coherent beginning, middle, and end. This is especially true when stories are short, lasting less than five minutes. I have a friend named Steven who will ramble on in all directions when telling a story. As he speaks to me, I find myself thinking, *Did I miss part of this story?* Steven's stories do not drive home a point because they lack structure and are difficult to follow. In advocacy situations, if the story doesn't make sense, don't tell it—it will only backfire and make you look unorganized.

Your story must be simple enough for your audience to follow without difficulty, but you must realize that a chronicle of events is not a story. It's also not interesting. ("The alarm went off. I hit snooze. I went back to sleep.") Most persuasive stories have an opening that sets the scene, introduces the characters, and gives any background necessary to understanding the story.

Think back to the story of the Good Samaritan. Jesus said, "A man was going down from Jerusalem to Jericho, and he fell among robbers, who stripped him and beat him, and departed, leaving him half dead." We are given the minimum information necessary to pull us into the story. We are not told what the man looked like, what his name was, or how many children he had, because these pieces aren't important to the story. In fact, as discussed earlier, perhaps such pieces would detract from the power of this particular story.

The middle of the story should help build the drama. Your story's protagonist, the main character, typically has a conflict with an antagonist—someone else (his wife, the IRS, a robber, his boss), something else (nature, illness, his car), or himself. This conflict is what will lead to the climactic scene where the tension of the story is resolved. Again, in our Good Samaritan example, "Now by chance a priest was going down that road; and when he saw him he passed by on the other side. So likewise a Levite, when he came to the place and saw him, passed by on the other side." This sets up suspense or dramatic tension, so that when the Samaritan arrives we know that others have not "done the right thing," and we can be thankful for the Samaritan and his goodness.

The suspense builds to a climax, and the story reaches a turning point. The protagonist, who wants something, realizes that he is either going to win or is going to lose the fight. The ending of the story serves three purposes: It presents the climax, shows the results of the climax, and gives closure. Or in the terms of your case, it asks your juror to give the story closure by deciding in your favor, recognizing and acknowledging the justice of your argument.

Make It Memorable

Rather than using notes when telling my stories, my secret is remembering the series of images that tell my story. The essential meaning and words are stored in those images. You can also use the fact that a picture is worth a thousand words to your advantage. If you memorize the opening and closing sentences of your story and the sequence of images in between, your story will spill forth with vitality and you will have the freedom for spontaneity. Your story will be more effective because there won't be barriers between you, the storyteller, and your audience.

Before making your case, you've arranged the setting in advance, are dressed comfortably, and are well prepared—but what about nerves? I find it actually helpful to be a bit nervous. It keeps me alert and on my toes. After a couple of years of television appearances, I still find myself nervous every time I walk into the studio. I told my producer this once, and he said, "Great! Never lose that. It keeps you fresh for the audience." I cherish that comment, and have realized that focusing on the audience helps me forget about stage fright. In the end, as I'm explaining a story on TV or telling my story in making my case, I try to remember that the goal is to help my audience, or my juror, understand what happened or to communicate what I want to happen.

* * *

You should spend a great deal of effort coming up with a powerful and evocative story that illustrates or explains your case. A great story will definitely affect your juror. And no matter what your theory of the case, lying just below all the facts, evidence, and order of events is a story waiting to be told.

And if you tell it well, you and your case will live happily ever after.

SKILLS OF A LAWYER FOR THE TRIALS OF YOUR LIFE

LEGAL BRIEF: STEP 7

GREAT STORYTELLING

As you shape a story to tell as part of your advocacy, consider the following guidelines:

- What stories do you remember from childhood? Why do you remember them?
- What stories are powerful to you now?
- What is the story of your case?
- Is this story easy to understand?
- Is it relevant to your theory of the case?
- Is it applicable to the facts at hand?
- Will this story foster empathy and identification in your adversary?
- Does it avoid excess sentimentality or self-pity?
- Do the facts of the story speak for themselves, without excess emotion?
- Will this story bring home your key arguments and truly help you win your case?

Chapter 8

Step 8. Sum It Up:
The Closing Argument

> *The closing argument is your opportunity to wrap up your case in a neat package and give it as a present to your juror.*

When I teach trial advocacy, the first class of the semester is closing argument. Why closing first? Because you have to know where you're headed in order to figure out the way to get there. Your closing reiterates your theory of the case and asks for closure—where you've been heading during your entire case. If you think of your case like a road map, the closing argument is your destination, where you want to end up, and your theory of the case is your starting point. Between the two there are a lot of forks in the road, and in order to get from Point A to Point Z successfully, you'll need to be confident at each fork that you're choosing the route to a successful verdict.

Your closing should be the deal clincher. In a tight courtroom battle, the best closer will win. The goal of a closing is to help your juror look at and understand your case as a whole and empower her to make a decision on your behalf. The closing argument synthesizes your entire presentation into a powerful and effective narrative, and provides a tour of the strong house of bricks you've built with your facts and evidence.

The Final Present

The closing argument is your opportunity to wrap up your winning case in a neat package and give it as a present to your juror. But as with any present, you want the recipient to like it, and you want it to fit. The purpose of your closing argument is to help your juror remember your key evidence, place him in a position to understand the case as a whole, and motivate him to make a favorable decision. Condensing the crux of your case can be tricky—it is human nature to overexplain and to want to repeat evidence that backs up your argument. If you stick to the following five points, your summation will be concise, powerful, and effective, and will help you wrap up your case with a presentation that fits perfectly:

1. Start with your hook.
2. Sum up your most important evidence.
3. Resolve any weaknesses in your case.
4. Highlight the empathetic element of your argument.
5. Justify and ask for the verdict you seek.

Start with Your Hook

One mistake young trial lawyers make is to start their closing with the perfunctory thanks to the jurors: "Thank you all for serving on the jury and taking your civic duty seriously." Meanwhile, the jurors are snoring. You can also bet that if you begin with yet another "This is a story about the underdog/the need to do the right thing/taking responsibility," you will have lost your jurors in the first sentence. No doubt they have heard that line numerous times throughout the case and will hear it as an announcement that they can tune out on what comes next; they've heard it before.

It's much better to start your summation with a bang, using a fresh approach to briefly reiterate your theory of the case. The key words here are *fresh* and *briefly;* keep in mind that the juror's attention span is short, and she is expecting something important to be stated.

Be blunt as you begin—ask yourself what you want your juror to remember. I once tried a case in Seattle in which the defendant was a Boeing engineer named Harry Jacobson. During the hearing the grand jury had learned that Harry was a methodical man, compulsively neat, who had planned the murder of his wife, Carla, by inventing a remote control device that would disable her car. They also learned that he had hired a hit man from Tennessee to do the dirty deed. During my closing, I didn't sugarcoat it. Using testimony from the hit man and phrases the jury had heard during the trial, I briefly explained my theory of the case using a fresh hook:

"Harry Jacobson, always a stickler for neatness, thought of a way to get rid of his 'five-foot-four problem.' And it wasn't by divorcing her. No, as we've learned, Harry engineered a way to knock off his 'five-foot-four problem'—he'd get her a little tipsy, and then a hired hit man would use the remote control device Harry invented to drive his wife 'into the drink.' That's right. Harry didn't want to get his hands dirty, and rather than divorcing his 'five-foot-four problem,' he'd have someone kill her, make it look like an accidental drowning, collect the insurance money, and live happily ever after. But you, ladies and gentlemen, know what really happened. And you're not going to let Harry get away with it."

That same directness works outside the courtroom. Nicole, the mother who was trying to get her child transferred to a different classroom, began her closing argument with the same strategy. She made herself very clear: "Mr. Holden, I have a little boy who is eager to learn and is looking for a teacher who will give him the guidance and structure he needs to be successful in school. Brad is at a pivotal point where he's either going to decide that he loves learning or that he hates it, for the rest of his life. It's up to us to make sure he makes the right decision—don't you think?"

In both cases, the theory of the case wasn't just restated, it was brought to life. And in both cases, it worked. Harry Jacobson is behind bars and Brad is in a new classroom.

Sum Up Your Key Evidence

By the time you reach closing statements, most jurors have already developed a version of the case they believe is most likely to have occurred. As explained in Step 4, research shows that often jurors make their decisions about the case during opening statements, and then filter all the evidence thrown at them through this decision or their life experiences. Most likely, your juror has already decided his position on your case—but doubts may linger.

By summing up your key evidence in a manner consistent with his life experiences, you are reinforcing that his decision is the right thing to do (if he has already agreed to support your case) or giving him the motivation to erase his doubts and "do the right thing" by siding with you (if he is still on the fence).

Sometimes you need to point out that not everything is as it seems. Remember the movie *My Cousin Vinny,* where the sheriff gets on the stand and says the defendant confessed to shooting the store clerk? The sheriff testifies that the defendant said "I shot the clerk" twice. The movie flashes back to the scene of the "confession," where the sheriff lays out the scene of the crime to the defendant (who is innocent) and says, "And then you shot the clerk." In shock, the defendant says, "I shot the clerk?!" The sheriff repeats: "Yes, you shot the clerk." And the defendant repeats: "I shot the clerk?!" On the stand the sheriff turns the shocked question into a declarative statement—a confession.

Closing argument is *not* the time to repeat all the evidence you unearthed in discovery, direct, and cross. To do so would simply be redundant, and again, the juror at this point is ready to resolve the situation. Stick to your key evidence—use only the pieces that will keep your closing argument simple, clear, and concise.

Defense attorney Mickey Sherman was representing a man accused of knifing and murdering a drug dealer who had sold drugs to his pregnant girlfriend. Mickey started his closing with, "You know when they [the prosecution] lost the case. It happened like that [snapping fingers]. You all saw it and felt it the moment Officer Smith took the stand and told you that the cops could have tested the murder weapon—a knife—for fingerprints, but elected not to. As they say in the business, the police looked at this crime as a 'misdemeanor murder'—just one more black guy killing another black drug dealer—and they couldn't be bothered to do a twenty-minute fingerprint test to see if the defendant's prints were on the knife to make sure they got the right guy." (Result: The defendant was declared not guilty.)

Rather than recapitulating all your evidence, this is the time to explain the reasons why you presented the case as you did, referencing the appropriate evidence and your theme as you go. When you're planning your closing argument, lay out the strategy for telling the juror what you believe she knows—which, if you have followed Steps 1 through 7 correctly, is to agree with your theory.

Your closing argument is a time to summarize what has been learned about the case throughout your presentation, telling it in a fresh way. If you're arguing with your spouse about his faulty record of paying the bills and during the case you've shown him copies of the late statements, you might summarize by saying, "The late payments we've incurred over the last six months add up to $340, and if you include the extra interest we've paid, the total is double that amount. Either you need to stay on top of the bills, or we need to reevaluate our domestic duties."

When, in your closing, you organize the information of your case in a simple and clear manner, your juror can see the big picture.

Your most important job during the closing statement is to provide your juror with the tools he needs to support your case.

Resolve Any Weaknesses in Your Case

It is rare that a case will go 100 percent your way. Weaknesses, differences of opinions, and disparaging evidence will always exist and need to be addressed in a manner that best supports your case. Therefore, you should always address your juror's nay-saying with the skill of a trial lawyer; by doing this, you showcase your own confidence and provide your juror with the opportunity to doubt her own convictions.

During a DUI case in which the defendant, Bill, had a prior DUI conviction, a defense lawyer said in closing, "When Bill first came to see me, he worried about his prior DUI conviction. He worried that you all would convict him for this crime because of his record. I told him not to worry, that you would realize that when he was accused of driving while drinking, he took responsibility, stood tall, and pled guilty for what he had done. But in this case, he can't take responsibility for something he didn't do. He has to stand up for his rights." Thus Bill's prior conviction was sandwiched within a story and reinforced his case by highlighting the man's history of taking responsibility for bad actions.

In your personal cases, it may also be effective to address with your juror potential snags in his decision making. For example, when Peggy was applying for a job as a personal assistant, she had recently been accused of stealing and had been fired by her previous employer. In her job interview, her final remarks addressed this accusation. "As you know, I worked for Ms. X for three years," she told her potential employer. "She trusted me with all her personal matters, her finances, her bank cards, and I cherished that trust. As I've shown you, I have numerous notes and letters of commendation from her for my outstanding work and other terrific references. It's unfortunate the way my relationship ended with Ms. X, but I want to personally tell you that any accusations of stealing are unfounded. In fact, when her necklace disappeared, I asked Ms. X to call the police because I wanted to prove that I had nothing to do with its disappearance, but because of some personal situations in her life she didn't want to." Peggy showed that even after her former boss tarnished her reputation, she would still take the high ground and maintain the woman's secrets. She said *I'm honest* without having to say, "I'm honest."

By addressing your adversary's rebuttals and the weaknesses in your case, you imply that you do not fear and are not ignoring evidence that appears to diminish your theory. Your conviction will be contagious—your juror will begin to release any doubts about your case and find himself in the position of having to fight hard to find a reason not to give you the verdict you want.

Highlight the Empathetic Element of Your Argument

The most challenging part of your closing argument will be to give your juror the incentive to give you what you want. It is human nature for people to want to do the right thing, and your juror or adversary is no exception. It is your job to express your closing in a manner so that the "right thing" is the favorable outcome you request. The easiest way to achieve this is to appeal to your juror's sense of empathy and morality.

As discussed in Step 4, we all make judgments based upon the morals and values we learned as children and have adapted, based on our life experiences, in adulthood. It makes sense that the individual experiences belonging to jurors will play a large role in their decision-making process. If the summary of your case coincides with their view of the world, then naturally they will believe that you are correct and support your theory. If your summary appears to go against what they believe is true, however, then you are fighting an uphill battle.

Carrying the theme of your case (which you set before your opening statement) into your closing statement is an effective way to stir empathy in your juror. Themes play on the need for the juror to make a just decision, and phrasing your summary in a manner that allows your adversary to sympathize, protect, or help you will enable her to make a decision that coincides with her feelings of righteousness.

After having been sent to an optometrist by our family pediatrician, I learned that my daughter, Danielle, had what's known as a "lazy eye" and that the condition would only worsen if she didn't undergo "eye coaching." When I explained to her teacher I needed to take her for a half day each week for eye coaching, I was informed of the strict school attendance policy that would require the teacher lower Dani's grade if more than three days were missed during a grading period. The coaching was not an excusable absence under the school's strict policy.

Wanting to do the right thing for my daughter, I decided to appeal to her principal. Before meeting with him, I read the school handbook, gathered my facts, and did my research. When I made my case to the principal, I presented my evidence and appealed for empathy in my closing argument:

"Dani is a terrific student. She loves school, and I know both of us want to see her succeed and to do what's right by her. I've discovered that many children with lazy eyes end up developing learning disabilities as they get older, and I'm fearful that if we don't do something now to correct her vision, this will grow to be a serious problem—one that might make Dani's grades suffer and cause her to not like school. As you know, I'm a working mom, so this is also going to require me to miss work a half day each week, but I'm willing to do it because I know medical prevention will in the long term greatly benefit my daughter. Neither of us wants to do anything but what's right by Dani. I'm going to have to put this decision in your hands." I put the heavy burden of a decision on him, knowing his conscience would have to live with the outcome. By encouraging the principal to be empathetic, I helped him identify with my situation and make an exception to the rule.

In the final argument, you must relinquish your power to the juror to do something meaningful and important—therefore you must relinquish control and inspire her to care about what you are saying and feel satisfaction and closure about the decision to support your theory.

Justify and Ask for the Verdict You Seek

During your closing argument you are placing your juror in a position of authority to make a decision for your theory of the case. When you ask the juror to do the right thing and reach a verdict that is favorable to your case, he finds himself empowered. In constructing and delivering a powerful closing argument, your final appeal should be structured so that your adversary is not cornered, doesn't lose face, and has the incentive to give you what you want. If you are a savvy advocate, you can even make your adversary think that the verdict you want was actually his idea all along, rather than something you have convinced him to do.

My friend Martine, while making a push for flexible hours to the CEO of the software company she worked for, summed up her case in a manner that allowed the CEO to arrive at her conclusion. "Five years ago I chose to work for this company because I had a vision of how we could increase our competitiveness by providing employees with flexible hours. Since then, our productivity has gone up in three of the last five years, and despite the increased number of hours employees must work, our employee absenteeism rate is half the average for our industry. I believe we owe it to our employees—and their families—to expand that program company-wide. And I feel you'll agree." In her closing statement, Martine skillfully reiterated her theory, repeated her strongest evidence, and justified the verdict she sought. She left the CEO in a position to feel that he'd made the decision himself. As a result, Martine got the outcome she wanted, and the CEO was able to appear heroic and act as the advocate for employees.

By presenting evidence that supports your theory of the case (thereby convincing your juror you are correct), you are halfway to the objective of getting what you want. When you inspire your juror to take action, consider your job done.

When I moved from Seattle to New York to take the job at Fox News, I decided to rent a furnished house in New York and rent out my house in Seattle. After my new tenants signed a lease, I flew back to Seattle to get what I needed. My sweet neighbor, who had helped me place the ad, interview potential renters, and make all the arrangements, met me at my house with "stickies." "What are those for?" I asked.

"To say what you're going to ship to New York, and what you're going to store," he told me. "The tenants have decided they are going to bring their own furniture."

After discovering that storage fees were going to cost more than two hundred dollars a month and rereading both the original ad and the lease to see that they indeed stated "furnished," I decided I needed to make my case. I explained to the tenants that I had also taken a furnished house in New York and pointed out that the lease said "furnished." Then I made my closing statement that I couldn't move my furniture out and asked that they abide by our "furnished" agreement. "I'm glad you are renting my house," I said in closing, "and feel very comfortable with you doing so, but quite honestly it's impossible for me to move my things out. That's why the lease and the ad said 'furnished.' But I'll understand if you decide this is not the house for you and be glad to refund your deposit."

My renters, realizing I was trying to be fair, agreed to take the house furnished. We compromised by agreeing that I would store my furnishings in the garage and a closet—saving me the storage costs and the effort of moving out, and giving them the room they needed.

After constructing a closing argument that does not repeat itself but instead allows you to make a compelling appeal for your objective, consider inspiring your juror to take action using the following steps:

1. **Justify the action by linking your needs with the needs of your juror.** By tailoring your conclusion to the interests and needs of your juror, you can justify the verdict you seek. ("... but quite honestly it's impossible for me to move my things out. That's why the lease and the ad said 'furnished.'")
2. **Show that you're fair and trying to do what's right.** It's human nature to want to agree with someone who is trying to do the right thing. ("I'll understand if you decide this is not the house for you and be glad to refund your deposit.")
3. **Identify the specific action you would like the juror to take.** State bluntly and clearly the verdict you seek—your theory of the case. ("I hope we can work this out, because I'm glad you are renting my house and feel very comfortable with you doing so.")

Make your story stop short of a resolution—like a "to be continued." Ask your juror for resolution to the theme or story you have woven through your case, and then rest your case. If you phrase your closing correctly, your juror will conclude your story happily and punctuate it with "The End."

Three Ways to Ruin a Final Argument

1. **Apologize or butter up.** No one wants to hear you say you're sorry that you've taken so much of their time—especially when you've already taken it. It won't serve any purpose but to make your juror resentful. The same is true with pouring syrup over him as if he's a pile of pancakes. Nothing is more transparent than hollow praise and phony thanks. Be wary about gushing

praise on someone you're asking to make a decision. It will only backfire and discredit all the work you've done.

2. **Say something that is either unrelated to the case or inappropriate.** You have a limited time to make your final argument, so choose what you say carefully. When you're making a case to your insurance adjuster for a higher settlement, he doesn't want to hear your opinion on politics or the weather. I once saw a prosecutor get up for his closing argument and say, "Ladies and gentlemen, I have never seen a person lie so much as this defendant." The judge interrupted him and said, "Mr. Prosecutor, you can't say that." The prosecutor replied, "Your Honor, I'm sorry." He then turned back to the jury and said, "But it's true." Funny, but inappropriate. The case was thrown out of court.

3. **Ramble.** The primary complaint of jurors in trial training programs is that lawyers keep repeating what the witness has just said. It's not helpful to your case to blather on and on about the testimony and facts, trying to remind the juror of every point. He gets it already.

Three Ways to Make a Better Final Argument

1. **Rehearse.** In talking to your juror, you're the most important witness in your case. Rehearsal gives you a chance to smooth out the rough spots in your argument and help it gain strength. Prepare thoroughly, remembering that an actor would never take the stage without a rehearsal, a football player wouldn't enter a game without practice, and you wouldn't want a surgeon cutting into you without working on a cadaver first.

2. **Focus on your first few sentences.** Make a powerful statement as you begin, grabbing the juror's attention. Perhaps repeat to the juror something she's told you that reinforces your case, and tell her something important that rewards her for her attention.

3. **Be heartfelt.** Take a deep breath, look at your juror, and establish

a final rapport. When you speak from your heart with conviction and knowledge about your position, your juror will be willing to invest in your argument. If you relax and be yourself, you'll deliver a powerful closing argument and surpass expectations.

Closing is your moment to shine—your moment to showcase all the preparation, hard work, and thoughtfulness that have gone into making your case. It is the time to infuse your hard evidence with your passion and underscore the theme—the moral—of your story. In a courtroom, lawyers are never allowed to attest to their personal beliefs, even in closing, but in your case you can depart from this protocol. In your closing, say loud and proud, "I believe you should see it my way because of all the evidence and moral authority behind what I've said."

Waiting for a Verdict

After you've asked for a verdict, all that's left to do is wait. Hopefully, your juror will render it quickly and not keep you in suspense long. This is my most nail-biting time in court—I fall into a fuzzy zone where I can't think of anything else. I once went to the grocery store while waiting for a verdict and walked out, got in my car, and drove back to the courthouse, leaving my purchases behind at the checkout.

If your case is for a new job, a promotion, admission to college—anything that doesn't call for a quick verdict—the only thing you can do is wait. While waiting, congratulate yourself on a job well done. You've presented a great case and have summed it up well—be confident that when your juror unwraps it, the only thing he'll return is a favorable verdict.

*   *   *

So What Happened to Jennifer?

Remember Jennifer, my paralegal friend whose undeserved negative review gave me the idea for this book? Jennifer and I prepared her case using the Eight Steps you've just learned.

Armed with her evidence, she plotted out what she was going to say. Jennifer took a deep breath and arranged to meet Michelle in the conference room where they would have privacy and no threat of distractions. Clearly and tearlessly, she began her opening argument by declaring she was concerned about the review and wanted it to be rectified. She presented her supervisor with her direct evidence and went through it point by point.

"The reviews are only part of the process," Michelle retorted quickly.

In her cross-examination, Jennifer produced the passage in the employment manual that defined who was responsible for performance reviews—thus impeaching Michelle's claim but deflecting her ire from Jennifer herself. Jennifer kept from making any missteps by keeping to the evidence at hand and not diluting her case by making last-minute charges, such as asking if Michelle thought Jennifer was after her job. Then Jennifer allowed herself to advocate from the heart, saying that the situation was so upsetting to her because she loved her job so much. "I just want to keep my attorneys happy," she said with a smile—thus implying that she wasn't gunning for her supervisor's job, though she didn't have to come right out and declare it. Then Jennifer summed up her case in her closing argument:

"Michelle, I'm good at what I do and should be recognized for it. I've worked here for ten years and my performance reviews have always been outstanding. This year, the lawyers gave me the same outstanding reviews. If there were any complaints about my work—that I drove the night word processor too hard to get a project done—I did so at the direction of the attorney I was working for. As you know, in law a deadline is a deadline. My reviews show

how much I love and care about my job. I only want to do the best job, and if you or anyone had issues with my work, I wish those issues could have been brought to my attention before this review was printed. I hope I've earned that right. So I would like to start from scratch on this review, and I hope in our relationship. Do you think that's possible?"

"It looks like a mistake was made here," Michelle said simply. "What I'll do is amend the final job review and resubmit it to the partners."

Jennifer had to stop herself from cheering out loud.

An Unfavorable Verdict: *The Appeal*

Sometimes life isn't fair. Sometimes even your most shining closing will not give you the verdict you want. Let's say you didn't prevail—that your juror rendered a negative verdict. There is often the opportunity to make an "appeal." You may take your case to a higher authority, or present your position in a newly persuasive way to the same juror you initially addressed. In the United States the highest court is the Supreme Court. At your office it may be the board of directors (in the case of a whistleblower), but with your spouse, the highest court is probably the only court.

I'm reminded of the movie *To Kill a Mockingbird,* in which Gregory Peck as Atticus Finch delivers a powerful closing argument, perfect in its form, in its delivery, and in its passion. He asks his jurors not to assume that whites tell the truth and that black people lie:

[Start with Your Hook]

The state of Alabama has not produced one iota of medical evidence that shows the crime Tom Robinson is charged with ever took place. This case is as simple as black and white.

[Sum Up Your Most Important Evidence]

Miss Ewell did something that in our society is unspeakable: She is white, and she tempted a Negro.

[Resolve Any Weaknesses in Your Case]

Mr. Robinson is accused of rape, when it was [Miss Ewell] who made the advances on him. He put his word against two white people's, and now he is on trial for no apparent reason.

[Refer to the Empathetic Element of Your Argument]

A court is only as sound as its jury, and the jury is only as sound as the men who make it up.

[Justify and Ask For the Verdict You Seek]

Review without passion the evidence you have heard, and re-store the defendant to his family.

Atticus Finch delivered a perfect closing, but he lost. Sometimes even if you've delivered a winning case—have done everything right from soup to nuts—the jury comes back with the wrong verdict. Unfortunately, factors such as race, money, sex, gender, and other biases can sometimes prevent a successful verdict. There will always be those veils. We like to have a "we" and a "them" and an "us" and a "they." And I must be honest and say that sometimes, due to circumstances beyond our control, what is supposed to be, just isn't.

Perhaps the most recent example is the U.S. presidential election of 2000. After a process wrought with flaws and voting discrepancies in the state of Florida, the election went through appeals in various lower courts before landing in the hands of the U.S.

Supreme Court. In a historic 5–4 verdict, the Court ruled (by a one-vote majority) that George W. Bush would be president. Many people were upset by this decision, but most of the mainstream elected to adopt it, if not embrace it.

So, too, with your case. You may not be happy with the end result, but there are often steps you can take to appeal. At the end of your appeals, if you disagree, you'll have to decide if you can accept the results—and if not, how you're going to move on.

As you'll see in part 2 of this book, there are many ways to incorporate the Eight Steps into the trials of life. What matters most is that you face each situation, each difficulty, with a fresh eye, an open heart, and an eagerness to succeed. Sometimes in life, as in court, you win and sometimes you lose. But losing with the right attitude keeps you on track for a win.

My advice is to forge ahead—make your appeal. There's a difference between perseverance and obstinacy. The first is a strong will, the latter a strong won't. Approach your cases, and your life, with perseverance.

> And many strokes, though with a little axe,
> hew down and fell the hardest-timbered oak.
>
> —William Shakespeare

SKILLS OF A LAWYER FOR THE TRIALS OF YOUR LIFE

LEGAL BRIEF: STEP 8

THE CLOSING

1. Start with your hook.
   a. What's the most memorable image of your case?
   b. What will grab your juror's attention?

2. Sum up your most important evidence.
   a. Is there a way to briefly summarize evidence?

    b. Is there any evidence that bears repeating?

    c. Can you explain why your evidence is important?

    d. What is the overall big picture you want your juror to remember?

3. Resolve any weaknesses in your case.

    a. What are the weaknesses in your case?

    b. How can you reframe those weaknesses to your advantage?

    c. Is there a way to sandwich the weakness within strengths?

4. Refer to the empathetic element of your argument.

    a. What is the undeniable "right" part of your case?

    b. How can you express to your juror the importance of doing that "right thing"?

    c. Is there a story that you could briefly tell that illustrates your theme?

5. Justify and ask for the verdict you seek.

    a. What is the verdict you want?

    b. Is there anything stopping your juror from giving you that verdict?

    c. Be strong and sincere as you ask your juror to give you that verdict.

DON'T

- Apologize or butter up.
- Say something that is unrelated or inappropriate.
- Ramble.

DO

- Rehearse your final argument.
- Focus on your first few sentences.
- Be heartfelt.

Ten Steps for Your Appeal

1. Is there someone else to whom you can present your case?
2. If not, can you go back to your juror?
3. What reason did your juror give for a negative verdict?
4. What elements of your case didn't work?
5. What elements of your case did work?

6. What mistakes did you make?

7. Did you leave out any steps?

8. Is there any evidence you missed?

9. When can you present your case again?

10. What will you do differently?

PART II

Winning the Trials of Your Life

Introduction

The more you can trust your inner advocate, the sooner you will master the skills you need to chart the course of your own life. You now know how to evaluate the best approach to a particular audience, "judge," or jury"; gather the evidence you need and figure out how to use it effectively so it doesn't rebound against you; choose the time and situation to make your case; tell the honest truth, but in a way that persuades; and speak from the heart without losing your head. (And of course you can always take a sneak peak back at Steps 1 through 8 in part 1 in case you haven't memorized them!)

"Okay, I understand the Eight Steps," you say, "but how do I know they'll work for me in my life?"

Did you ever see the movie *Hoosiers*? In it, a small-town Indiana basketball team wins the state championship. Before the state finals, Coach Norman Dale, played by Gene Hackman, takes his boys to see the enormous arena where they will play. The players are overwhelmed by its size and intimidated by how different it seems from their small gym in the country. So Coach Dale asks one of his players to measure the distance from the line behind the basket to the free-throw line.

"Fifteen feet," he announces.

Next, he asks his shortest player to climb on the shoulders of the tallest and measure the distance from the basketball rim to the floor. "Ten feet, Coach."

The coach looks at his players and smiles. "Just like at home," he says.

It was the defining moment in the movie. All his players had to do in the championship game was keep in mind that the court was no different than the one they knew. The game of basketball is played the same whether you're in your hometown gym or a fancy arena with stadium seating, electronic scoreboard, and bright lights. The Eight Steps works like that—with equal strength whether they're applied before the Supreme Court or your human resources manager. They work whether you're fighting for equal rights in the workplace or equal rights at home; they will hold up in negotiations for a new position or a new car. And most of all, as you embrace them as a part of your life, they'll help you develop the self-confidence, positive attitude, and skills of persuasion required to stand up for yourself in any personal or business situation—with the determination, direction, and passion that the best lawyers bring to their top cases.

If your life is anything like mine, you may at times feel discouraged, overwhelmed, or helpless, but if you use the Eight Steps to positively approach your situations and difficulties, you'll be as successful in your life as Perry Mason is in the courtroom. These techniques are a proven formula for success. They've worked for hundreds of years and in millions of cases in this country, so why wouldn't they work when applied to everyday life?

I've interviewed and worked with many people, introducing them to the Eight Steps and watching these skills bring positive results to their lives. What I've learned is that by becoming familiar with the Eight Steps, you find yourself reflexively using them in situations both routine and extraordinary. At work, at home, in relations with friends and with authority figures, in all your daily interactions, they become part of your personal toolbox. No matter your trial, the Eight Steps will help you win your case every time:

- **The Workplace.** You will be prepared to present an effective argument to obtain the job you want, get a raise, win a promotion, develop projects for managers and clients, make effective sales presentations, and manage difficult or contentious coworkers.
- **Consumer negotiations.** Instead of losing your temper with a service representative or salesperson, you will organize your evidence to make a measured and powerful case to the phone company or to the mechanic who replaced your transmission without permission.
- **Business negotiations.** You will enter the biggest deals of your life, such as buying a house or car, with a coherent plan, using these tools to effectively negotiate buying a home, enter a business partnership, or even deal with an attorney.
- **Parenting.** You'll be a better parent when you cast aside the "because I said so" reflex and instead logically present facts to your child, calmly argue your point of view, perform an effective but subtle cross-examination, and share stories to create empathy—whether you're negotiating homework tasks or confronting a child's possible drug use.
- **Friends and family relations.** Often we approach the issues in our closest relationships reactively, with more emotion than argument, more sentiment than sense. These newly learned skills can help you manage your in-laws at Thanksgiving, deal with a friend's problematic behavior, or plan a vacation with your spouse.

Now, let's look at the evidence . . .

Chapter 9

Winning at Work

> *Never stand begging for that which you have the power to earn.*
>
> —Miguel de Cervantes

The workplace is probably the arena where we routinely encounter some of the most intense interpersonal conflict. The Eight Steps work optimally on the job, where the conflicts we encounter often resemble the drama of the courtroom—with the added challenge of having to maintain positive, long-term working relationships with supervisors, coworkers, and clients, and where winning a case often means achieving consensus.

Perhaps workplace advocacy is so challenging because it's not just our livelihoods that are bound up in our careers—our identities are, too. In fact, what we "do" seems to be of central focus whenever we encounter new people. Learning to advocate for ourselves in the workplace is of primary importance—emotionally, financially, and even physically. Since most of us don't want to be lone wolves, winning Pyrrhic victories at the expense of relationships with our superiors and coworkers, the workplace is an especially fraught arena in which we need to advocate with confidence and consistency.

There Are Just Eight Steps to Success in the Workplace

When you are part of an organization, you are part of a mix of many personalities. Since the personalities can be complex, whenever you have an issue it's important to think it through, line up the facts to support your case, and consider your juror. When you are thoroughly prepared, your argument will be more cogent and you will be more self-confident.

Presenting in a self-confident manner can also reduce or eliminate emotional reactions. You certainly don't want a negative or apathetic response from your juror. It is always helpful to bounce ideas off another person. That person can contribute ideas, including things you may not have thought of, and provide a testing opportunity before you go to your jury. Depending on the organization or the person you have to deal with, if you have to deal with someone at a higher level on the organizational ladder, it can be helpful to have a superior join you as an ally.

You can't yell "do over" like kids in a street game. So when you are dealing with important issues in the workplace, carefully plan your case:

• **Know what you want.** Clearly define your goal, your theory of the case, so that it can't be undermined by the prospect of immediate gain (temporary satisfaction rather than a long-term solution), the pull of personal relationships (your dislike of a coworker, your desire to score points or please the boss), or being convinced that your goal is not as important as you think. Then find a way to make that theory a capsulated theme throughout your presentation. For example, if you're arguing that your company should have an Internet presence: "Bigger exposure equals bigger sales." Or if you're negotiating a raise: "I'm worth it."

• **Choose your juror.** Think through who the best person to approach might be and how to approach that juror. At work, many of us do not stop to judge who might be the best person to hear our case. Instead of reflexively going to a boss, a coworker, or supervisor, assess who has the authority—and the disposition—to give you the best chance of winning the verdict you seek.

• **Do your discovery.** Assemble evidence and be prepared to support any position you need to fight for. There is power in knowledge, so it's particularly important to conduct careful and complete discovery in the workplace, where it's easy to see your position "shot down" by an envious coworker or a condescending boss.

• **Challenge hearsay, bias, motive, and prejudicial evidence.** If you're sure of your facts, you can confidently challenge flimsy statements, whether they're conjectures from a boss or prejudices of a fellow worker.

• **Speak from the heart and tell your story.** Even on the job, a case presented with passion can be quite effective. Such stories are effective when they are directly relevant to your job and the issue at hand, and you maintain a professional demeanor as you deliver them.

• **Personal goals advance your company's goals.** Learn to present your case so that your personal goals advance your company's goals. Your case is immeasurably strengthened if you can show how the verdict you seek contributes to your company's increased success.

The Eight Steps can help you get a job and keep a job; negotiate an initial salary, a raise, a relocation package, or a severance agreement; achieve flexible work hours or the right to work at home; refute negative responses in a performance review; resolve personal issues with colleagues and bosses and maintain productive bonds with them. The Eight Steps can be effective not only in "trial" situations, but also in making all kinds of presentations, structuring oral and written reports, and promoting a product or service.

Let's look at some areas in the workplace where the Eight Steps can be effective and learn from actual people who have put the techniques to good use.

Salary Negotiations

Salaries are one of the most emotional issues in the workplace, because people often tie their self-worth and their value as an employee to how they are compensated. According to labor negotiator Caryl Mahoney, the majority of people are satisfied with their salaries when they accept a new position, but often become disillusioned after exceeding expectations and having their salaries stay the same. She suggests that salaries, as well as compensation systems, should be reviewed on a regular basis in order to make sure that your salary remains competitive and, if you are a long-term employee, that your loyalty is fairly compensated. Using the Eight Steps can help you review your salary with your superiors without becoming emotional.

Crystal, Receptionist

When Crystal started her new job as a receptionist and general office helper for a manufacturing company, she was eager to make a great impression. Crystal was ambitious and hoped to someday run her own business, but she knew she had a lot to learn and was happy to pour herself into her work, putting in long hours accomplishing her tasks and even working weekends. Nobody at the company had ever seen anyone work so hard.

After several months, a woman who'd been with the company

for more than thirty years dropped by Crystal's desk. "You know," she whispered, "you're entitled to overtime if you work more than forty hours a week."

"I am?" Crystal said. "Nobody told me that."

"I know," the woman said in a hushed tone. "They've been breaking federal labor laws for years. I tried to warn them a long time ago, but they told me I was wrong. I told them to look it up, but I don't think they ever did. Or maybe they don't want to know. You're putting in massive hours, and you should be paid for it."

Driving home that night, Crystal thought about what the woman had said. She didn't want to be a troublemaker, but the law was the law. When she got back to her apartment, she turned on her computer. Using several search engines, she found out her coworker was right—under the Fair Labor Standards Act, she was entitled to overtime pay anytime she worked more than forty hours in a week.

Rather than make her case prematurely, she carefully kept track of all her hours, the compliments her superiors gave her, and her accomplishments. At the end of the year, after she received a very positive formal evaluation, Crystal made an appointment to see the head of human resources. "I have been working overtime all year," she said nicely, "and I'd like to be paid the appropriate overtime."

The human resources director smiled but shook his head. "We don't pay overtime," he answered.

"Actually," Crystal responded, calmly handing him a copy of the federal law, which she'd downloaded from a government Web site, "I think you'll find that federal law requires that you pay overtime to any employee who works more than forty hours in a single week, unless that employee is a manager or otherwise exempt from the law." She also gave him an article from a business magazine explaining how the law applies to small companies. The human resources director read the applicable sections Crystal had highlighted.

"I've worked 413 overtime hours over the past year," she said. "I have it all documented right here." Crystal handed him her carefully kept notes, showing when she arrived each day, when she left, and the weekend hours she had put in. Then, came the critical moment for Crystal's advocacy.

"It's always been my dream to work at a company like this," Crystal said. "I majored in marketing at college, but afterward I couldn't find a job I wanted. I worked as a waitress and also as an office temp. I was so excited when you hired me, and this is the first time I've had a job where I'm learning how to run a successful business. This company has been around for fifty years and has very loyal employees. It has a great reputation in the community for fairness and quality work, and I am very glad to be a part of it. I have no complaints about working overtime—I want to make that clear."

The human resources director nodded. "I'll have to talk to some others about this and get back to you," he said.

"Thank you," she said. "Thanks for taking the time to evaluate my position."

Her request was a wake-up call to the company, which for years had operated under the misconception it didn't have to pay overtime. Of course, her managers had never really made an effort to find out—and before Crystal, no one had pushed them to do so. The following week, Crystal received a check for several thousand dollars.

She made a winning case not by accusing her company of ignoring the law and not by threatening to report the company to the authorities. She told her story compellingly, framing it in a way to which her audience would be receptive, and presented her evidence clearly and succinctly. She knew that the company and the human services director saw themselves as fair and honest, so she fit her story into their conception of themselves and appealed to their sense of fairness.

Crystal made it easy for the company to give her the overtime pay to which she was entitled without alienating anyone. Afterward, the human resources director sent out a company-wide memo informing employees that federal law entitled them to overtime if they worked more than forty hours a week. Like many companies, however, it also instituted a policy whereby workers needed permission from a supervisor to work more than forty hours in a given week.

* * *

Sometimes, particularly in large organizations, a raise might fall between the cracks or not be addressed. Knowing that any organization is its people and any good organization recognizes this fact, leaders will typically address issues of inequity. Keeping this in mind, don't be afraid to request an evaluation of your job and compensation. Salaries, as well as benefit plans, should be reviewed on a regular basis to ensure that not only are new positions and starting salaries competitive and fair, but so is the pay of the loyal long-term employees.

Stephanie, Nurse

Stephanie was a nurse with eight years of experience, all at one hospital. The nurses on her unit were so busy they barely had time for lunch. One day during a rare break, Stephanie was chatting in the lounge with a newly hired nurse who also had eight years of experience. She would never ask anyone about their salary, but in the course of conversation she discovered that the new nurse was hired at a higher salary than she was paid herself.

Stephanie immediately went to her supervisor and anxiously asked why she was making less than a new hire. He said she should speak to someone in the human resources department for an answer. Rather than approach human resources emotionally and unprepared, as she had her supervisor, Stephanie decided to figure out what she wanted and gather her facts. Though she was upset that as a long-term employee she was less valued salary-wise than someone from the outside, she realized that this was a red herring. Her case wasn't about the others, it was about her. She had worked at the hospital for eight loyal years and was well aware that nurses are a scarce resource. In fact, her hospital, as well as others, depended on temporary agency nurses and overtime to fill the void. There were times when even these steps did not meet the needs.

Stephanie called several other hospitals in the area and learned that not only would she receive a higher salary if she transferred there, but she would also be given up to five thousand dollars as a sign-on bonus. One hospital invited her to an open house and a catered dinner with the hospital president and other executives. Armed with all this information and feeling confident, Stephanie decided to bring her case directly to someone who could make a decision and rectify her problem—the new human resources executive. She listened to Stephanie's case, which she presented factually and unemotionally. When she provided the backup salary and bonus data she had assembled, Stephanie indicated that she hoped she would not have to leave the hospital; she believed the mission of her longtime employer complemented her own tremendous compassion for her patients. She recounted a story about training there as a student, and said she respected her supervisor and had developed friendships with many of her colleagues.

The human resources executive thanked Stephanie and indicated she would have an answer in a few days. She then audited the salaries of all eight-year nurses and found that Stephanie and several others were paid below the appropriate rate. A formal audit was then done on all nurses, and a large number of other pay inequities were discovered. Stephanie had won—the inequity was resolved. Stephanie's salary was raised, as were the salaries of the other nurses, who thanked her profusely.

Employees in an organization should understand its compensation system, as well as where and how they fit into it. As an employee, you should never be afraid to request an explanation, particularly of something as important as salary. Mistakes do happen, and if one goes unaddressed you could be experiencing a great financial loss.

*   *   *

Employee satisfaction surveys consistently reveal other areas of concern in the workplace besides salary, including finding a job, lack of challenge, space, and the future. The Eight Steps can provide winning results in each of these areas as well.

Losing a Job, Finding a Job

Organizations today are less stable than they were before the challenges of mergers, acquisitions, reengineering, downsizing, or restructuring. Whatever the situation or the nomenclature, cost-cutting efforts usually result in the elimination of jobs. As a result many good employees (as well as bad) find themselves without a job, and those who remain find themselves doing as much or more work with fewer resources and less support.

If you've been "downsized," how do you explain to potential new employers the reasons you were let go from your previous job and why you'd be a needed asset to their organization? This was the case with Amy. She used the Eight Steps to negotiate a terrific severance package and to seek new employment.

Amy, Banking Executive

Amy is a petite, attractive woman in her forties. Married and a mother of two boys, she had worked her way up to a senior executive position at one of the largest banking institutions in the country, but after a merger she was told that her job would be eliminated. Rather than getting emotional, Amy applied the Eight Steps to her departure. Her theory of the case was to get the best severance package possible. After writing down everything she wanted—from a temporary office to secretarial help to letters of reference—she negotiated her departure. Being organized made her feel powerful in a difficult situation, and, after making her case to the vice president in charge of her division, she got everything she asked for.

Her next goal was to find a new job, and she believed that a search executive (aka "headhunter") would be her best route to finding the right job with the top compensation. Before meeting with several headhunters, she decided that her goal, her theory of the case, was to convince the headhunter that she was the best in the industry—not that she should get a particular job available right then. She wanted to distinguish herself from other applicants and set herself up as the better candidate so that the hunter would remember her and think of her when the ideal position presented itself.

Amy felt the main red herring to avoid was showing her anger about being let go from the bank. She knew that this would not do her case any good. She also decided that she didn't want her career in the hands of hunters who talked about themselves, concluding that if a hunter talked about himself—how he got into the business, where he went to school, and so on—then he wasn't talking about her. In her discovery, she learned that the good ones don't have time or inclination to talk about themselves, but instead focus on the issues of their clients: in this case, Amy and her search.

In developing her case, she gathered credentials proving to herself and potential employers that she is the best in the industry at what she does, and then she tried to anticipate every objection or question a headhunter (or prospective employer) might have. For example, she thought she might be asked if she's detail-oriented. "I'm not, but I make up for it in drive." And she knew an obvious question would address why her position had been cut. "The bank wanted someone with a more forceful ideology—someone like my male counterpart, who would say, 'That's a stupid idea.' In the officers' minds, I was too nurturing to the people under me for the direction that they wanted the bank to go."

She also tried to think of the questions she would ask in return, and decided that if she wasn't sure of what someone wanted, she'd ask, "Can you give me more details about what you're asking?" She used the Eight Steps to catalog the hostile things that were said about her or her work during her years at the bank, and how she'd handled them. ("My department had higher stats and was more productive than any in the company.")

She was proud that her preparation had helped her anticipate an objection from a headhunter who told Amy that the salary she was requesting was too high since she didn't have a lot of human resources experience. "I was ready to counter in my low, slow, forceful way that I had indeed a lot of experience in running my own business, was responsible for compensation, and knew how to assess profit and loss both from a management and a human resources perspective. I don't just know about human resources, but I also know about being an expert in leadership." He was so impressed with her answer that he went on to represent her.

Rather than head into the downward spiral of stress often associated with losing a job, Amy reported that the Eight Steps allowed her to ask herself what she wanted and set up a case for why she deserved it. The Eight Steps gave her the discipline to prepare so that during her meetings she was grounded and empowered. As of this writing, she is being courted for an executive position by two competitors to the firm that downsized her.

Lack of Challenge

On the opposite end of the spectrum to losing your job is having one that provides no satisfaction, just boredom. Many employees are frozen by the lack of challenge they feel in their jobs. We all want to live up to our potential and feel more willing to work hard when we feel challenged and interested in what we're doing, especially if we believe our efforts are making a difference.

Colette, Boutique Salesperson

I met Colette in my favorite gift shop. For the first six months on the job, Colette showed up every day eager to work. When the store wasn't busy, she'd spend time reorganizing the storage room, rearranging the displays, and getting to know the merchandise. She became an expert in how and where items were made, came up with ideas about new uses for some of the merchandise, and even found suppliers that provided products at a savings to the store owner.

After the busy holiday season was over, Colette's job grew dull. She found herself sitting around a lot waiting for customers to come in. One day, while she was redoing the store displays, I came in to pick up a quick present, and we got into a discussion about life. I mentioned that I was writing a book. "Oh," she said, "that sounds so exciting. I want to find something exciting to do."

"Why?" I asked her. "You're great at what you do."

"Yeah," she said, "but I've sort of done this. How many times can I rearrange the soap?"

"If you could do anything," I asked, "what is it that you'd want to do?"

"Well," she said, her eyes widening, "I suppose I'd love to use my computer skills and design Web sites."

"Then that's your theory of the case," I said.

"My what?"

"Your goal." For the next few weeks, Colette and I corresponded by e-mail. I explained the Eight Steps in detail, and she had some amazing insights. What she discovered was an idea that would merge her love of the gift shop with her love of designing Web sites. After carefully preparing her presentation, she went to Louise, the owner of the store, and made her case.

"I've done a lot of research into online shopping, and I think we could increase your business exponentially if you launched a Web site associated with the store." Colette presented a chart depicting similar businesses and how their sales had increased once they had an online presence.

"It seems like a great idea," Louise said. "But I can't afford it. In this economy, I'm barely meeting my overhead now."

Knowing that this would be a concern, Colette had an answer. "I could continue to work at the store, and work on the design and the programming of the Web site during slow times. I'd be willing to do the work for a percentage of the sales that come as a direct result of the Internet business. That way, it wouldn't cost you anything to start, it would keep me at the store, and it would, hopefully, increase your business."

Louise hesitated, and Colette launched into her prepared questions to help lead Louise to her desired verdict.

Q: Haven't sales in the store hit a plateau?
A: Yes.
Q: But aren't you continually getting new products?
A: Yes.
Q: Are you doing the same amount of advertising?
A: Yes. If anything, I've increased my advertising budget. You know that.
Q: Has the population increased in the area?
A: Slightly, but I think we're about at our saturation point.
Q: How can you expose more customers to your merchandise?
A: I don't know.
Q: When was the last time you visited the Internet?
A: This morning.
Q: And what were you doing there?
A: Looking to buy my husband a set of golf clubs on eBay . . .

Louise's face broke into a smile. "Okay, how do we start?"

Colette pulled out some sample sketches she had done. "The first thing we do is decide on how we want the home page to look . . ."

Today the store's Web site is up and running, and it's already started paying off for both of them—showing one way that career boredom can be solved by applying the Eight Steps.

Space

A professor in an MBA program once told his students that they probably would not remember a lot of what they learned in his class some years down the road. But he assured them they would remember one thing he said: "Perhaps some of the most difficult problems you will deal with when you enter management are the allocation of space and parking, and raising the price of coffee in the employee cafeteria. All can be emotional issues."

Stuart Brown, Employee Relations Manager

Stuart Brown worked in a heavily unionized facility as the manager of employee relations. His job was an important one since he had to hear the cases that both management and the union brought before him for resolution. He held some meetings in his office, but having more than two additional people there was a squeeze. Stuart's office had been carved from part of the food storage area for the cafeteria, which was on the other side of the wall. It was rectangular in shape with a miniature desk that had one side flush to the wall. He had just enough room to get up if he backed his chair against the wall behind him and swiveled his legs toward the door. In front of the desk were two small chairs that had to be pushed close together in order to fit. People over five foot eight had a real challenge positioning their knees. As a result, taller people often stood.

Stuart was always looking for empty conference rooms, or trying to persuade people to give up a conference room they had booked if they had reasonable-sized offices in which to conduct their business. For the first two years of his office relocation from across the street, he had done all right in obtaining conference room space, but now it was getting harder to schedule due to the growth of the company and the employee population. Some of the conference rooms had been converted to office space.

At times Stuart felt as though he was groveling for space, which he found humiliating. Still, some of the situations employees and union representatives were subjected to in his office were even more humiliating. Stuart prided himself on being professional and hearing grievances and resolving problems quickly. When he didn't have the option of a conference room, he had to rely on the goodwill of people, which was not always dependable. With tensions running high, the goodwill was running thin. There was certainly discomfort when knees kept touching during a heated discussion between a supervisor and a surly employee he had just disciplined. Eye contact was also difficult to maintain when sitting shoulder to shoulder, particularly when a third chair had to be squeezed in. Never mind the difficulty Stuart had writing his notes when the standees were wrapped around his wall and someone was reading over his shoulder, sometimes sweating profusely because of the lack of proper ventilation.

Stuart had a chance meeting with the company director of facilities, Rick, outside Stuart's office one day as they both headed for lunch in the cafeteria. Rick was responsible for the growth and renovation projects for the facility, and Stuart seized the moment to invite him into his office and explain his problem. As he listened, Rick quickly looked around, and before he hurried off he told Stuart he would see what he could do to help.

Weeks went by, and Rick had not contacted Stuart. A number of the executives and engineers had been bragging about their new space, so Stuart knew renovation plans were moving forward. He also knew of Rick's reputation for having the "need-to-please disease"—being unable to say no to anyone or anything and often saying or implying a yes, then not following through. Rick's ego was huge. He projected a nice-guy image of caring and listening, but his management style was a source of frustration throughout the organization. The issues would either disappear amid frustration, or, if they were important enough, would be addressed by the president or other executives. Rick then often took credit for the accomplishment.

Stuart had a very real need, but he was not a high-level executive who was likely to get Rick's attention. Stuart was not sure about what his next step should be in getting a response from Rick, so he shared his dilemma with his superior Karyn, the executive responsible for human resources and several other departments. She had experienced her own frustrations with Rick and suggested that they develop a compelling case that would win his attention as well as enhance his image in the organization.

Karyn and Stuart put together data showing the growth of the employee population over the past four years and the percentage increase in the numbers of grievances. Added to this was information reflecting the generous amount of conference room space initially available to them versus the waning amounts over the past year. They obtained a copy of architectural plans showing the dimensions of Stuart's space as well as adjoining spaces. During their planning, they decided that it was important to have the office remain near the cafeteria, since it was convenient for employees and supervisors to stop in for benefits or policy information, medical forms, and other employee relations material, which was supplied by the clerk occupying a small space in front of Stuart's office. (Previously, employees had to go across the street.)

In reviewing the options it became obvious that the best alternative was either to expand into the food storage space behind the office, or to create new space on the other side of the corridor—which would give Stuart more space plus a window. This would also not infringe upon anyone else's space. Karyn had learned years before from a labor attorney representing unions that the best way to assess the environment where a grievance occurred was to visit the site. She and Stuart wanted Rick to witness the crowded conditions for himself, but thought it might put him, as well as others, in an awkward or embarrassing position to look in on or be present during an actual hearing. They opted instead for pictures that simulated a hearing. The simulation with volunteers from the human resources department avoided the need for consents and explanations to others.

Stuart and Karyn scheduled an appointment with Rick, and together presented the case. Rick was annoyed to have to be dealing with this issue when in his mind he had more important people to accommodate, but nonetheless listened and then reviewed the photos, which seemed to get his attention. "Look," he argued, "I gave this space to human resources three years ago, and you were happy to have it. I've got your solution: If you want a bigger space, you can move back across the street."

Karyn and Stuart had anticipated this argument, and countered with all the positive reactions they had received from employees after human resources services were brought to the main building. "This eliminated the need for employees to trek across the street on limited lunch hour time, in all sorts of weather," Karyn explained. "In fact, Stuart and I have been in the process of preparing a proposal to provide computer kiosks so that employees could directly access benefits and other information. This would improve services to the fifty to a hundred employee walk-ins per day, but would also pose a question regarding space."

"Supervisors have begun to complain to me that they resent having to deal with their issues knee to knee in my office," Stuart added. "They have even told me that they believe it reflects a lack of caring and respect by upper management for their employees. This is a space needed by employees and management to air disputes and resolve conflicts, and is of crucial importance to good relations within this company. One supervisor told me last week that it's obvious how much money was spent on individual executive offices, and it was laughable how little was spent on the employee relations space. The new space isn't a benefit simply for me, but also for the employees and management who benefit from my services, and I believe that such space should be as welcoming and accommodating as any executive office."

This argument persuaded Rick, who always preached the importance of quality management and staff recognition. He invited Karyn and Stuart to join him, and they reviewed the options with the space engineer. Other places were found for food storage, which freed up space for the expansion of Stuart's office. In fact, there was enough space to expand the front office as well and put in the much-appreciated kiosks. Rick was, of course, pleased to be invited by Karyn and Stuart to host an open house when the renovations were completed and give a speech to employees on "the new center of excellence he had been striving to contribute to them."

The Future

Employees naturally question their job, especially in times such as now in which the economy is sluggish, the stock market volatile, and geopolitical issues uncertain. We all want to be assured about our income, feel secure in our jobs, and know that we're going to be able to send our children to college and retire comfortably. We want to know that opportunities will be available to us in the future.

Susan, Billing Clerk

Susan worked in a financial services company. She was the first one at her desk in the morning, had no absences in three years, and worked diligently striving to have her work be error-free and completed by the end of each day. Susan's computer and interpersonal skills were excellent. She was often requested by customers, and also given the most difficult people to deal with. Mr. Wilson, Susan's superior, had acknowledged his appreciation in her excellent performance reviews.

Susan wanted to move up within the company, both in income and position, but to be able to do that she needed to complete her degree. Unfortunately, she found herself in a catch-22. The courses she needed were offered at times that conflicted with her work schedule, and her current salary didn't enable her to take the night classes at the private college in the area. She needed to increase her salary to ensure a better future.

She decided to make her case based on her personal strengths, her performance review, and the letters of praise from customers. Although she considered it, she decided not to offer opinions of or comparisons with her coworkers. A digression might put Mr. Wilson on the defensive, and he might think less of her for pointing out the faults of her peers. Instead, she focused on facts directly related to her issue. She did, however, remind Mr. Wilson that she was a single mother of two teenaged girls and had a part-time job on Saturdays.

With partial tuition support from the company, Susan had been trying to complete her degree for several years, and she had relied on the consistency of the bonuses she had previously received to pay the difference in her tuition. The company had had a bad fiscal year and gave minimal increases to staff. The theory of Susan's case was that she did not want to leave the company and hoped to one day be a part of management, but in the meantime she deserved a raise.

Mr. Wilson was supportive and quite complimentary about her work, but had to turn down her request because her job duties had not changed and financial resources were limited. "Mr. Wilson," Susan asked after his verdict, "would you be willing to accompany me to human resources to appeal my case?" He agreed, but human resources confirmed Mr. Wilson's explanation—funds were tight at the company and the value of Susan's job had not changed. Still, after hearing her case, the head of HR told her that she was a valued employee and since the company did not want to lose her, perhaps they could work out a flexible schedule so Susan could put in the hours she needed for her job and complete her degree more quickly by being able to take advantage of more of the college's course offerings.

Susan was delighted, and recently, with her degree in hand, she was promoted to a new position within the company, which she feels is an ideal stepping-stone for her future career.

You Have the Power

The skills of advocacy allow you to be proactive in dealing with workplace issues and to transcend your feelings of powerlessness, even if the "other side"—the coworkers, the boss, the investors, the board of directors—seems to have all the power. When I was representing the Democratic minority on the House Judiciary Committee during the Clinton impeachment proceedings, we had no real power. The Republicans were the majority, which basically gave them the right to call all the shots. When the Republicans wanted to release to the public all of the evidence submitted by Kenneth Starr in support of his report, the Democrats were strongly opposed. My clients wanted to redact passages that were needlessly hurtful to the first lady or Chelsea, that unnecessarily invaded people's personal privacy—such as the mention of Monica Lewinsky's credit card number—or that could threaten national security, such as photographs and drawings of inner White House offices used for national security meetings.

The Republicans were jurors over whom it was going to be really difficult to have any leverage. Nonetheless, my goal—my theory of the case—was to convince them it was in their best interests to allow these limited redactions. I had to anticipate the Republicans' objections and then deal with their resistance by showing them that their own position (favoring complete disclosure in the Starr report) would actually damage them in the long run. I pointed out that Americans were eager to read Starr's supporting evidence, but after digesting it, they would question the relevance of some of it, especially information that could compromise America's security. I told them that Americans would realize—because the Democrats would make sure of it—that it was the Republicans who'd insisted on a full-scale release.

Even with absolutely no negotiating power, I convinced the Republicans that my goal was in their best interests, and my clients got what they wanted. Over the next several days we painstakingly redacted selected materials before the evidence was released to the public.

* * *

No matter how powerful or distant or inflexible your superiors may seem, implementing the Eight Steps will enable you to deal successfully within the workplace hierarchy and embolden you to seek out the experiences and opportunities that you really want to have in your job.

Now get back to work so you can win every time!

THE TRIALS OF LIFE

LEGAL BRIEF: WINNING AT WORK

Step by Step

Step 1. What is it that would make work better for you? What do you need that you currently don't have? What's your goal?

Step 2. Who can help you reach that goal and when is the best time to approach this person?

Step 3. What "evidence" do you have that you deserve your goal? (Examples: letters of commendation, years on the job, great reviews, sales records, awards received, press clippings.)

Step 4. How are you going to start your case? What is the first thing you are going to say?

Step 5. What questions can you ask your juror to reinforce your goal?

Step 6. How can you avoid being emotional, pointing fingers, or belittling someone else to make yourself look better?

Step 7. Is there a story you can tell to reinforce your case, explain the importance of your goal to either you or the company, or illustrate your point?

Step 8. What's the last thing you are going to say and how are you going to ask your juror to grant your wish?

Chapter 10

Winning in Business and
Consumer Negotiations

> *Always define your terms.*
>
> —Eric Partridge

The skills of a lawyer will help you succeed in all sorts of business and consumer negotiations, giving you the strategies and support you need in order to (for instance) get liability provisions in the contract your company is negotiating with a client; lease a new office space for the firm you help manage; buy a car for your family at a fair price; return a consumer good even if "all sales are final"; confront a mechanic who did unauthorized repairs; get the best phone rates; or successfully challenge a doctor who doesn't listen or an HMO that stonewalls you.

Before I show you the Eight Steps in action in this context, you should know some basics of contract law. If you're aware of what is generally required in a contract, you will be more successful in dealing with your life cases involving everything from buying a teapot on eBay that matches the plates you inherited from Grandma to knowing what to get in writing from a moving company.

Key Issues in a Contract

Most conflicts arise when two parties have different expectations of the same situation. *I thought you were going to . . .* and *Why didn't you . . . ?* are two examples of statements you hear when one side's expectations aren't met. You don't want these phrases to be part of your vocabulary—either speaking them or answering them. When you understand that a failure of expectations is at the root of most disputes, you will find solutions to problems before they arise by setting the parameters of what is expected from the other party in any circumstance.

• **Offer and acceptance.** Whether you're purchasing a used refrigerator from a neighbor or selling a Picasso on eBay, it's always critical to make sure there's clearly been a "meeting of the minds" between the parties on what is offered and what is to be received. Ideally, this offer and an acceptance will be documented in writing.

• **Performance obligations.** If you're hiring someone to do or create something for you, what range of goods or services or requirements does the deal cover? If you're offering a good or service, what obligations are you willing to agree upon? These questions are at the core of almost every business negotiation.

• **Quantity.** If the arrangement involves goods or services that can be measured by quantity, what is that number? How do you confirm whether it has been satisfied?

• **Payment obligations.** How much is owed, and when? What happens if the payor is late in a payment or thinks the payee hasn't properly performed its obligations? If you are owed a percentage, commission, royalty, or similar "contingent" payment, how can you confirm that you've been paid properly? Does either party have a right to see the other party's books?

• **Timing issues.** When is the good or service supposed to be provided? Are there penalties for lateness? How long is the term of the consumer/business arrangement? When does the term end, and what happens at the end of that term?

• **Representations and warranties.** What legal representations and warranties is each party making? If you are sued by a third party because the other party breached a representation or warranty, will that other party *indemnify* (cover the costs) of your losses and attorneys' fees? Will you have to indemnify the other party?

• **Liability issues.** What constitutes a "breach" of the arrangement that you are entering? What happens if the good or service you're offering, or obtaining, is delayed, is defective, fails, or causes damage or harm to somebody or something?

• **Termination issues.** Under what circumstances can you decide to terminate the deal? Under what circumstances can the other party decide to end it? What procedures must be followed to end the arrangement following an alleged breach? Is written notice required? Does each party have a chance to cure the breach?

• **Dispute resolution.** If a future dispute arises between you and the other party and you're not able to resolve it amicably, will you go to court? To an arbitration panel? To a mediator or an expert in alternative dispute resolution?

Real-Life Contracts

Suppose you're hiring someone to paint your house. Let's look at the points of a legal contract and see if you and Mr. Painter have answered each point.

√ **Offer and acceptance.** "You have offered to paint my house, and I have accepted your offer and agreed to pay you $3,000." By putting these terms in writing, you will both be protected later.

√ **Performance obligations.** "You are going to use Sherwin-Williams paint exclusively—flat 'Gettysburg Gray' for the house, semigloss 'China White' for the trim. You have suggested that the house will only need one coat, but if that coverage isn't sufficient (if the application doesn't provide complete coverage of the current blue color), you will apply a second coat." The more specific you are at the outset about what each side is supposed to do, the less likely you will have conflict later.

√ **Quantity.** "You estimate that the house will require twenty gallons, and the cost of the twenty gallons is included in the $3,000 payment. If any paint is necessary over that amount, we agree to split the cost equally. If there is damaged wood or insect infestation, I agree that I will have a handyperson fix the problem at my expense." Does "house" mean doghouse, outhouse, or the main house? Does this include the trim?

√ **Payment obligations.** "I agree to pay in personal check $1,500 before the project begins, and $1,500 when the project is completed." Notice that the method of payment is specified, so that the painter can't say "You told me cash" and you can't say "I want to pay you in stock options."

√ **Timing issues.** "You agree that the project will take fifteen workdays, weather permitting. The project will begin on Monday, May 5, and will conclude fifteen business days thereafter, but that period will be extended one day for any day that rain or weather conditions prevent painting. The period will also be extended by the same amount of time required to perform any repairs that are needed for the house." Should there be a reduction in the price owed if the work is not completed on time?

√ **Representations and warranties.** "You will be personally performing all of the work and will not need to hire any subcontractors to assist you." Think through what you want the other side to promise or guarantee about the work. Perhaps you want to request that the painter meets the standard he did on

Mr. Jones's house down the street. Can he take on other jobs while he is working on your house?

√ **Liability issues.** "If you fail to perform the obligations of this agreement, it will be considered a breach of this contract and you will refund any moneys paid you. You are bonded and insured by Acme Insurance and will be responsible for any damage and hold me harmless of any injuries that may occur." Are there other consequences if the painter or you don't live up to the terms of your agreement?

√ **Termination issues.** "If either of us decides to terminate the arrangement, all obligations of this contract are still in effect unless we have written changes, signed and agreed to by both parties." Who will pay to complete the work if your painter decides to walk away from the job?

√ **Dispute resolution.** "If a dispute arises between us and we can't amicably resolve it, we agree to have it settled by Joe Smith, a mutually agreed-upon mediator." Are you free to find someone else to finish the work during the dispute?

Contracts prevent trouble before trouble happens. When you think through, talk through, and then work through these issues *before* the painter picks up the brush, the entire experience will go more smoothly because both parties know what the other side expects.

Similarly, when you handle these types of issues *before* you make a commitment in any aspect of your life—whether it be with your credit card company or your real estate agent—you will find the entire experience easier and typically more successful. Armed with the Eight Steps and these contract and business law basics, you will feel confident to stand up for yourself, so that you can win every time.

For example, let's imagine that you are working for a small, family-owned company that sells imported antiques from countries like France and Belgium, and it's up to you to find the best telephone and Internet service for the essential work your company does via telecommunications. Your journey through the Eight Steps might go something like this:

Step 1. Know What You Want: *The Theory of the Case.* Before you contact your three target providers—let's assume they're AT&T, Sprint, and MCI—you need to determine what your case is truly about and establish your final objective accordingly. You decide your theory of the case will include these criteria: You are seeking a telecommunications provider that is responsive, communicative, and reliable (even at the cost of a few extra dollars) rather than a company that may offer you discounted rates but doesn't seem as open, straightforward, or trustworthy—and might actually force you into a long-term deal that, in the end, is even more costly.

Step 2. Choose and Evaluate Your Juror: *Voir Dire.* When you approach each of the three companies, you'll want to make sure that the person with whom you're talking has the experience, and the authority, to respond meaningfully to what you want and to your "theory of the case." Thus, if you explain to the sales representative at AT&T that your company does a lot of international calling and then inquire what program he recommends, and he replies, "Well, I can send you our rates, but we really just have one program," your immediate next step should be to ask to talk to his supervisor or to someone at AT&T who specializes in international rates. Likewise, if you say to a sales representative at MCI that you'd like to "create a long-term relationship in which people at our company will be able to call one person and get immediate attention" but that sales representative says that she does not have a direct number where she can be reached, and then puts you on hold for five minutes, you'll either need to look elsewhere or find a contact person who will be directly responsive and responsible.

Step 3. Marshal Your Evidence: *Discovery.* Rather than cold-calling the companies, you'll want to conduct "discovery" beforehand about their rate programs, the services they provide, the terms of their standard contracts, and how you could terminate a service if you are unhappy with it. You can consult consumer and trade groups to check out the quality of the three competitors' programs; you might also canvass other companies similar to yours to find out their experiences and the terms they negotiated. You may be able to request copies of the three competitors' standard contracts, study their terms, and discuss with your colleagues or other businesspeople you trust what provisions you might seek to delete or change and what "red herrings" to avoid.

Step 4. Advocate with Confidence: *Making the Case.* Let's say that among the contracts' key provisions (rates, billing methods, penalties for late payment, length of contract, contract termination options, and repair service), you learn that most of these contracts allow the phone service companies to change their calling rates every three months—without informing you! When you begin to make your case, you may decide to say something like: "I've studied your contract, and the contracts of some of your competitors, and I'm going to need a signed contract with you that promises me and my company that if you change your calling rates, you'll send an advance letter to my attention and we'll have a chance to terminate our relationship with you. I'll also need a provision that says that you'll send us notification at any point that you lower rates, and that we'll have the chance to benefit from those lower rates for as long as they're available. Before we go any farther, I'll need to know you can help me out on these things . . ." Having done your discovery and knowing just what you want, you'll be able to advocate point by point, confidently, and effectively.

Step 5. Counter the Claims: *Cross-Examination.* If the representative on the other end of the phone says, "Well, we don't usually commit to these sorts of special requests," you'll be ready to use your cross-examination skills. "But I know that Litchfield Antique Imports just signed a deal with you last week, and you promised them that the rates they paid would always be your lowest, and that you'd send them quarterly e-mails updating them on rate changes. This is something that you'd feel comfortable offering our small import business, too, then, isn't it?" or "Didn't you say you could beat any other phone company's rates? Well, it would make sense that you could do so not just now, but throughout the term of our contract together, wouldn't you agree?"

Step 6. Stay True to Your Case: *Avoid the Seven Deadly Spins.* You may have discovered (based on your due diligence) that most phone companies offer a flat national long-distance rate of between six and eight cents per minute. Perhaps after much research, you've found one company that charges only five cents, but learned that the company doesn't offer reliable service and may actually be in bankruptcy. When the sales representative at Sprint tells you, "We can offer you an eight-cent flat rate for all your national long-distance calls," you may be tempted to reply, "Oh, come on! I can pay five cents at most companies!" Arguing from such a false inference, however, may backfire—the sales rep may see right through your strategy. Instead you can say, "Why, eight cents seems very reasonable, but I've looked into these rates, and I understand I can actually, at least at some companies, get a rate as low as six cents per minute. Do you think this rate plan might become available soon at Sprint? Because you guys really do have such a great service record." If you can effectively use the real information at your disposal, rather than arguing from a false inference—or engaging in browbeating or threats—the sales representative's response is much more likely to be flexible.

Step 7. Advocate with Heart: *Let Me Tell You a Story.* Even in a no-nonsense business encounter, telling a story can be a very effective, humanizing strategy. Thus, you might say to that aggressive telecommunications salesperson, "Let me tell you why the terms of your repair policy are so important to us. Our sales in European-based antiques compete directly with dealers whose stock is in the United States, which means that we have to use the Internet to show our clients photos of the items they are considering. Once I had a client come in to look at a grandfather clock in England, but when our connection crashed for the whole day, I couldn't get the photos I needed. We lost the sale—and the client. I can't let that happen again." Using an apt story such as this, especially following your presentation of the hard-boiled facts, you'll help the other party relate to and respect your position.

Step 8. Sum It Up: *The Closing Argument.* Having gone through the first Steps 1 through 7, you'll be surprised at how succinctly and powerfully you can sum up your position: "Look, we want the lowest rates you're offering, not just now, but throughout our relationship. We need a contract that we can cancel if we realize that we're overpaying. And we need to work with a company with representatives we can call day or night, and solve any issues quickly and efficiently, so we never lose a deal or an opportunity. If you're that sort of company, we'd like to hear about it and know about the very best contract you can offer us." In this closing argument, in addition to restating your theory of the case, you want to refer, again, to the key evidence supporting it ("I've asked around, and I'm told that Sprint will work with our company along these lines"); remind the decision maker of the story you've related ("I want to sell a lot of English grandfather clocks!"); and state exactly what you are seeking ("So along with Internet service, we'd really like to sign a contract at no higher than seven cents per minute for state-to-state calls, and no more than fourteen cents per minute for our calls to Europe; we'd like to be able to end the contract whenever we feel we need to; and we want it in writing that any service interruptions will be resolved the same day on which we report them to you").

Eight Steps in Action

In consumer negotiations, control your witness by making sure you know what answers you'll get to your questions before you ask them, and by asking closed-ended questions whenever you can. If you've done your discovery correctly and gathered all relevant facts, you'll know what information the particular witness has to offer—and you'll be able to extract from the witness the information supporting your case.

Rental Cars

When my friend Joe in New York recently reserved a car with Thrifty Car Rental, he was quoted the cost over the telephone. But when he went to pick up his car at midnight at O'Hare Airport in Chicago, he was charged a higher rate.

After he returned to Manhattan, Joe effectively documented the who, what, and where of the situation in order to build his case. He had noted the names of the sales representative who initially gave him the quote over the phone as well as that of the service agent in Chicago. He called and inquired how many years each of these employees had been working at Thrifty. When he called the national manager of customer relations to discuss the matter, the man told Joe, "I'm sorry. The sales representative you spoke to is really new and she didn't remember that we no longer offer those discounts at the Chicago airports."

Joe didn't miss a beat. "Are you talking about Ms. White?"

"Yes," the manager said.

"And Ms. White has been at the company for more than seven years, isn't that about right?"

"Well, it has been a while, now that I think about it," the manager conceded, clearly embarrassed. Before Joe could complete his cross-examination, the manager offered him a complete refund and a coupon for a free weekend car rental.

Frequent Fliers

Devin wanted to surprise his wife, Monica, for their tenth wedding anniversary. He decided to plan ahead, and three months before their anniversary he made a reservation at the hotel on St. Lucia where they had honeymooned. Knowing he needed to conserve money, Devin wanted to cash in some of the many frequent flier miles he had accumulated in his job, but after just a few minutes on the phone with a huffy airline booking agent named Patty, he realized she had no desire to help him.

"So," he asked, "am I to understand that there are no frequent flier redemptions available to St. Lucia for the entire month of March?"

"That's right, sir," Patty said. "Those are limited seats, and we do take reservations for frequent flier redemptions up to eleven months before the date of travel."

Devin had the wrong juror. Rather than arguing with Patty or asking to speak with her supervisor, he just said, "Okay, thanks," and hung up the phone. He had a case to prepare. After gathering his evidence, he called the airline back, late at night rather than early in the afternoon.

"Hi," he said cheerfully to Liz, a new representative, "I'm hoping you can help me."

"I'll try, sir."

"I would like to travel to St. Lucia in early March with my wife using my frequent flier miles," he said, stating his theory of the case. "As you can see from my account, I travel a great deal and have accumulated a lot of miles."

"Yes, you have," Liz said, "In fact, you have enough to take several trips to St. Lucia!"

"But I was told earlier today that all the seats available for frequent flier travel are booked . . . for all of March."

Liz checked his preferred date, March 4, and a week before and a week after, and came back with the same results that Patty had earlier: There were no frequent flier seats available. "That's so disappointing," Devin said, telling his story. "It's for my tenth wedding anniversary, and I'm already breaking the bank to surprise my wife with a week at the hotel where we honeymooned. I just don't think I can afford the two tickets on top of it."

"Your tenth wedding anniversary?" Liz said. "With all those points, it is a real shame you can't use them. It seems like the problem is the connecting flight in San Juan. Everyone wants to go to St. Lucia on that one-thirty PM flight."

"I looked up on your Web site the seat availability, and it seems like the flights aren't even half full," Devin said, laying out his evidence. "Is there a time when the airline will release the seats?"

"Sir?" Liz asked. "Do you mind holding on for a minute, and let me see if I can do some shuffling?"

When Liz came back, she had a solution to offer. "Well," she said, "there is an early-morning flight out of San Juan, but it wasn't coming up on my screen because it would mean you would have to take a flight the day before to San Juan. But if I were you, rather than spending eight hundred dollars on each ticket, I would fly down the day before, tour Old San Juan, stay in one of the beautiful hotels there, and take the early-morning flight. It might give you the day to decompress before your real vacation begins. And we're running a special today that saves five thousand miles a ticket, so you could actually use those saved miles for maybe a free hotel night at one of our participating hotels."

Devin won his case by knowing what he wanted; realizing that the first juror wasn't going to give it to him; discovering his evidence; laying out his case; telling his story; not getting irate, accusatory, or emotional; and asking for a favorable verdict. He says his tenth-anniversary trip was even better than the honeymoon.

Car Dealers

Besides a house, a car is perhaps the second most expensive purchase you'll ever make. Unfortunately, if you've gone down this road, you also know it can be more painful than a trip to the dentist. My friends Ann and Greg learned this lesson on their last car purchase. They walked into a Volkswagen dealer in California and proclaimed, "We really need a new car and love that white Golf sitting out there in front of the showroom. How much is it?" shortly followed by, "We'll take it," and "What will you give us for our old car?" Though they loved their new car, they didn't love the deal they got, especially when their neighbor got the exact same car from the exact same dealer for two thousand dollars less. For that purchase, they weren't working with the Eight Steps. For their more recent purchase of a Honda Element, however, they were.

Before going into a dealer, Ann went online to learn everything she could about the car. Using edmunds.com and www.automotive.com, she found four dealers in their area willing to compete for their business, and got price quotes from each sent to her via e-mail. Greg found information from critics at sites such as carreview.com, epinions.com, and forbes.com. Armed with this information, they went for a test drive.

Since Ann had given her name and personal information in order to get price quotes, they decided that at the dealerships Greg would take the lead. At the first dealer (the dealer closest to their house), they listened to the salesman's pitch before taking the test drive. On his discovery mission, Greg had learned that talking to the salesperson can provide a feel for a dealership—how the people there are going to treat you once you buy the car and drive it off the lot. He also walked over to their service department and, as suggested, asked a customer how he had found the service.

During their test drive, they discussed privately their theory of the case. They decided that rather than "We want it," they'd try, "This is a great car. We'd like to get it at your best price."

Back in the sales office, they heard numbers as much as three thousand dollars higher than the lowest price they'd gotten on the Internet.

"Okay," Greg said, "Thanks for letting us drive it. We're going to shop around."

The salesman stopped them at the door. "We offer the best deal in the state," he bragged.

Greg was ready with his cross-examination.

GREG: Oh, really? Better than Handy Brothers?
SALESMAN: Yes.
GREG: Better than Jim Johnson Honda?
SALESMAN: You bet.
GREG: Do you guarantee that your price is lower?
SALESMAN: Absolutely.
GREG: What will you do if it's not?
SALESMAN: I'll give you $250 cash if I can't beat their deal.

Greg then presented the price quotes he had in writing, including the quote from the dealer he was talking to, which online was nineteen hundred dollars less than the "best deal" he had just offered. The salesman looked at the numbers and said, "If you'll excuse me, I'll go present these to my manager." When he returned, he boasted, "We can match it."

Greg quickly asked, "Are you offering 0 percent financing?"

"No," the salesman said, "the lowest we can offer is 3.9 percent."

"All right," Greg said, "May I have my $250? Johnson is offering your price and 0 percent financing."

"Just a second," the salesman said, and once again left to "talk to his manager."

When he returned, he delivered a winning verdict. Ann and Greg won their case and got their dream car at the lowest price in the state by being prepared, by thinking through their "trial" from start to finish, and by standing up for themselves rationally, logically, and confidently.

Be Nice

No one wants to pet a growling dog. In the context of consumer and business negotiations, presenting your case in a nonadversarial way—what I call the "velvet assassin" approach—is particularly important in helping you win the verdict you want. Patience and kindness go a long way.

When my friend Rick recently got bumped from an airline flight, he decided he would be the only bumped passenger not screaming in the gate agent's face. Instead, he quietly focused on his facts, the theory of his case. When it was his turn in line, he nicely said, "I'm a doctor and have to get back home for an emergency room shift tonight. Is there any way you can help me?" Rick got on the next flight—bumped up to first class.

Always remember that the person you're dealing with is human, too. Everyone has feelings, so approach as you'd want to be approached if the tables were turned.

Proof Is in the Putting It into Action

Take the Eight Steps out for a test drive in your consumer and business negotiations. You may be surprised by the results. By implementing these techniques, you will learn that effective advocacy is not about "bullying" the other side—it's about getting what you want in as positive a way as possible. You take strides toward your goal by approaching what you want simply, stating your point succinctly, backing it up with proof, calmly countering your "opponent's" arguments, and above all treating the opposite side with respect and dignity, not intimidation.

You reach a successful verdict in consumer negotiations through preparation. In fact, lack of preparation is the biggest mistake people make when advocating for themselves. Asking for your money back or trying to persuade the telephone company to drop a hidden fee without preparing is like fighting a battle without a weapon. How does that make you respond? Defensively, rather than offensively. When you get defensive, you get emotional and upset. And let's face it: Being upset is not persuasive.

The bottom line on the bottom line: If you don't use the Eight Steps, you aren't on your way to getting the best deal.

THE TRIALS OF LIFE

LEGAL BRIEF: WINNING IN BUSINESS AND CONSUMER NEGOTIATIONS

A Few Great Phrases to Get You Started

- "A positive outcome to this situation is important to me because . . ."
- "Are you the one who can authorize . . ."
- "Based on what I found out reading the terms of the health plan . . ."
- "Sir, that's not the point. I have just addressed that issue. The point is . . ."
- "Thanks, I've been listening to the phone menu—it's great to finally hear a real voice . . ."
- "Let me tell you a quick story about why I need . . ."
- "I am feeling frustrated. Can you help me?"
- "I've talked to several other people who've gotten a better deal from you. Can you offer me . . ."

ATTENTION MEN:
Turn to chapter 12!
Chapter 11's secrets
are for women only!

Chapter 11

A Woman's Voice

> *Forget it! I'm staying put, right where I am. It's gonna take you and the police department and the fire department and the National Guard to get me outta here!*
> —SALLY FIELD, playing the title character in *Norma Rae*

In case you haven't heard, the Equal Rights Amendment was never passed, and what that means, ladies, is that, as Aretha Franklin sings, we're going to have to "do it for ourselves."

Remember Erin Brockovich, the twice-divorced woman with three children and no money who took on Pacific Gas & Electric and put together a case that was awarded $333 million—the largest settlement ever paid in a direct-action lawsuit in U.S. history? While doing her discovery, she needed to photocopy specific records at the county water board, and as she headed out the door to accomplish the goal, her boss asked, "What makes you think you can just walk in there and find what we need?"

She quickly answered, "They're called boobs, Ed."

Admittedly, one of the surefire ways we women have historically used to get what we want is sex. We bat our lashes, expose our cleavage, pucker our lips, and swish our hips. Why is that? Is it because men are really the weaker sex and can't withstand our beguiling power? Or is it perhaps that sex is the one weapon we've gotten stuck using?

Eleanor Roosevelt shared her woman's voice in her syndicated newspaper column, "My Day." Six days a week from 1936 to 1962 she discussed her views on social and political issues, current and historical events, and her private and public life. In one column in 1939, she addressed womanly wiles after receiving an article written for a men's magazine, in which a Dr. S. N. Stevens said: "Women are generally more intuitive than empirical. In other words, they play hunches instead of examining facts in the evaluation of a situation. And I have never yet seen one who, in a tight spot, didn't try to take advantage of the fact that she was a woman."

In addressing the second part of this statement, Mrs. Roosevelt agreed that some women do prey on men with their womanhood, but argued that those women won't ever go far in their jobs because the act of using their womanhood becomes a job in itself. Mrs. Roosevelt made her case that women should train themselves to examine the facts and evaluate the factors in any situation, so that paired with their intuition they'll have the distinct advantage over men. She added, "A woman may use her woman wiles to help her in tight spots, but she isn't trading on being a woman, she is just handling the job which is hers, and frequently it is the job of handling a man and making him think he isn't being handled."

What do we possess besides our womanly wiles? We have our intuition. We have our empathy. We have great skills of communication. But when we have to stand up for ourselves, social expectations and ingrained conditioning often cause us to press the brake and the gas at the same time. We are told to be assertive but not aggressive, savvy but not sneaky, feminine but not weak, well spoken but not soft.

We've made great strides at home, in the workplace, and as consumers, but we still face unique challenges as women—from not being taken seriously to being resented when we speak our minds. As a prosecutor, I faced daily battles in dealing with macho federal agents who were not always pleased to report to a woman. I once had to deal with a rather surly agent who seemed to be resisting my authority. Using humor to disarm him, I told the agent that I couldn't cook or sew, but that I would do the best darn job possible in court. At the end of the successful trial, the agent presented me with a gold plaque with the inscription: CAN'T COOK, CAN'T SEW, SURE CAN LITIGATE.

Your gender is inevitably part of how you are perceived. I was aware of this each and every time I walked in the courtroom, and on occasion, I admit to using it to my advantage. I was once in trial with a particularly cantankerous judge who snapped at all of the lawyers, including me. I knew that his daughter was pregnant. Luckily for me, I was four months' pregnant with Jacob at the time. So, a few days into the trial, I began wearing my maternity clothes for the first time. On the first day I wore my tentlike dress to court, the judge asked me during a recess how I was feeling and suggested I rest in his chambers during the break.

Find Your Voice

As I mentioned in the introduction to this book, there are four ways to approach situations that arise in our life, but *now that no men are around* let's reexamine these approaches and how we can implement the Eight Steps to find a strong, but gentle, woman's voice.

Four Ways to Approach Difficulties or Problems That Arise in Life

1. **Ignore them and hope they go away.** As women, we often bury our own problems and difficulties and instead caretake for

others. Our children need us; our spouse needs us; our elderly parents need us; the school PTA needs us; our job needs us; the house needs us. And with all those needs, who has time to deal with our own crises?

2. **Assign them to someone else.** In our times of real crises, we turn to a spouse, a colleague, a parent, or a friend to be our knight in shining armor and come save the damsel in distress. We're Lois Lane and need our Superman. We turn to someone else to rescue us, to pull us back from the abyss, to say to us, "You're okay. Everything is going to be all right."

3. **Contend with them irrationally.** We get emotional; we yell; we cry; we say we don't want to talk. Does this accomplish anything? Rarely. And even if we succeed with the emotional approach, we've also said, *I'm weak.*

4. **Face them head-on.** The Eight Steps give us a method to assert ourselves in a way that is both comforting and comfortable to us, allowing us to handle our distinctive concerns with concrete strategies and become more confident asserting ourselves, nurturing our advocacy skills, and effecting positive changes. Using the Eight Steps, we can approach our difficulties logically and thoughtfully, with thorough preparation, scoring winning results—both for ourselves and for those we care about.

I imagine you've often tried to face your problems with options 1, 2, and 3. Like you, I've dabbled in those "techniques" myself, and I've met with little success. (When I have found success, it's often been at too great a long-term cost.) But when I face my problems head-on and apply the skills I've learned as a lawyer to the trials in my life, I achieve the same kind of results in my personal difficulties as I do in my courtroom cases.

Let's see how the Eight Steps can help us overcome our conditioning and take a stand for ourselves.

Not-So-Dear Terms of Endearment

As women, we can't jump up and scream every time a man casts his eyes on certain parts of our anatomy. (We'd be screaming a lot!) But there are times when we have to take action because the price of not saying or doing something is just too high.

During one case, I had a wonderful lawyer as my trial partner, a fatherly man named Ken who was incredible in the courtroom, but a little unaware on the sensitivity front. Throughout our first morning's preliminary hearing, Ken consistently referred to the judge's clerk (a woman) as "hon" and "darlin'" and to me as "sweetie" and "sugar." I realized quickly that the judge's clerk was rattled by it, and I knew from the hairs on the back of my neck that his references would grate on the women of the jury—and that would be detrimental to our case.

I decided my theory of the case was to gently educate my trial partner, not lose his friendship, and successfully win our case. I didn't think for a minute that Ken meant to be demeaning or rude to women by his references. In fact, I'm sure he didn't have a clue that his words might be offensive. So as we prepared for our upcoming trial, I did my discovery by jotting down the "cutie-pie" remarks he made to me and others in the office, literally keeping a written log of all these references for a few days.

I chose my time to talk with him carefully—over a cup of coffee during our usual midmorning break, where we would be out of the office, and he would be fresh and relaxed. I also anticipated his cross, knowing he would probably say something like, *But I don't mean any harm* or *That's just my way of being friendly.*

As we sipped coffee and discussed our case, I asked kindly, "Ken, do you mind if I talk to you about something?"

"Sure," he said. "What's up?"

"I want to mention something to you that I think will help our case."

"Great."

"I've noticed that you often make references to women in a way that you intend to be nice, but are actually condescending. Being referred to as 'sweetie' and 'hon' makes some women uncomfortable." I was ready with my "evidence"—the reference log—but I didn't actually show it to him; I just gave him a general catalog of the terms I had heard him use and when he had used them. "I don't take offense to them because we're friends, but I'm a little concerned it might not be good for our case in front of the women of a jury."

"But that's just me being friendly," he said.

Having anticipated his defense, I was able to deliver a powerful closing argument. "I know that, Ken," I said, smiling reassuringly. "But think about your two daughters. Would you really want a man twice their age calling them 'honey' and 'darling'? Even if he was *just being friendly*?"

Ken went cold turkey. That was the last time I ever heard him refer to anyone, besides his wife, as 'honey.' Several months later, Ken came to my office and said he wanted to thank me for making him aware of something hurtful he was doing in a way that did not try to threaten or hurt him in return. He also said his performance in the courtroom had improved, and he attributed it to the fact that the female jurors seemed to like him more.

Equal Pay

The feminist community believes that women should be allowed to do anything men do. I agree, up to a point. I believe that we should be *allowed to,* but sometimes we might have to admit we *can't* do. For example, there have been long debates in fire departments about lessening the physical standards so that women can join. But a two-hundred-pound man in a burning building isn't going to get lighter just because a woman has come to rescue him. He's still going to be a two-hundred-pound man in a burning building.

I do think we should spend our energy vehemently arguing for equal pay for equal work, and I have used the Eight Steps to challenge my employer over the issue of receiving pay equal to my male peers. As a professor at the University of Washington Law School, I became director of the trial advocacy program, one of the largest programs in the school. After a short time on the job, I learned that I was being paid five thousand dollars less than the director of another, smaller program, who happened to be male. The unfairness of this incensed me, and I had to figure out what to do.

I determined that my theory of the case involved the injustice of being paid less than a male coworker who had less experience and ran a smaller program, but also the fact that I was a role model for women students at the school and could not in good conscience accept being paid five thousand dollars less than a man for the same work. In fact, I was willing to resign over it.

I did my research and found out that the pay disparity (which I'd first found out about as hearsay) was indeed true. I assembled my facts regarding salary rates, the comparative experience of my fellow director and me (mine was greater), and the amount of work involved for each of us (my program enrolled more students). I organized my evidence point by point and rehearsed my presentation, from opening argument to summation. Then I went to the law school dean—my juror in this case—whom I had pegged as a fair man reluctant to get tangled in intercollegiate warfare.

He listened carefully, nodded when I said that the issue was equal pay for equal work, and was properly taken aback when I said I couldn't in good conscience keep a job where I was not enacting my own values. When I finished my summation, he informed me that salary issues were the domain of the provost. I decided to appeal. "Will you accompany me to the provost?" I asked. He agreed.

I presented my case again to the university provost, laying out the evidence of the wage disparity, comparing my credentials with those of the other program director, and showing class lists that compared the different enrollments of our programs. I concluded with my own story, declaring that as a lawyer I had learned—and now was teaching to my students—the importance of obtaining justice. I couldn't honorably instruct my students—especially aspiring women lawyers—if I didn't now seek justice for myself. When I concluded, the provost agreed to grant me the five-thousand-dollar raise that would give me parity with my colleague.

Body Issues

Often the seemingly smallest moments in life present opportunities for us to advocate for ourselves in ways that will have big effects. In fact, sometimes the most important things in life to advocate for are the seemingly little ones that are a part of a woman's everyday life. Remember the story "The Princess and the Pea"? She couldn't sleep all night because of the annoyance of that tiny pea lodged twenty mattresses below her. If something is bothering you, find the voice to take a stand and say so, but approach it rationally rather than responding emotionally.

Heather, a woman in her early twenties, had recently lost her mother to brain cancer. Her mother's long sickness and recent death had caused great sadness and pain in Heather's life, and, whether psychosomatic or due to illness, Heather was having almost daily headaches. She decided to go explain her symptoms to her doctor in the hope that he would be able to prescribe something that might provide relief.

Like many women, Heather dreaded the moment when, in every doctor visit, the nurse would guide her down the hall and tell her to step on the scale to get weighed. She didn't just dread it; she hated it, because in her view its only purpose was to serve as a painful reminder of an issue she'd rather not be reminded of—namely, her body image and the self-loathing that occurs when she's confronted with weight. She also has found the scale in her doctor's office to invariably be off by as much as ten pounds, only adding to the misery of the experience.

For years Heather had taken issue with her weigh-ins at the doctor, but each and every time she went, she succumbed to the request and hopped on the scale. As the nurse wrote down her weight, she always stood there in her paper robe feeling "like a pig at auction." But like so many others, Heather never even thought that she might have a choice in the matter. She simply didn't question the reality of the doctor's office weigh-in and conformed to their requests.

Still, the death of Heather's mother gave her a new perspective on many things in her life. Before this doctor's visit, Heather decided she'd had enough. When she got to her appointment and the nurse asked her to get on the scale, she almost chickened out on her plan and once again stepped on the scale, but, remembering her "case," she stood strong.

"You know," Heather said, stopping short of the scale and looking the nurse firmly in the eyes, "I'd rather not."

"I need to get your weight," the nurse said, "for our records."

Heather smiled, and then delivered her theory of the case: "It's not necessary for you to take my weight today."

"I need to know your weight to complete the preliminary information in your file," the nurse said, pointing to Heather's chart. "Look, there's a blank there that needs to be filled in."

Heather was ready for the nurse's argument. "Is that actually necessary?" she said, smiling at the nurse. "I'm here for a reason that has nothing to do with my weight, and I do not want to get weighed today. What's going to happen if that blank is left blank?"

The nurse started laughing. "You know," she said, "you're right. It really isn't necessary. You don't have to get weighed today. That blank will still be blank the next time you come in."

Heather and the nurse then shared a good laugh. As they walked back down the hall, the nurse said, "I wonder why more women don't say that?"

Heather sailed through the remainder of her appointment—answering the doctor's questions, letting him check her pupils, take her pulse, and perform other diagnostics that might explain her headaches. The diagnosis was that her headaches were most likely stress-related and not caused by brain cancer. When he offered her a prescription for antidepression medication, Heather turned him down. "You know," she told him, "I feel like a weight was just lifted off me." The nurse chuckled. "As long as you don't think I have brain cancer, I think I'm going to be okay."

Keeping the Peace

Advocacy sometimes takes a form quite different from laying out "your case" for someone and being explicit about your needs and desires. Sometimes simply establishing a communication style that is calm, open, and forthcoming can work to alleviate a situation that is drenched in lies, misinterpretations, or misunderstandings. Many times, when you are being lied to or about by someone, those lies are stemming from insecurity that the person ("the liar") may have about himself or about you.

Heidi has an older brother, Justin, to whom she is very close. Justin had recently ended his relationship with a girlfriend who had very much become part of their family, and shortly thereafter began dating quite seriously a woman named Lisa who was incredibly difficult to get along with. Lisa, unfortunately, was completely uninterested in getting to know Justin's family at all. In fact, she seemed determined to separate Justin from his family altogether.

She would lie to Justin about her interactions with members of his family, telling him that when she'd called the family home and asked to speak to Justin, his family members were extremely rude to her. Justin, of course, felt protective of his girlfriend and was quite accusatory with his family. Lisa repeatedly told Justin that she was being talked about by members of his family and was simply being mistreated.

Justin approached Heidi and then the rest of his family, upset and confrontational about the situation. Heidi was extremely hurt by his accusations and felt defensive, as she had never been anything but kind to Lisa and resented being accused of such behavior.

She was incensed that Lisa would make up such lies, and was also very concerned as to why she would do this. She quickly realized that it was Lisa's intent to upset the family and cause friction between Justin and his family.

Heidi realized that to react defensively, to grow angry, or to simply overlook the situation would not be in the best interests of herself, Justin, or her family—it would allow the strife to continue and result in Justin being estranged from the family. Instead, she did something that was very difficult. She asked Justin and his girlfriend to sit down and talk with her about what Lisa had suggested about the family. Immediately, Justin said that Heidi should speak with Lisa alone. Heidi, though, realized that this would not accomplish what she desired because it would allow Lisa to relay the conversation they had to Justin in whatever fashion suited her interests. She could assert that Heidi was, in the conversation, "mean" to her, "rude" to her, or any number of things. Additionally, it wouldn't accomplish her real goal—her theory of the case—which was to help mend the family problems that had arisen as a result of Lisa's accusations. Heidi wanted Justin there for the conversation. They agreed to all be present.

This was an extremely hard conversation for Heidi to have because in actuality she was very angry with Lisa for telling lies, and also angry with Justin for believing them and not giving his own family the benefit of the doubt.

When she sat down on her family sofa with Justin, Lisa sitting on his lap, she was filled with hesitancy. Heidi told Lisa that she had been told she'd done some things that made Lisa feel uncomfortable and unwelcome in their home. She apologized to Lisa—telling her that she had no intention of making her feel unwelcome and was very sorry for whatever she had done. By starting the conversation this way, Heidi noticed that a lot of the initial tension that seemed to exist between the three of them dissipated somewhat. It seemed to melt the barriers between them a little bit. This was a hard apology for Heidi to make, because she really felt that these allegations were completely untrue—yet she knew an apology would go a long way toward establishing open communication among them. She then asked Lisa to please tell her what it was that Heidi could do to make her feel more comfortable and welcome in the family. Lisa detailed ways that she thought Heidi was excluding her, and Heidi nodded and tried to be as responsive as possible.

Then Heidi, after listening to Justin and Lisa, told them both that she really wanted Justin and Lisa to feel comfortable and welcome. She told them they really needed to talk to her directly and right away about things that were a concern to them—about issues they were experiencing. She expressed that she wanted them to be able to communicate with her honestly and effectively, in a calm and adult manner.

The results of the conversation were profound. Regardless of Justin and Lisa's reason for animosity and distrust, they became much calmer, more direct, and more adult in their communication style with the family. Additionally, Lisa seemed to stop telling Justin fabrications about her communications and interactions with the family, and actually began spending more time with them.

Heidi discovered something important to note about your "juror." Sometimes a situation calls for others to be present for the conversation, even if ultimately it will only be a conversation between two people. This will work to alleviate problems of interpretation of the conversation that may take place if only two of you are present, and will prevent your case from ending up at a she said–he said impasse. Open, difficult, but honest conversations can work to defuse a situation that is being exacerbated by gossip, hearsay, and "he said–she said" communication.

Woman to Woman

Women can be so tough on other women. If we don't have it hard enough, we often make it hard on ourselves. If I'm prosecuting a date rape case, I don't want women on the jury, because they are much more likely to jump to the "she asked for it" conclusion. For some reason, some women who've succeeded in a "man's world" often don't want to help up-and-coming women (referred to as the "Margaret Thatcher syndrome," for the former prime minister of Great Britain who wanted only men as her highest advisers). According to a recent *USA Today* finding, there are only six female CEOs of Fortune 500 companies, and of the twenty-four best-paid executives working for these six CEOs, only three are women. Unfortunately, having a woman in power doesn't seem to guarantee that she will propel many other women to the top—in fact, just the opposite might occur.

When I was practicing corporate law, there was a woman partner in the group who had a reputation for being really tough on women. I wrote many research briefs for partners and received many great reviews until I wrote a brief for this woman. She tore it apart. I rewrote that brief at least five times before she found it "passable." Also, it's common practice for a partner to bring along the junior associate to meet clients for strategy and trial preparation sessions so that the associate can be a "known" face for the clients in case they have questions down the road. This woman shut me out of meetings—literally locking the door while speaking to the client in the conference room. So I tried a little experiment and wrote a brief for her, but had a male colleague submit it under his name. She raved about "his" work and accepted it without changes out of the block.

Sometimes we also have one-sided relationships with our women friends. Anne Marie, a senior in college and close to attaining her teaching degree, struggled in school and in her life. She worked hard to maintain a positive outlook despite the fact her finances were tight, her relationship with her boyfriend tenuous, and her living conditions close to squalid. Anne Marie cared very much about her friend Emily. They had been friends for several years and had grown very close. The only problem with the friendship was that Emily—while very good at "taking" in the relationship—was very bad at "giving."

Their friendship and conversations always revolved around Emily: Emily's frustrations, Emily's problems, and Emily's depression. While Anne Marie never minded discussing these things, she was also aware that Emily could go weeks before asking Anne Marie how she was doing. Anne Marie accepted this because she knew Emily battled a depression that she never seemed to be able to shake, and she felt uncomfortable expressing to Emily her dissatisfaction with their friendship because she felt Emily's emotional needs were more pressing than her own. She allowed this one-sided friendship to continue for a long time.

Then one day, something clicked. Anne was sitting in the dog-haired, cluttered living room of the house she shared with four other girls near her college campus when Emily came by. Anne Marie had had a terrible day—she'd been up late writing a paper the evening before and not gotten enough sleep. That day, irritable and tired, she'd had a small spat with her boyfriend. She decided to take a bath and relax but instead came home to find that her female roommates had taken over the two bathrooms to get ready for a night out. When Emily popped in to visit, Anne Marie should have been happy, but instead she got wearier just thinking about talking with Emily.

Emily sat down and asked Anne Marie, "How was your day?" But before she could answer, Emily plunged into a conversation about herself: about her day, about how depressed she was, about how she was feeling. Anne Marie decided she couldn't deal with it anymore. She interrupted Emily and said, "Emily, there's something I've needed to talk to you about for a while, but I've got a few things I have to get done right now. Could we have breakfast in the morning?" Although Emily wanted to hear it right then and there, Anne Marie said it could wait until morning.

The following morning, they met for breakfast at the local diner. Emily was eager to hear what Anne Marie had to say. "I need to be honest with you," Anne Marie began. "And I hope you'll not interrupt me and know that I'm telling you how I really feel because I do care for you."

"Okay," Emily said, her manner uncharacteristically quiet.

"I've listened to you talk about your depression for a long time now, and it has become a burden for me. Your problems are more than I can handle, and I think you are chronically depressed. You've been depressed since I've met you and you seem to create problems in your life and make things more difficult. I really think that you need someone in your life to help you besides me. Perhaps a psychiatrist might think you'll benefit from being on an antidepressant."

"You're putting your nose where it doesn't belong," Emily said.

"Emily, your depression is defining your life—even to the point that it prevents you from having fulfilling relationships, including a good friendship with me because you're so upset all the time that you never get outside yourself enough to care about what others are feeling, to care about my life." Anne Marie laid out her "evidence," relaying back to Emily numerous conversations that Emily had dominated and important things in Anne Marie's life that Emily knew nothing about.

Emily was incensed. "You have no business telling me I need therapy, no business speculating on my medical needs, and I think you're selfish for bringing up this subject at all!"

Anne Marie had figured Emily would respond that way, and rather than combating emotion with emotion, she stayed calm and on her case plan. "Emily, I care about you," she said. "I think you're a very special person, and that's why I'm your friend. But in being your friend, I have to be honest with you, and I can't continue our friendship this way."

Emily threw down her napkin and stormed out of the diner. Nonetheless, Anne Marie felt she had done the right thing. She could no longer accept the friendship as it existed, and while she preferred not to hurt Emily, she knew that she had reached her limit and would, if made to choose, decide to lose the friendship rather than have it continue as it was. She needed to have people in her life whom she felt cared about her in some real sense.

Several months later, Emily came to see Anne Marie. They had not seen or spoken to each other since that morning in the diner. "I came by to thank you," Emily said. "After our conversation, I was really mad, but in the end I realized you were right." She told Anne Marie that she had made an appointment with a psychiatrist, and after a month of evaluation, he had prescribed an antidepressant medication and continuing psychiatric care. As a result Emily was feeling much better about herself, her life, and her future. "No one had ever been honest with me before, and I'm grateful to you. You were right about our friendship. I hope you'll give me another chance."

Anne Marie and Emily were able to rebuild their friendship, but Anne Marie points out she would have been content leaving the friendship with the conversation in the diner that day. She says that for her, finding a strong woman's voice means being willing to care enough about herself, and value her gut instincts enough, to walk away from things in her life that are hurtful or unfulfilling even when there is a risk she might be losing something else as well.

Being an advocate means being honest with yourself about your needs and caring about yourself enough to assert those needs—even with those who may not be receptive to them.

Woman to Man

For the twenty years of her marriage, Joan felt the reins of power were in the hands of her husband, Ross. Far from advocating for herself, Joan had fallen into the role of "appeaser" in the marriage, much like her role at work as a secretary to a powerful businessman. She had married Ross when she was twenty-five years old, and it wasn't until her mother's death that Joan realized she'd never been honest with herself about her own needs in the marriage. In fact, everything in their marriage had become about making Ross happy, and now she was watching him exert the same kind of control over their two teenage sons.

Her mother's death was an awakening for Joan. "I realized I was unhappy, the kids were unhappy, and really Ross was unhappy—though he'd never admit it—and I came to the conclusion that I was not going to remain unhappy the rest of my life."

She began preparing her case. She determined that it wasn't worth staying in a bad marriage just for the sake of staying together. Though Ross had had two affairs during the marriage, she had worked through them at the time and didn't want to bring those up as the issue now. She thought about talking to the boys first, but realized that wouldn't be fair to them or to Ross, and basically, it would have been her shield. She needed to stand up to Ross and communicate with him directly.

When she'd gathered her evidence—all the things she'd needed to say for a long time but, because of Ross's dominance, had remained quiet about—she decided she'd ask Ross out to dinner and talk to him then. She felt that neither of them would be able to raise their voice in a restaurant, and hoped this would allow them to talk calmly. The night she had worked up the courage to have the conversation, Ross came home in a rage. He wanted to know why she'd allowed their younger son, Ben, to have a friend stay at the house without asking his permission.

"I didn't realize I needed to get your approval," she said calmly as Ross yelled.

"This is *my* house!" he roared. "You need to ask me what goes on in my house!"

"I thought this was *our* house," Joan said, deciding to delay her "case" for a less tense time. "Haven't we both worked to pay our bills for twenty years?"

"Yeah, if we counted on what you make, we'd be living in a shack!" With that, Ross grabbed his keys and walked out, slamming the door behind him.

As his car backed out of the driveway, Joan was glad he left. She didn't want him to see her cry.

The following night, the boys were at a school event, and when Ross got home Joan asked if he'd join her out for dinner. "There are a few things we need to talk about."

At dinner, she calmly told Ross that she thought their marriage had come to a point where it wasn't good for either of them. She explained that she had felt subordinate for too long, had tired of his control, and knew that she was a strong, worthy, independent woman. "You're nothing without me," her husband said. "Don't you forget that."

"That's what you've wanted me to believe for the last twenty years," Joan said. "And the sad truth is I believed it—I bought into that nothingness. But I'm not 'nothing.' I've succeeded at my job—"

"You're just a secretary!" he interrupted.

"I've succeeded at my job," she repeated, "as a secretary. I have helped my boss move up to the top of the firm and have had my benefits increase exponentially. I'm a good mother to our two sons. I'm a dedicated volunteer for several terrific organizations. I am something. I am worthy, and there are only two things I'm sorry for: one is that it took my mother's death to make me realize that, and the other is that you've never realized it. Ross, I think you're a good man. You have provided for your family, and I don't want to sell that short, but I think the time has come for us to end our vacant marriage."

"This will kill the boys," he said, as she had expected.

"You know, Ross, I've given that a lot of thought, and I think this will be really good for the boys. I don't think it's healthy for them to see their mother continually put down by their father. It doesn't serve them well for their future relationships. And I don't think they are happy with how much you control their lives."

"Control their lives?" Ross said, starting to raise his voice, and then realizing he was in a restaurant. "I don't control their lives. Give me just one example!"

"Okay, you always insist Cody goes fishing with you, not even realizing that Cody hates fishing. You wouldn't let Ben do the science fair project he wanted, you made him do the one you wanted him to do."

"That's enough. Fine. Let's separate. You'll regret it."

The next day Ross moved in with his mother, and in the six months they've been separated, contrary to Ross's opinion, both Joan and the boys have made great progress in their lives. The boys' grades have improved at school, and they've established strong friendships that they weren't allowed to when Ross was home. Joan's life has blossomed. She wakes up happy to go to work and comes home eager to see her boys. Though she's still waiting for her divorce to be final—trying to be "nice," she wanted to allow for the two of them to file a joint petition—she has remained positive to the boys about their father and strong in her decision. She's also realized that she is indeed *something* without Ross.

Man to Woman

No matter how strong a woman I think I am, I have to admit I'm smaller and weaker physically than most men. It's just a fact of nature I have to face. If I call and threaten a man, it's a lot less intimidating than a man calling and threatening me. And if it happens, this is a time that we may have to rely on someone else to advocate for us.

I was in the middle of prosecuting a rape case against a man who, after being released from prison, was harassing his victim again. She came to the U.S. attorney's office and was able to bring a federal complaint against the man, because he had used the mail and interstate phone to threaten her.

One night I was alone working late in my office and the phone rang. When I picked it up, a man on the other end of the line said, "I'm going to kill you, but before I do I'm going to tie you up and f**k you, just like I did Nancy. Only with you, I'm going to kill you, and I'm going to enjoy it."

My heart was pounding as I hung up the phone. I recognized the voice as that of the rapist. He'd been in the courtroom for initial appearances and arraignment, but was out on bond. Rather than panicking, I began typing. I typed exactly what he had said to me, the time I received the call, and what I was doing. (Keeping a record of events is crucial, not only because it allows you to recall a series of occurrences in detail, but also because it adds credibility to your version of events.)

I could have gotten hysterical. Or worse, my fear could have caused me to minimize the severity of the threat, and I could have not reported it. I knew two things: I could no longer be the prosecutor on this case and I needed help in advocating for myself. Still, I applied the Eight Steps, resolving that my theory of the case was to stop this man and send him back to jail. I asked myself whom in the U.S. attorney's office I should go to. Whom should I ask to help me?

I chose an attorney named Mark because I respected him in the courtroom; because his wife, Ana, was also a prosecutor; and because they also had two small kids. I knew he would understand both how frightened I was and how much I wanted to do the right thing. I felt that if I had chosen a woman, she might be prone to the very same thing that had happened to me. Mark got right to the case, the FBI was in the office within fifteen minutes, and he launched his discovery into the whereabouts of this man on the night of the threat and tracing phone records. About two days later, I fortuitously received in the mail a death threat made up of cutout letters from the newspaper. Mark traced the postmark and sent it off to the crime lab for print recovery.

I knew it was not going to be fun sitting on the stand and having to look at a person who wanted me off the face of the earth. It was a very disturbing few weeks, and I was angry that this person could have such control over my life. Mark went over with me the possible cross-examination questions that would be thrown at me.

"Ms. Wiehl, how do you know that the voice you heard was the voice of my client," the defense attorney asked as we'd expected and prepared for.

"Because I've listened to his voice when he threatened other people," I said, damaging his case with my answer since he'd thrown me an open-ended question rather than a yes or no.

We also anticipated that the defense attorney would try to make me emotional, catch me in an inconsistency, or get me to damage our case. He goaded me; he riddled me with emotionally charged questions; he tried to get me to overstate what had happened, but I remained calm and referred back to the notes I had taken right after the threat.

Mark told the story of how I had hired a babysitter so that I could work late on the case against this man, because I knew he was a danger and desperately wanted to protect his victim from further harm.

I couldn't make my closing for myself, but as he made the closing, Mark advocated for me. "Ms. Wiehl is a federal prosecutor. As you know, Judge, we take these jobs because we want to see justice done. Ms. Wiehl was doing her job, following the law, diligently working to prove the truth in this case, and this man, Mr. Smith, didn't want her to find the truth. He told her he was going to sexually attack her and then kill her. We can't let people like Mr. Smith take her dedication to the law away because of his threats. Ms. Wiehl should not have to live in fear because she was doing her job."

The government met their burden of proof. The defendant pled out before trial and went back to jail where he belonged. I won my case not by ignoring it or becoming emotional. But under these kind of circumstances, I did win my case by asking for help.

What's Your Theory of the Case?

In discussing the Eight Steps with women, I realized that often we, as women, fall back on our emotions during difficult confrontations in our lives. When we're in a "fight," we allow it to escalate to verbal shouting matches. And, particularly in our confrontations with men, as his voice grows louder, ours, perhaps unconsciously, grows weaker until we're reduced to tears. Often as women, we use tears to defuse confrontations—hoping that the vulnerability we demonstrate will cause the anger to ebb, stop the yelling, and perhaps curb the argument.

We've grown reliant on our tears to try to reverse the power dynamic. But these tears disempower us and empower those with whom we're having the conflict. That's not to say, never cry. Our emotion is certainly something that makes us empathetic, caring, nurturing beings. But by applying the Eight Steps, we can turn our emotions and intuition into an unbeatable resource. If properly allocated, personal feelings, especially as expressed through a narrative of facts, can be powerfully persuasive and help us stay clearheaded, strong, and in control. We can reverse the cycle of dominance.

A few years ago I was on a big highfalutin legal panel with a slew of federal judges and well-known lawyers, including Gerry Spence, the plain-talking, cowboy-hat-and-fringed-coat-wearing lawyer from Wyoming. Gerry was the keynote speaker, and he ended his speech saying this: "I've tried a lot of cases and had a lot of fancy opponents, and I've always won. I'm sitting up here on this panel with these esteemed jurists, and I've got to tell you ladies and gentlemen, as I look at this group of legal luminaries, I'll tell you who I'd be afraid, really afraid, to face in the courtroom. No, it's not these silver-haired judges or the fancy-suit-wearing lawyers with their years of experience and fancy legal briefs. It's that little lady right there." He pointed at me. "I wouldn't want to try a case against her. You know why? She's sincere, honest, and doesn't posture. The jury will believe anything and everything that little lady says." And he meant it.

Ladies, we've got our intuition, we've got our womanly wiles, but as Eleanor Roosevelt reminded us, if we combine these with an examination of the facts and evaluation of the factors in any situation, we'll have an unbeatable advantage over men—whether we're facing a Gerry Spence in the courtroom or a chauvinistic boss in the office.

What Do You Want in Your Life?

Whatever it is, walk through the techniques described in this book to find your authentic voice. Do your adversaries see you as a competitor, a little girl, an avenging Amazon, or a seductress? No matter what your juror's projection about women in general and you in particular might be, you can adjust how you make your case accordingly—from how you dress to how you present facts, cross-examine, rebut an argument, and tell your story.

Men may be stronger, but we're smarter and live longer! And even though the Equal Rights Amendment was never passed—shame on you Alabama, Arizona, Arkansas, Florida, Georgia, Illinois, Louisiana, Mississippi, Missouri, Nevada, North Carolina, Oklahoma, South Carolina, Utah, and Virginia!—we have become the clear majority. According to the 2000 Census, there are 143,368,343 females in the United States and 138,053,563 males. We're now more than 50.9 percent of the population, ladies. We're taking over!

Put the Eight Steps to work, find your voice, and get out there and win every time.

THE TRIALS OF LIFE

LEGAL BRIEF: A WOMAN'S VOICE

My Top Tips for Advocacy, Woman to Woman

- Rehearse your arguments in front of a mirror or to friends, the way lawyers often do, to help hone your arguments and to receive feedback you trust; this is called *mooting an argument*.

- Do a "self-portrait" of yourself as advocate to assess how you present yourself, asking, *What image am I trying to present?*
- Memorize opening and closing arguments in situations where you are doing your most significant advocacy.
- Maintain a low pitch to your voice to help maintain physical control during your presentation.
- Use hand gestures sparingly. They can be distracting and reduce your power.
- Remain determined not to let yourself get interrupted.
- Remember to state emotions ("I am frustrated"; "I am angry") rather than express them, so that you remain in command of your feelings, even under pressure.
- Believe with all your heart that what you're saying is interesting, important, and relevant.

Chapter 12

Advocacy with Loved Ones

> *To love you have to learn to understand the other, more than she understands herself, and to submit to her understanding of you. It is damnably difficult and painful, but it is the only thing which endures.*
>
> —D. H. Lawrence

Thirty-two-year-old Josh had grown up in difficult circumstances that haunted his adult life. He was raised—inattentively—by Brenda, a single mother, a woman whose fragile psyche was traumatized by the stress of parenthood and poverty. Even as a young child, Josh would have to get up and go to school without any help from Brenda. Josh's older brother, equally neglected, was also emotionally disturbed; he would beat Josh regularly, and several times Josh ended up in the hospital. Yet Josh managed to attend college under his own power, and he had become a highly successful salesman of sophisticated computer equipment. "I wish I could deal with my family in the same direct, accountable way I do with people at work," he told me.

Even after he got married and put some emotional distance between his family and himself, Josh remained troubled by his mother's ever-worsening moods. Brenda would stay awake for days at a time and then remain in bed for weeks afterward. She was unable to keep a job or even take care of herself. Josh's wife helped him realize that his mother was most likely suffering from a bipolar condition, had been most of her life, and that something had to be done. But what? "The last thing I wanted was to send my mother over the edge or drive her away from me," Josh said. "How do you tell someone you love that she has a psychotic condition?" In the past, whenever he had gently suggested she get psychological help, his mother rebuffed him angrily. But after a particularly bad episode, Josh decided he had to advocate with his mother.

Establishing his theory of the case (Step 1), Josh resolved he just wanted to get his mother to see a shrink and would not make her relive her past behavior; nor would he be distracted by any of her indignant accusations. Because he knew Brenda (his "jury") so well, he was able to approach her at a relatively serene moment, and he knew he had to talk to her directly, eye to eye, in a public place that would temper her reaction (Step 2). He marshaled his facts and was able to discard the evidence that was prejudicial to his case—he would not recount all of his mother's transgressions. Instead, he would focus on the evidence of how unhappy Brenda claimed she was; how painful life could be for her. And when she cross-examined him, he would be ready with his own gentle rebuttal (Step 3).

Josh met his mother for lunch at the neighborhood café. Nervous, he managed to start his carefully prepared presentation of the evidence with his mom when the entrée arrived. He told her that he was very concerned about her and worried she wasn't happy (Step 4).

"You think I'm sick," Brenda said. "I'm not. I'm fine. I'm having lunch with you, aren't I?"

"Mom, last Thursday you called me up and cried on the phone for an hour," he said, sticking to the facts.

"I was just upset about money. You have a lot of nerve—that's *your* problem."

Responding to his mother's charges (Step 5), Josh said very gently that he believed his mother suffered from a chemical imbalance. It wasn't her fault, but she needed—and deserved—professional help.

As Brenda protested, Josh ignored her counterclaims and did not let himself succumb to the temptation (Step 6) to add in more claims about her mental health that would damage his ultimate intention, to get her treatment. He reached for Exhibit A—medical pamphlets about bipolar disorder and its treatment. He pushed them across the table and described what they were. "Mom, please. Just read through the list of symptoms there. Do they fit what you've been feeling and doing?"

It was a risky strategy—he knew the answer, but he wasn't sure whether his mother would be honest about it. Brenda glared at him, then picked up the pamphlets and began looking through them.

Josh watched her face evolve from resentment to skeptical interest. He went on to tell his mother that he would go with her to the doctor and—anticipating her main concern—would be by her side the entire time and pay for the visit himself. Brenda looked doubtful. "I don't know any doctor."

"I got the name of a doctor who is very good," Josh said. He knew that if this process was to work, Brenda herself would have to commit to making the call.

"But what if the doctor just laughs at me?"

"He's very kind and respectful," Josh said.

As his mother listened with surprising attentiveness, Josh made the emotional truth of the mother-and-son story part of his argument (Step 7). "Mom, you've always been so brave. For years, you've been a single mother who had to do everything to keep our family together. I know how hard it's been for you to raise sons, keep us fed and clothed, try to keep a job—even how hard it can be to get up some mornings. It hurts me to see how brave you've had to be." Then, closing his argument (Step 8), he reiterated the facts that his mother's behavior showed she needed help, that help was available, and that he would be there for her. He wove his case for care into a coherent whole. "You deserve better than this," he concluded. "And I think you're brave enough to see a doctor and let him treat you."

Both mother and son were close to tears. Finally, Brenda agreed to call the doctor and see him, "just once, to hear what he says." And as it turned out, after living with bipolar disorder all her life, fifty-five-year-old Brenda was able to find some balance and security in her life. She has been able to hold down a part-time job and attend school during the day. Josh has found the mentally and emotionally grounded mother he'd never had.

Using the Eight Steps

As Josh's story reflects, our most complex and challenging advocacy is often with those we care about the most. When we advocate for what we need from family, romantic partners, and friends, we often feel like prisoners of our personal history, our needs and emotions, and our ingrained patterns. It is natural for our preconceived and often disabling thoughts and attitudes to underlie our feelings with the people closest to us. The Eight Steps actually make advocacy with our loved ones easier by changing our thought patterns and altering our behavior. The Eight Steps allow us to be proactive rather than reactive; to ground our arguments in facts, not wayward emotions or opinions; and provide a point-by-point plan that keeps us from getting our buttons pushed and instead moves us toward the goals we seek.

Because we have to live with, care for, and otherwise maintain personal relationships with those we love even when we advocate with them, the entire concept of "winning" an argument expands, ultimately becoming more generous and empowering. "Winning a case" with a loved one requires that we allow ourselves to be open to others' arguments, too. We need to express our feelings and needs, and listen and remain openhearted as we do so.

The Eight Steps will help you build a win–win consensus among family members and friends in order to, for instance, negotiate with your spouse on where to spend a vacation or how to improve your marriage; confront a backstabbing buddy and lay out a plan to restore or end the friendship; or successfully manage sibling rivalries. Let's explore advocacy with loved ones step by step.

Step 1. Theory of the Case

In advocacy with loved ones, it's often important to have both a long-term and a short-term theory of the case. You want to achieve a specific objective (persuading your husband not to read the paper at dinner) that supports your larger goals (better communication and having more mindful time together). But it is crucial to make sure you are operating from a truly sound theory of the case so that red herrings don't distract you from your goals. You can subvert your own best intentions if you get entangled in the minutiae of evidence and the short-term emotions they stir.

Mona, a busy screenwriter and mother of three children, realized this belatedly when she was fuming to her husband, Jeff, how little he did around the house. "I was so caught up in bargaining with him to make the bed and supervise the kids' homework that I lost sight of what I really needed to achieve with him—more involved parenting and a fairer and more caring relationship for the two of us. I was addressing the symptoms instead of the cause."

When we shoot from the hip, reacting out of anger, hurt, or frustration, we confuse "scoring points" with achieving defined and positive goals. We have to keep our eyes on the real prize. When Mona realized her mistake, she formulated her theory of the case and reminded herself of that theory as she approached each discussion with Jeff. The results were that Jeff understood Mona's needs and was able to address them, rather than defensively fighting back.

Step 2. Know Your Audience

We can't choose our family and we want to remain committed to our spouse and friends, so we are stuck with our jurors. But we can use the familiarity with our loved ones to develop an approach that will fit their predilections and character. Since we know them so well, we can also select the time and place that our advocacy will have the greatest possibility of success.

"I've learned that the best time to approach my wife about something important is when we're working together on a project," my friend Rich said. "Some of our best conversations have been while pulling weeds."

"I agree," his wife, Eileen, said. "And if he tries to change my mind about something in the middle of a messy kitchen, the answer is an automatic no."

When you're advocating with loved ones, you know when they are in their best frame of mind. Make your case then. Any other time is asking for disaster.

Step 3. Marshal Your Evidence

In advocacy with loved ones, since our emotions and relationship bonds are so much in the foreground, it is all the more important that we advocate based on the facts. If your sister has a habit of borrowing things and not returning them, the next time she wants to borrow something, rather than saying a hurtful *No, you never give anything back*, marshaling your evidence allows you to say, "Sure, I'd love to loan you my Sting CD. Have you finished with Norah Jones, Macy Gray, and my white skirt?"

Knowledge is not only power, it's also a whole lot easier on a relationship than errant emotions and accusations. Taking the time to do your research will save you time in the long run. For months, Eddie had been complaining that his wife's spending had gotten out of control. "You're throwing our money away!" he'd yell in the middle of one of his endless fights with Judy. By implementing the Eight Steps and deciding his theory of the case was to get their spending under control, he pulled out the receipts from their tax records of the same period the previous year. What he found was astonishing. "We were spending 30 percent more and bringing in basically the same thing. When I approached Judy and showed her the receipts and the numbers, she was shocked. For months, I'd been wasting my breath. When she saw it on paper—the proof—the reckless spending immediately stopped. We're back on track."

In dealing with loved ones, evidence is psychologically (and occasionally financially) liberating.

Step 4. Make Your Case

Your tone, especially with those with whom you are familiar, is critical to your success. Those who know you can pick up every flinch, every crook of the brow, every "huff." When you're dealing with a loved one, make sure you're prepared. If you're prepared, you will be relaxed. If you're relaxed, your juror will relax.

Make sure you state clearly what it is you want. My friend Marlene laughed that during a recent argument her poor husband tried everything to appease her: He went and got her aspirin, he called the babysitter, he took out the garbage, he even said he liked her mother . . . but nothing worked to cut her anger. She scowled, she slammed doors, she called him an "oaf," she did everything but say what she really wanted—"I never said, *I don't want to go to your boss's house for dinner.*" Often a case can be won with the ones we love if we just tell them what we want.

Step 5. Cross-Examination

Remember, you have to live with these people after your advocacy is over, and I cannot stress enough that a cross-examination need not be cross. In fact, the best cross-examinations are strategically nice. By asking leading questions and maintaining control of yourself and your argument, you can gently but firmly challenge your loved ones' contentions without even having them realize what you are doing.

> WIFE: Will Fred be there tonight?
> HUSBAND: Yes.
> WIFE: Is he still buying all his suits from Barneys?
> HUSBAND: Yes.
> WIFE: Do you think this dress is nice enough for the night?
> HUSBAND: Yes, honey, you always look good.
> WIFE: How about my shoes?
> HUSBAND: Your shoes are fine. Wow! In fact, you look really great. Do you think I should wear something a little nicer than jeans and sneakers?
> WIFE: I'll be happy to help you pick something out if you want.

Notice that no feelings were hurt. And going to the party with a husband who reached his "own" decision will be a lot more fun than going with the one who feels browbeaten into wearing what you told him to wear.

Because you are grounded in a sound, long-term theory of the case, you can also find yourself open to your loved one's responses—without feeling that such a counterargument will undermine your overall advocacy.

Step 6. Avoid the Deadly Spins

Since we know our friends and relatives so well, it's easy to get distracted by their complex motives and personalities, not to mention our own. Remember, no one knows your weaknesses like your spouse, other family members, and close friends. Often, your loved one will bring up other issues that may be important but are extraneous to your theory of the case. If you are well prepared and have facts as your foundation, however, you'll be less likely to spin off the path to your goal.

Stay true to your theory of the case, say only what you know you can back up, and rather than making statements that are open to interpretation—"You're so irresponsible"—make statements that can't be refuted, such as "You said you would pick me up at eight o'clock."

There's nothing worse than missing your goal because you've been sideswiped by your own goof. With personal relationships, you have more of a chance of getting your buttons pushed and damaging your case by getting sucked into another argument. Don't let them get you emotional. If they bring in your faults, take the wind out of their counterarguments by admitting to the faults, but controlling how you do it as part of your overall theory of the case: "Yes, I do sometimes unnecessarily overreact, but I don't think in this instance I am overreacting. The fact is, you left our three-year-old alone in the car and a stranger called the police."

Step 7. Tell a Story

A story told from the heart is often the best way to reach loved ones. They feel your pain or your joy like no one else, and a story might help them instantly identify with and better understand where you're coming from. Randy was trying to convince his wife, Kathy, to let his mother stay with them while she recovered from hip replacement surgery. Kathy was nearing the end of finishing her dissertation, and Randy knew the thought of his nagging mother in the house was far from peachy with Kathy. He used a story to convince his wife to open their home.

"After the twins were born, we needed help. We were really

struggling, financially and emotionally. Remember the day Mom showed up with that carload of diapers, blankets, and that whirl-pool attachment for your baths? She gave up her vacation to stay and help us for a few weeks ... and that really saved us. Even though at times she's overbearing, she needs us. I can't imagine her all alone in that house with all those stairs, even if she has a nurse a few hours a day. She showed her love for us. I know it will be hard on you, but could you find a way to let her stay for a few weeks?"

Kathy couldn't say no. The power and truth of Randy's story helped her remember the well-intentioned heart of Randy's mom. With loved ones, stories communicate your message and reach them directly.

Step 8. Sum It Up

Hopefully, by the time you've reached Step 8, you're feeling confident that your case is on track for a win. Certainly, by the time you reach your closing, most jurors, including your loved ones, will have reached their decision. The closing statement is your chance to clinch the deal. My advice is to tell jurors what you believe they know—"You know I'm overextended. I'm working a forty-hour week, taking care of the kids, cleaning, making sure everyone gets clothed and fed . . ."—admit the weaknesses of your case—"I know finances are tight"—and then remind them what you want—"But if we could hire a housekeeper just one day a week, it would take such pressure off me."

The great thing about winning verdicts from loved ones is that when they give you what you want, you can give them a kiss. (I was never able to do that with my jurors!)

Is It Worth the Win?

Sometimes in dealing with loved ones, you may decide that "winning" is not worth the fight. Take, for example, the story of Amos:

Amos came from a very religious Chinese family. His father was a Christian minister and his mom worked diligently as the preacher's wife, but after years of hearing the teachings of the faith, Amos realized that he didn't share in his parents' beliefs. When Amos began dating Laura, he found someone who shared many of his personal and political convictions. Like Amos, Laura was not religious and also believed very much in issues of feminism, so when they decided to get married, Amos agreed with Laura that by taking his last name she would be subsuming her identity for Amos's. Amos suggested that they take each other's last names—he would keep his last name but hyphenate it with Laura's, and she would do the same.

They happily announced their decision to Amos's parents, who became distraught by the idea. They told Amos that it was the name of their ancestors and that they felt it was tremendously disrespectful to change it. His mother cried and his dad was extremely distressed. Later, in an attempt to sway his parents' attitude, Amos and Laura formulated their theory of the case. The following week, over a nice dinner with his parents, Amos and Laura decided to once again address their name decision.

Amos thanked his parents for being wonderful about his life decisions: his career, his choice of partner, the way he lived, even his decision not to embrace their faith. (He kept the red herrings off the table.) Then he quietly, but confidently, conveyed his position to his parents—he and Laura were merging their last names as a symbol of their union. His parents listened and expressed understanding for his side. They discussed with him the enormous cultural issues of being Chinese and the importance his name held in a cultural context. Ultimately, his parents would never insist that he and Laura do as they ask, but Amos had never seen his parents so upset.

In thinking about their theory of the case, Amos and Laura realized that this issue meant much more to his parents than it did to the two of them. They weighed his parents' request, thought about alternatives, and in the end decided to have Amos keep his last name and have Laura keep hers. Sometimes by working through our theory of the case and listening to our loved ones' side of the story, we see that we might actually want to agree with them. For Amos and Laura, this was not a battle worth fighting.

In your advocacy with loved ones make sure you're going to be able to live with the results.

Do You Have All the Facts?

Before you wage battle with those you care about, make sure you really know what you're talking about.

Linda, a young mother in a close-knit group of moms whose children played together, was warned by her friend Pam that she had overheard Molly, Linda's best friend, telling people that Linda was cheap. "She says that when you go out with her you never tip and that you often stick her with the tab," Pam informed her. Linda was deeply wounded by hearing that Molly was telling lies about her. Her first urge was to find Molly and give her a piece of her mind or a poke in the eye. Then she centered herself, realizing that what she'd been told was hearsay, and decided her theory of the case was to get all her friends to tell her the truth.

After asking a few friends in their circle if they thought she was "cheap," Linda realized that it was the first time they'd heard such a statement. She went back to Pam and gently, almost offhandedly, cross-examined her. By asking some questions based on her theory of the case (that she wanted all her friends to like and trust her), Linda realized that Pam was jealous of her bond with Molly and was out to sabotage it. Linda saved her close relationship with Molly—and made it clear to Pam that she cherished her friendship, but she required honesty and openheartedness from all her friends.

Pam apologized profusely to Linda, and also went to Molly and told her she had done something she regretted and asked her to forgive her. Through the experience, the group of friends became closer and learned the importance of honest communication.

And How About Sex?

Yes, sex. Even your sex life can be assisted by the Eight Steps!

Michael and Valerie had been married for seven years, had two kids, and each had a successful career. Their sex life had gone cold. "Not cold," Michael said. "Frigid." Michael wasn't sure whether Valerie even noticed or cared that they weren't having sex, but decided he was going to make his case to get the intimacy back in their marriage.

Michael planned his case carefully, but simply.

• **Know your audience.** He secretly hired a babysitter, packed an overnight bag, and put it in the trunk of his car. He called Valerie at work and asked her out on a date to their favorite restaurant, like old times. At dinner, they talked about the kids, about their jobs, and then he said, "Let's talk about us. I've been thinking I've gotten to see so little of you lately that I'm forgetting what you look like."

"What?" Valerie asked, her brow raised. "You see me every day."

• **Theory of the case.** "I mean *see* you," he winked. "I want to put the life back into our bedroom." Michael saw Valerie's cheeks flush as they used to do when they were first dating.

• **Evidence.** "The last time we had sex was a Tuesday night five weeks ago. And it lasted eight minutes start to finish." Valerie laughed. "And that's including taking off our shoes! When we were first married, we had sex every day. Sometimes twice."

• **Make the case.** "I love you. I'm proud to be your husband and find you incredibly attractive, even more today than when we first married. We work so hard in our life, and I need intimacy to reassure me that everything is okay. I've found my eyes wandering lately and that scares me. There's no reason I should look elsewhere. I've got the most beautiful wife in the world."

"What do you mean, your eyes have wandered?" Valerie asked defensively.

• **Cross-examination.**

Q: That's not to say I've acted on it, but I have fantasized. Haven't you?

A: I suppose.

Q: Do you still find me attractive?

A: Yes.

Q: Do you love me?

A: With all my heart.

Q: Don't you need a little lovin'?

A: Yes, but I'm always so tired.

Q: What could we do to make you a little less tired?

A: We could go out every once in a while by ourselves.

Q: You mean like tonight?

A: Yes.

• **Avoid the spins.** Rather than bringing up any of his buddies, or trying to make his wife feel guilty about the hearsay exploits of others, Michael kept the case on track—talking about them.

• **Tell a story.** Michael then reminded Valerie of a few of their sexual adventures that, well, are too racy for these pages. But I'm sure you get the picture.

• **Sum it up.** "We've got a lot of fun years ahead of us, and I don't want them wasted. I'm tired of putting it off until 'later.' Our careers are doing fine; our children are old enough to be left with a sitter." He took Valerie's hand. "I've got a hotel room reserved, the babysitter is staying the night, and I've got some fun stuff packed for us. What do you say?"

• **Verdict.** Valerie called the waiter over and asked for the check.

Try It. You'll Like It.

Perhaps one of the most important uses of the Eight Steps is interacting more successfully with those we love. It's certainly one of the easiest ways to try them out and test their benefits—more than likely, if you approach someone you love with openness, eagerness, and a goal of making things better, you won't be spurned.

Those around you usually are the first to benefit when you make your life better. Give it a go. It's a real opportunity to affect your own fate.

THE TRIALS OF LIFE

LEGAL BRIEF: ADVOCATING WITH LOVED ONES

Top Tips for Advocating with Love

- Stay on topic: Throughout your advocacy, keep to your theory of the case by reminding yourself of your short- and long-term goals.
- Choose the timing and the place—don't have them chosen for you.
- Evidence, evidence, evidence: When in doubt, stick to the facts.
- Maintain control through your reliance on the facts and your use of leading questions.
- Prepare your cross-examination or counter-rebuttal beforehand—if you're intimate with people, you usually know how they are likely to respond.
- End by asking for what you want—put the decision in your loved one's hands.
- Remember the Golden Rule—approach the trials with your loved ones with an open heart. You'll want them to do the same.

Chapter 13

Eight Steps to Effective Parenting

> *Any child can tell you that the sole purpose of a middle name is so he can tell when he's in trouble.*
>
> —DENNIS FLAKES

Parenting involves the challenging task of teaching children the difference between right and wrong, teaching them the importance of responsibility, and setting boundaries as they search for the limits. The Eight Steps will help you advocate effectively *to* and *for* the children in your life, whether it's getting their homework done without a battle, helping them right a wrong, or convincing them to get off drugs.

The Eight Steps give families a practical way of providing the structure that child psychologists recommend. Dr. T. Berry Brazelton, in the classic *Touchpoints* and most recently *Discipline: The Brazelton Way*, stresses the importance of giving a child the security of having boundaries. Brazelton says that children are "searching for limits." They don't want to be mini-adults; they want parents to provide the strictures and structures of defined behaviors and rules. In my own role as a mother, I have found that the Eight Steps are a way to give useful and flexible form to the kinds of parent–child interactions that Brazelton sets forth. Having a procedure to guide parents in connecting with their children over specific issues allows adults to work from reason and care—and also gives the child a stable and predictable system within which to respond.

Not long ago I had a touchy incident with one of my children—and found myself in the kind of situation a lot of parents might find familiar. Preparing to do a load of laundry, I found several candy wrappers in my son Jacob's jeans. I knew I hadn't bought him the candy, and thinking back over his activities over the last couple of days, I had an unsettling idea of where he had gotten it. Because ten-year-old Jacob prides himself on being a good kid, I knew that it would be of limited value to accuse him directly. He would clam up and deny everything, then agonize about his lying in a way that would ultimately be counterproductive. Instead, when he came in from playing that afternoon, I showed him the candy wrappers and asked him if we could figure out together where they had come from. He went along with me, but as I asked him leading questions he agreed that yes, they could have come from a certain neighborhood store we had gone to, which sold this kind of candy. "Were they paid for?" I asked.

Jacob said no. As I'd feared, he had shoplifted them. I was angry, but then he told me, "Mom, I wanted the candy, but I didn't want to ask you for it—I didn't want the guy at the register to think I was spoiled."

His motives for swiping the candy tempered my reaction, but together, we agreed that, difficult as it would be, he had to go back to the store, tell the manager what he had done, and pay for the candy from his allowance. He went, painfully, but with some pride that he was doing the right thing.

Be Gentle and Patient

As a trial lawyer, I have learned the art—and the importance—of questioning people gently. I did this in the most difficult of cases, including those involving children who had been molested by their relatives. I used gentle cross-examination to elicit important information from the children without traumatizing them once again. In talking with a child for the first time, I always tried to go to the home or to a place that was especially comfortable for that particular child. Sometimes I took the child for a walk in the park, so that we weren't just staring at each other over a table. Having done my discovery ahead of time, I was able to talk about things the child was particularly interested in—sports, movies, music. Since most of the children were not eager to talk about what had happened to them, I always tried to dance around the subject until I felt that the child was comfortable with me. And when I asked that child about the experience, I made sure to do so in a soft, calm manner saying simply, "Can we talk about what happened to you?" Sometimes I would ask the child to draw me a picture or write me a letter to read later.

As a parent, I know firsthand that managing your advocacy with a child takes practice, discipline, a willingness to listen, and an open heart. Different kids respond differently to different approaches and techniques. For example, when your child misbehaves, you might find it best to address your concerns to her immediately; however, if she is someone who is likely to resist discipline implemented too quickly or arbitrarily, you might instead say something like, "I'm concerned about what you did. I'd like to talk with you about it in an hour or so, once you've had the chance to calm down and think about it for a while." Through your familiarity with your child's temperament, you can get the outcome you seek—without tears and slamming doors. I've found one of the best times to talk to my son Jacob is while out riding our bikes. Some of the best communication I had with him while I was going through my divorce was while riding our bikes. He was open and relaxed, and our conversations were heartfelt and meaningful.

"Not Me"

The Eight Steps might also protect your children from false inferences, if wrongly accused. When Kate came home from her nursing job to find a broken heirloom lamp and all three of her children (age seven, nine, and fourteen) claiming innocence, she interviewed each child separately, using direct examination techniques, methodically asking each child a series of questions: "What time did you come home from school?" "Who was home when you got there?" "What did you do next?" She then gathered them all together and slowly spoke to each child in turn. Ultimately the verdict was rendered on who had broken the lamp: Jasper, the family dog.

I had a similar instance at home in which I accused the wrong party. I had invited six little girls over for a two-hour party celebrating my daughter's fifth birthday. I love throwing parties for my kids, although I must admit I get more stressed out about putting on one of these parties than I do going on national television and debating Bill O'Reilly. My worries are typical mom worries. Will the girls get along? Will any of them feel left out? Will they like playing pin the tail on the donkey? Will they be able to bring down the piñata? Will it rain so the kids won't be able to play outside?

The one thing I didn't worry about was food. No one would go hungry. I had made plates of peanut butter and jelly sandwiches and had bought a beautiful chocolate cake with a rich pink frosting and plastic figures of ballet dancers. So about an hour before the party was to begin, I went to my home office, where I had hidden the cake. When I opened the door to my office, I almost keeled over. I couldn't believe my eyes. The cake looked like a lunar landscape. The frosting had been completely decimated by someone's fingers.

I immediately suspected my son (based solely on weak circumstantial evidence). After all, he had torn out of the house a few hours earlier, saying he was going to play baseball with his friends (after promising me he would stick around for his sister's party). And who else could have done such a thing? There were no other people in the house. It was just Jacob, Dani, and me. He must have done the dastardly deed.

Shaking, I gathered up the bruised cake and ran to the bakery where I had bought the cake. "Please help me," I begged, putting the ravaged cake on the counter. Fortunately, they took mercy on me, and the damage was successfully repaired. I rushed home to get ready for the arrival of a battalion of little girls. My son pulled his bike into the driveway as I got out of the car. I mercilessly presented my theory of the case and asked him what he had to say for himself. I could tell instantly, just by looking in his eyes, that he had no idea what I was talking about.

I found Dani in her room, being unusually quiet. "Danielle?" I said, walking into her room. "Did you touch your cake?"

"No," she said.

"Not even for a second?"

"No."

"Good. I'm a little worried you might not like the icing."

"No, I like it," she said, getting caught like a lobster in a trap.

When I calmed down, I asked her why she would ruin her birthday cake. The simple answer: "I knew you would fix it."

Aaargh. To be a parent.

I have found the best way to give advice to your children is to find out what they want and then advise them to do it.

—HARRY S. TRUMAN

Homework Negotiations

Bob, a work-at-home single father, was tired of waging the homework battle every night with his eighth-grader, Blake. Completely unmoved by any activity that included the word *school,* Blake was interested only in playing video games, talking on the telephone, and resisting any suggestion his father made. "I was ready to give up on him and send him to reform school," Bob told me, half jokingly. "Every night I felt I was negotiating with an alien clone who had kidnapped my real son."

By using the Eight Steps, Bob was able to keep his emotions in check and maintain control of the argument. His theory of the case, of course, was to get Blake to do his homework without a nightly hassle, and Bob determined that the best way to approach his juror was to sit down and play a video game with him. "Hey," he said to his son one afternoon, "you think you could teach me how to play?"

"Why do you want to play Mario Brothers?" his son asked suspiciously.

Having done his discovery, Bob said, "I want to free the Princess Toadstool from the clutches of Boozer."

"That's Bowser, Dad," Blake laughed.

"Yeah, him. That's what I want to do."

They sat down and Bob's son taught him how to play the game. "See, that's Bowser. He's the King of the Koopas. There's a fire-breathing monster protecting each one of the castles and you have to defeat the dragon and find the princess. Unfortunately, she's not easy to find. Usually what you get is one of the princess's minions who tell you, 'Our princess is in another castle!'"

"How'd you learn all this?" Bob said, gently leading his son toward his goal.

"It takes practice, and I've played a lot."

"So this is what you want to do for a living, design games like this?" Bob asked after they finished a rousing game.

"Yeah," Blake said, "but not exactly like this. I'd like to use more mythical characters."

"How do you get to be a video game programmer?"

"It takes a lot of work," Blake said. "You have to know computers and engineering, graphic design, and that sort of thing. Also, if you're going to design, you'll need to be able to create the story."

"And where do you learn that?"

"College," Blake said, looking at Bob like he had three eyes.

"And you're going to go to college right after high school?"

"Yeah."

"What kinds of grades do you think you're going to have to make in high school to get into college?" Bob asked.

Blake turned to his father, a realization evident in his expression. "Probably better than I'm doing now. Hey, do you think you could help me with my pre-algebra?"

"Sure," Bob said. "And after that, I'll take you on in another game of Mario Brothers." Bob won his case by identifying with his son's precocious reasonability and leading him to make his own decision about his homework. Bob reports that Blake now seems to almost relish bringing his intellect to bear on his homework, perhaps making his own short-term theory (make good grades) to support his long-term theory (become a video game designer).

Practical Lessons

Laurel and her husband were responsible about their spending and wanted to instill in their children the same responsibility, but no matter what she said or did, she'd hand her son, Sean, his weekly allowance and he'd inevitably run out and "spend it on garbage." She tried buying a glass piggy bank, but after two weeks of "saving," Sean cracked open the piggy bank and bought some baseball cards. Laurel decided she'd try using the Eight Steps.

She found her best discovery in their backyard and decided that this would be where she'd make her case. One day when Sean arrived home from school, he asked for his allowance. "Your allowance is outside," she said.

"Outside?" he asked.

"That's right," she smiled. "Come with me, and I'll show you."

Sean followed her outside and they sat at the picnic table overlooking the backyard and its busy early-fall activities. She brought along the materials that would help her make her case. She got right into her gentle, but direct examination.

Q: Do you see those squirrels?

A: Yes.

Q: What are they doing?

A: Eating the walnuts.

Q: Are you sure? Really watch them.

A: Oh, they're taking off the outside part and carrying the nut back to their nest.

Q: And why are they doing that?

A: I don't know. Maybe they're saving them for later.

Q: Why would they do that?

A: Well, maybe because they know it's going to be winter soon, and they don't want to starve.

Laurel nodded. "How much money do we give you a week for helping out around the house?" she asked.

"Twenty dollars."

"And how long have we been giving you an allowance?"

"A long time," Sean answered. "I guess at least two years."

"And how many weeks are there in a year?" she asked.

"Fifty?" he asked. "No, fifty-two."

"That's right," she said, handing him pen and paper. "Now, multiply twenty times fifty-two."

His little hands did the calculations: "1,040."

"Now multiply that by two," she instructed.

He said, "2,080."

"And how much is that four-wheeler you've been begging us to buy?"

"A thousand dollars." Sean's eyes widened as the realization hit him. "You mean I could have bought it myself?"

"Actually you could have bought two," she laughed. "How much do you have of that $2,080?"

"None," he said.

For her closing, Laurel pulled out a twenty-dollar bill paper-clipped to the documentation for a kid's checking account that the local bank offered. "The squirrels don't have such a bad idea. If you want to fill this out, you can get a real checking account at the bank, and you can start saving your money for that four-wheeler."

Sean eagerly took the paperwork. Laurel reports that Sean now has his own checking account and has become a fanatic about saving.

> *You know your children are growing up when they stop asking you where they came from and refuse to tell you where they're going.*
>
> —P. J. O'ROURKE

Family Crisis

Mike had watched his sixteen-year-old son, David, grow more and more removed and noninteractive with the family. David, a happy, talkative, and fun child, was once the family entertainer, making up shows and performing in the living room. But he had become increasingly sullen and removed, opting out of family dinners and family vacations, choosing instead to isolate himself in his room. At first, Mike thought David's distance was just a product of adolescent separation. Then David became less interested in taking care of himself. His face was often unshaven, his hair long and unruly, his nails dirty.

Over time, the situation grew worse. Mike and his wife began to notice money missing from their wallets and items such as jewelry and other valuables missing from the home. They had been simply explaining these missing items as being misplaced or the money having been miscounted, but soon they became more suspicious. When Mike tried to talk to David about his life, David always said, "I'm fine. Let me live my life."

One day a fifty-dollar bill disappeared from Mike's wallet, and in a state of anger and worry, Mike went into David's room while he was out one evening. He hated doing it, but he was desperate for answers. His search proved very disturbing. In the bottom drawer of David's dresser, in a clear bag, David found a white, powdered substance. He knew it was cocaine.

Crying, he went to his wife and showed her what he'd found. They were devastated. They blamed themselves, they blamed David's choice in music, they blamed his friends, and then they realized that all the finger-pointing wasn't going to do anyone any good. They had to talk to David.

The first conversation was more of a confrontation. Mike fell victim to the Deadly Spins, losing control of his emotion, making false inferences, and threatening his son. David refused to admit the cocaine was his and was outraged that Mike would search through his room. Mike grounded David indefinitely—a sanction Mike knew was going to be impossible to enforce given his own work schedule.

After several weeks of hostility around the house, Mike decided he had to make a better case to his son, explaining his hurt and disappointment as well as encouraging him to change his behavior. While finding his evidence to support his case, Mike met with the school guidance counselor, who encouraged Mike to talk to the head of the theater department, Mr. Challen. It was, she explained, a nationally acclaimed program, and Mr. Challen had been known to change students' lives for the better. Mike met with the director, explained his circumstances, and asked if he would consider letting David join his production.

After several conversations, Mr. Challen decided that if David showed interest in helping with the play and demonstrated an ability to commit fully to the production, promising not to use drugs or alcohol, he would let him participate. Mike knew it was a long shot, but, knowing a few things David wanted, he thought he had a way to convince his son.

Mike gently knocked on David's bedroom door one night and asked if he could come in. "David," he began as they sat on the bed, "your mom and I really want you to be happy. I want that more than anything in the world. I know it's difficult being a teenager these days, and I want to do something to help you. I have an idea. Your school has an incredible theater program, and I've met with the director. He'd like you to try out for and participate in his program."

David looked at Mike skeptically and immediately launched into a million reasons why he couldn't do it. Mike interrupted. "David, I realize that this isn't high on your priority list right now, but I'm really sad about what's happened between us and what's going on in your life. Have I asked you for much over the years?"

"No, Dad, you haven't."

"Have I tried to give you everything that you've needed?"

"Yes."

"And have I worked to make a nice place for you to live and guitar lessons for you to take?"

"Yes."

"Will you please do me this favor and try this out? Look, I know you've been wanting a car, so I'll make you a deal. If you participate fully and completely in this production—including abiding by all the rules Mr. Challen sets—we'll get you a car when the production is over."

David, who'd been looking down, looked up at his dad. "Really? You'll do that?"

"Yes," he said, "I promise. And have I ever broken a promise?"

"No," David said. "Okay, I'll give it a try."

Mike left his son's room that night tentatively very happy. Though he didn't have extra money and getting a car for David would be difficult, he knew they had to reach David or the costs were going to be much higher. Mr. Challen lived up to his reputation, enforcing the rules he'd established and reminding participants if they disobeyed the simple rules, they'd be asked to leave the production. And for the months the production ran, David stuck with it, gained friendships, found a surprising talent to both sing and act, and has truly turned his life around. He didn't just give up drugs. After doing some soul searching, he changed his life.

In the end, David wouldn't accept a car from his parents—he bought his own with money he is making at a part-time job he has at the mall. David rejoined life.

> *We spend the first twelve months of our children's lives teaching them to walk and talk and the next twelve years telling them to sit down and shut up.*
>
> —PHYLLIS DILLER

Follow the Leader

Children learn by example. Just as they respond to real tales of real people and stories and illustrations that explain your case, children also watch and do as their parents do, much like the old game of "follow the leader." William Pollack, in his groundbreaking book *Real Boys,* suggests we teach lessons by showing them, rather than just telling them to our children. "Don't talk to your mother that way" is far less effective than observed behavior of your own treatment of and respect for your spouse. This also means that if you are a consistent advocate, you will stick with the terms of your case and the bargains you've made along the way. My son reminded me of this when he told me, "Mom, you said that if I cleaned my room we could go to the skate park, but you were doing your work and now the park is closed. So we need to go skating right after breakfast tomorrow." After I was impeached by my son's cross-examination, I knew I couldn't change the terms of my offer. He got his trip to the half-pipe right after his breakfast cereal.

Sometimes when you use the Eight Steps with your children, they might throw logic right back at you. Dani had been begging for a dog. I explained that with our recent move, we needed to settle in a bit before getting a pet. We discussed the evidence of how busy her life is—visiting her father, playing with her friends, and traveling back and forth to Seattle to see her grandparents. "A dog is a lot of responsibility," I reasoned. "And with our busy life he might get lonely."

"No, he won't," she said. "He'll love our life."

"You're going to have to prove to me that you can take care of a pet, show me that you're responsible. And the way to do that is by showing me little by little how you can take care of a pet. So why don't we start off by buying a fish, and if you take care of the fish, we'll get you a cat. And if you take care of the cat, we'll get you a dog."

"Great!" was her verdict. I figured I'd bought myself a few years.

Soon we were the proud owners of two goldfish along with their tank, pebbles, and little palm trees. After a few days I noticed that Dani wasn't feeding the fish every day and changing the water as she should. I asked her if she'd fed her fish, and with the reminder, she sprinkled some food flakes in the bowl and watched her pets gobble it up.

After a few weeks, I found a floater. I was grief-stricken over how to explain to my daughter that one of her pets had passed away. I took her in her room, scooped the nameless fish out with the net, and we had a "funeral" over the toilet bowl. As the poor little creature swirled away to that big pond in the sky, I asked Dani how she felt.

"Fine," she said. "One down. One to go."

"What?" I asked.

"Well," she said. "Once the other fish dies, we'll be able to get the cat . . ." In her logical plan, she was one step closer to having that dog! Just when you think you're all smart about how you're raising your children, they toss the logic right back at you.

Providing a Hand

One day recently I came home from work to find my son Jacob unusually quiet and withdrawn. When I asked what was wrong, he told me that the principal, Dr. Drier, would call me that night. Of course, I thought Jacob had done something to warrant the call, but he assured me it was something that had happened to him. At my urging, he reluctantly told me he had been beaten up in the schoolyard by a kid in his class, Max. Even as I reacted with anger and maternal protectiveness, I formulated what I needed to do to advocate for my son and his safety.

Step 1, my theory of the case, I had to protect my child from any further damage, either physical or emotional, and repair as best I could what had already happened. As for my theory of the case regarding what we sought from the outside world, after I ascertained the facts I had to make sure that the school understood the severity of what had happened and that Max needed to know he could not get away with harming my son—or harm anyone again. I also had to protect my son's pride and make sure he would not be vulnerable in the future.

When Jacob told me he had a substitute teacher that day and had gone to the principal to tell her what happened, I knew my juror (Step 2) would be the principal, even though I would go to Jacob's teacher first to tell her I was going to speak to the principal. I wasn't going to try to reason with Max's mother; by the bruises on Jacob's body, I knew this was way too serious for that.

I began the third step—gathering the evidence—and had Jacob tell me slowly and carefully the details of what had happened. Trying to see what discovery I could do, I asked Jacob who else might have witnessed what happened or whom else he'd told, and what time he had been assaulted. I called the parents of the two boys who'd seen or knew about the incident and explained what I knew, saying their boys may have been affected by what they saw or heard. (As it turned out, one boy—one of the smallest in the class—had approached Max and told him, "I'm mad that you hurt my friend!")

Both sets of parents spoke with their boys and called me back to confirm that what Jacob had told me was true. Then I asked Jacob to write an "affidavit" of what happened: the number of punches, where the punches hit, the number of kicks and where they had landed, and what Max said. He wrote it out in his own handwriting, spelling errors and all. I think the process was helpful to him.

Anticipating Steps 5 and 6 and possible counterclaims, I asked Jacob if he knew why Max would do such a mean thing. ("Did you have a long-standing feud? Did you provoke him in any way?") Jacob said that Max was a popular boy in class, but that Jacob was friends with a lot of Max's friends, and Jacob was seen as the class athlete. This had sparked Max's jealousy. "Did you hit back?" I asked Jacob. He said no.

So the next morning, armed with Jacob's affidavit (and, by the way, my son's gratitude that his mom was advocating so fiercely for him), I went to Jacob's school to present my case (Step 4). After making an appointment with the principal, I went to Jacob's teacher, told her the story, and showed her Jacob's affidavit. She was aghast and apologetic. She said she would make sure this would not happen again, and promised me she would also speak to the principal.

Next stop, the principal's office. In a cool, collected manner, I told her I needed to tell her the story of what happened on the playground: Jacob had seen two boys playing a "violent game," and when he went over to try to break it up, Max turned on him, punching him twice in the stomach then kicking him twice on the back and once on the thigh. At this point I took out Jacob's affidavit and showed her how he had cataloged the hits and punches (spelling *thigh* as "thy"). Jacob had not hit back but yelled, "Do you know what you are doing?" Max had responded with vivid curse words. I handed the principal the affidavit. She asked whether Jacob and Max had a long-standing feud; I was prepared and told her what Jacob had said. She said she was very proud of Jacob for coming to her yesterday; I told her I had always taught him to seek out the proper authority and confront problems right away.

As I summarized my case (Step 8), I told Dr. Drier that every child in the school deserves to feel safe and secure and that bullying should not be tolerated. Presenting the measures I wanted the school to adopt, I asked that Max's parents be told what happened, that all the teachers be informed of what had occurred and be specially attuned to Max's behavior so as to thwart any further outbursts, and Jacob be safeguarded while in the playground in a way that would not deny his dignity or autonomy. The principal gave me the verdict we wanted—and promised to follow up.

The Eight Steps had allowed me to advocate powerfully for my son.

Teach Your Kids How

You couldn't pay me to go back to school. Kids can be so mean and hurtful to one another, and much of what our children face each day, they never share and we never know. But the Eight Steps provides you with a system to connect with your children over specific issues, allowing you to approach them from a place of reason and care, and give them a stable and predictable system within which to respond.

In hoping to provide my kids with a way to make their lives kinder and their struggles easier, I've taught them these steps and encourage them to use them to think through their conflicts with their peers and in facing their personal struggles and desires.

Here's an actual "case":

Step 1. What do you want? (Theory of the case). As simple as, "I want two friends to spend the night."

Step 2. Who are you going to ask and when is the best time to ask them? (Voir dire). "First, I need to ask your permission. Then I need to ask them if they want to. Then we need to ask their moms."

Step 3. What reasons do you have that this should happen? (Discovery). "We haven't had a sleepover since school started. We don't have much homework this weekend. We just got *Finding Nemo* on video. You've been very busy with work. I've been keeping my room clean and helping around the house."

Step 4. What are you going to tell them? (Making the case). "My mom says it would be all right for you to spend the night Friday. She says we could order pizza and sleep in sleeping bags in the living room."

Step 5. What are you going to ask them? (Cross-examination). "Would you like to? Do you think your mom would let you bring some of your Nintendo games? Do you have a sleeping bag?"

Step 6. How can you avoid getting upset? (Avoiding the Seven Deadly Spins). "If you say they can't spend the night, I can tell you why I think it's important to me instead of crying. Or if they say they don't want to, I could ask someone else."

Step 7. Can you tell them a story about how you feel? (Telling a story). "I can tell them about how when we lived in Seattle and I got to have my friends spend the night once a month. We would build tents out of blankets and you'd make us popcorn, and we'd get to play video games until midnight."

Step 8. How are you going to end your case? (Closing). "I'm going to say, 'I hope you can come over. I know we'll have a lot of fun. If your mom needs to talk to my mom, she said she'd be happy to. What do you think? Do you want to?'"

I've found that when my two kids approach me, their friends, their teachers, and others with their thoughts firmly in hand, it makes both sides happier and the struggle of parenting a little easier. One thing is for sure: When they don't beg, whine, or nag, they've found they are much more likely to get what they want.

Raising children is certainly a delicate balance. We don't want to hold them back, but we need to provide defined behaviors and rules. Using the Eight Steps, we can teach them when they need to be taught, help them when they need to be helped, and empower them when they need to be empowered. Most of all, the Eight Steps provide a reliable backdrop that allows you to grant them the best verdict of all—love.

THE TRIALS OF LIFE

LEGAL BRIEF: EIGHT STEPS TO EFFECTIVE PARENTING

Questions to Ask Yourself Before You Talk to Your Children

- What is my theory of the case with my child in this instance?
- How does my short-term goal contribute to my long-term objective?
- How is my advocacy in this instance specific to my child? How would I make my case to a different child?
- What is the best order for my evidence? Is all of it appropriate to use in this instance? If, for example, I want to make a case to my daughter about not sleeping until noon, is it relevant to mention that she delays doing her weekend homework until Sunday night?
- Does my child need a "time-out" during our argument? Do I need a "court recess"?

- If I need to draw out the truth from my child about a situation, have I presented my questions so that they lead to a clear conclusion?
- As an advocate, am I setting a good example for my children?
- Am I allowing them the opportunity to advocate for themselves, both with me and with others?

Chapter 14

Closing Thoughts

> *Never be afraid to try something new. Remember, amateurs built the ark. Professionals built the Titanic.*
>
> —UNKNOWN

As clichéd as it may sound, life is short. We are not promised a tomorrow, only this moment. This hit home for me when I gave birth to my daughter a little more than six years ago. I'd had a fairly routine pregnancy and excellent prenatal care, but in the last few weeks of the pregnancy, my blood pressure began to rise to a dangerous level, and my doctor suggested I schedule a date for delivery.

I went into the hospital a few days before my due date and the nurses started me on a Pitocin drip to induce labor. No labor is easy, but mine was, again, fairly routine. After several hours my baby girl, Danielle, was born. That darling little face, tiny fingers—she was beautiful. For the first few moments after birth, I held her to my breast. And then, in an instant, everything changed.

I suddenly felt incredibly weak, then nauseous. I was scared. I couldn't hold on to her—I didn't have the strength. "Take the baby," I whispered. "I'm too weak." I watched the expressions of those around me turn from joy to anxiety. In the first few moments after my baby was born, everyone's attention had been on the baby, but their attention was now on me and everyone looked worried. I was very tired and groggy. I heard over the intercom, "Code Blue in Maternity." Within a few seconds I was surrounded by lots of people wearing white. I was dying.

I can't die now, I thought. *I have too much left to do. I need to be alive for my children.* I felt so tired, and yet I willed myself not to close my eyes. I could faintly hear one doctor telling another that I was "crashing." There was a nurse by my side. I reached for her hand and said, "Please, help me."

I like to think I have life under control—that things will work according to the great plans I make. But as I lay helpless on that hospital bed, I realized we cannot always dictate what will happen to us. All our plans can be made meaningless in a matter of seconds. As hard as we try, sometimes things are just out of our hands. Several pints of blood later, a doctor leaned over me and whispered, "You're out of the woods." Still too weak to move, I spent the night alone and strapped in that birthing bed. A few days later, I was well enough to go home with my brand-new daughter.

But it was that night—the night of my daughter's birth and my near death—that I realized I had fallen into the habits of life, fearful of taking any risks that would put me out of control of my world. I was in the moment in the courtroom, but I was somewhere else in my life.

Out of the Woods

I've used that lesson and the Eight Steps to change my life.

You now know the secrets and techniques lawyers use every day in the courtroom to win cases from traffic court to the Supreme

Court. Don't wait until it's too late to realize you shoulda, woulda, coulda. You have little control over when your life will end, but you have great control over how your life is in the present. This very moment. What do you want? How can you improve your life? What do you need that will make you happier, healthier, safer, richer?

You're out of the woods—you have the steps to handle any situation, any difficulty that arises, and handle it as a winner. You have the power to face your fears, take risks, and stand up for yourself every day. Life *is* too short to allow your personal insecurities, your weaknesses, or your fears to keep you from attaining what you want. Face your difficulties head-on—don't wait for someone else to rescue you. You now have the advantages and strategies the best lawyers use to win their most difficult cases. Use these Eight Steps to rise above the helplessness you feel when you are met with difficulties and confront situations of conflict.

One Caveat

Remember, I said this is not a book to make a litigious society more litigious. The Eight Steps should be your way to solve problems without the drama and without the need for a courtroom fight, but sometimes things happen that render us out of our league. If, for example, you're pulled over for drunk driving or accused of shoplifting, your bank is foreclosing on your house, the IRS is auditing you, or you're in a child custody battle, you're going to need assistance. There are times when you should hire outside counsel—when your winning strategy is to know you need help.

I couldn't advocate for myself when I was seeking a divorce. I hired a divorce lawyer because the situation was too emotional for me. I had done everything I could to try to make the marriage work, and when I faced the fact that it wasn't going to—I had to seek outside help.

I suppose the way to think about it is, if you were seriously ill, you wouldn't think twice about going to the doctor, so if you're in "legal trouble" you don't want to handle it yourself. Though it is everyone's right to serve as his or her own attorney—*pro se,* as it's called—as a friend of mine says, you are also entitled to practice pole vaulting in a thunderstorm. If you find yourself headed to court, my advice is that unless the penalty for your offenses is of no concern to you, it is reckless to serve as your own attorney. Still, you can use the Eight Steps to find a good attorney and assist her in making your winning case.

And in Closing . . .

Please keep in mind that effective advocacy is not about "beating" the other side. It's about getting what you want in as positive a way as possible. Lawyers who bully people in the courtroom often lose their cases because jurors can't stand that kind of posturing. And even if you win—do you want to put your head on the pillow at night knowing you've done someone wrong? The best lawyers treat their opponents with respect and dignity. Great lawyering isn't about intimidation—it's about persuading someone to come to your side.

That's not to say there won't be bumps in the road. There will certainly be times when you doubt yourself. A few days after receiving the call from Roger Ailes, the head of Fox News, while standing on the courthouse steps with my divorce attorney, I was doubting whether I should take the risk and give up my stable job and comfortable life in Washington. I was in the bathroom of a Seattle television studio putting on my makeup for a TV appearance, and my cell phone rang. It was Bill O'Reilly. "Lis," Bill said, "I know you must be afraid to move you and your kids three thousand miles from home, but in life, you've got to be willing to take risks."

"What if I fail?" I asked, while staring into the bathroom mirror.

"You won't," he said. "And even if you do, you can say you tried."

What he said reminded me of my resolve on that hospital bed. "Thanks, Bill," I said. "I'll see you in New York." I faced my fears, got on a plane with my two kids and my mom (who had generously offered to help us out for a week), and headed across the country to New York to start a career in national television, leaving everything I knew behind in Seattle. We arrived in the middle of the night, took a long taxi ride from JFK Airport to Westchester, and were dropped off at the house we were renting only to discover we were locked out. When we finally got in around three in the morning, there was nothing to eat, we had no sheets, and there was a gas leak.

Shortly after finally getting to sleep, the phone rang. It was six AM and a producer at Fox told me the Washington, D.C. sniper had been caught and they wanted me on air by nine commenting on the case. I started crying. I was overwhelmed. My car was being shipped, and I had no idea how to get to the city. I wiped away the tears and did what I had to do—I walked over, introduced myself to my neighbor, and asked him to take me to the train.

Were my first few days easy? No. Was it scary? Yes. Was it impossible? No. I used the exact techniques and principles I've espoused in this book to face my new job, empower myself, and change my life for the better. My life isn't always easy, as I'm sure yours isn't. But using these Eight Steps I solve my problems—everyday problems. That's not to say, when I'm at the Stop & Shop and discover I've left my wallet at home, I prepare and make an entire case—I don't. But I do say to myself, *What's my theory of the case? What do I need here?* And that keeps me calm and on track. When I realize that what I want is my groceries, I ask the manager if he can ring me up and hold them while I run and find my wallet.

Each personal success I have outside the courtroom is because I've had a working theory that successfully carries me through to a winning verdict. I say again, in your life, in your own personal cases—the trials and tribulations of your life—try, before you do anything else, to find the theory of your case. You will be amazed by the results.

I wish you the best of luck. You have the power to make your case and win every trial of your life.

Acknowledgments

I'd like to thank the following people. Bruce Littlefield, my collaborative editor, who brought his vision, smarts, and humor to make writing this book a labor of love. Bruce and I share the same "theory of the case," which is to help people win the trials of life, and if anyone knows how to tell a good story, it's Bruce.

My friends at Ballantine, including my editor, Maureen O'Neal, and Gina Centrello, Nancy Miller, Kim Hovey, Anthony Ziccardi, Johanna Bowman, and Laura Jorstad. Thank you for embracing the book and believing in me. And Sherry Huber at Random House audio books.

Roger Ailes, my boss at the Fox News Channel, who took a chance on hiring me and bringing me to New York. I'll always be grateful.

And my colleague Bill O'Reilly . . . it's an honor to call him my friend.

Todd Shuster at Zachary Shuster Harmsworth, my literary

agent, who believes in me and in the concept for this book. Anthony Lewis and Marjorie Dobkin, my teachers and friends.

And Robb, David, and Irving.

Kathryn Klemperer, Jayne Boelman, and Bridget Slavens, who opened up their hearts to me and used the Eight Steps in the trials of their lives. And all the people I spoke with who trusted me with their personal stories.

My favorite (and only) brother, Christopher.

And Mickey . . .